FRETBOARD BIOLOGY
COMPREHENSIVE GUITAR PROGRAM

"The Knowledge without the College"™

LEVEL 3

The textbook to accompany
the Level 3 course at:
FretboardBiology.com

©2021 Joe Elliott. Please do not distribute or reproduce this material. This program represents a lifetime of work teaching guitar players like you how to be better musicians. If you think this program is great, please encourage your friends to sign up for the course and go through it with you. They will get more out of the program, and you will feel better knowing that you aren't hurting fellow artists by just giving away their work. Thank you.

©2021 Fretboard Biology • Fretboard Biology.com

Music Biology Publishing

Copyright © 2021 Joe Elliott

All rights reserved. Except as permitted under the U.S. Copyright Act of 1976, no part of this book may be reproduced in any manner whatsoever without written permission from the publisher, except in the case of brief quotations in critical articles or reviews.

The paper used in this publication meets the minimum requirements of the American National Standards for Information Services - Permanence of Paper for Printed Library Materials,
ANSI Z39.48-1984.

ISBN 13: 978-1-7362942-0-8

DEDICATION

I would like to dedicate this to all the great teachers out there who are passing along their knowledge and experience.

ACKNOWLEDGMENTS

In any project like this, it is hard to thank all of the people who have been instrumental in its development and success. I've been fortunate to have the support and friendship of many people along the way. I've somehow been wise enough to listen to those who know more than me, too. I encourage everyone to live that way.

I would like to start by thanking my wife, Eileen, for all the support, encouragement, and freedom to take on this monstrous project—and the faith that it would be a success—as well as all the years of putting up with the stresses of being married to a professional musician. My interest in music was fostered and supported by my parents, Jack and Marian Elliott, who always had a house full of big band and classical music, and my older siblings, Dave, Mary, and Dan, who exposed me to a lot of great music growing up like the Trashmen, The Beatles, The Stones, Sergio Mendes, Chicago, Sly, and Crosby, Stills, and Nash.

There were several people who were very influential in my development as a musician and educator that I would like to acknowledge: Fred Brush for showing so many great musicians to me in my formative years. Glen Johnston for exposing all of us "Montana Boys" to the real musicians in person at Montana State. Kent Erickson for drilling me on theory on our long road trips. Carl Schroeder for your unique way of getting your points across back in the day when I was in your classes in LA. You certainly shaped my way of teaching and managing a classroom. Keith Wyatt for the steady example of professionalism in guitar education. Combining great guitar talent with an organized mind is a great combination for any student. Scott Henderson for your relentless intolerance of mediocrity. You still scare me into working harder. Don Mock for being such an egoless sharer of your knowledge and gifts. You'll probably never know how many lives you affected with your pragmatic approach. Howard Roberts for all the lives you changed teaching guitar players real-world skills and shaping the most innovative guitar program that's ever existed. Bruce Buckingham for feeding me the right information at the right time. Eric Paschal for always finding the best in all your students. And Dan Gilbert for the energy you pumped into every class and the motivation to practice more than I've ever practiced.

For this project I was very fortunate to be surrounded by a team of amazing and intelligent musicians and specialty experts such as Ricky Peterson, Sean Nilson, Eliot Briggs, Bill Lafleur, Luke Elliott, Carter Elliott, John Krogh, Harry Chalmiers, Kevin Sullivan, Tony Axtell and the McNally Smith College of Music "guitar department in exile"—Tim Lyles, Paul Krueger, Chris Olson, Mike Salow, Dave Singley, and Eva Beneke—for test-driving this Fretboard Biology method for seven years.

None of this would have happened without the dedicated work of my business partner in the Fretboard Biology program, Todd Berntson, and his wife, Monique. There's a lot of skill and talent in that duo and it was only through Todd's insistence that this project was launched.

Lastly, I would like to thank all the great musicians and students I have had the pleasure to work with over the past 40 years.

TABLE OF CONTENTS

LEVEL 3 INTRODUCTION — 1

UNIT 1 — 3
- Theory - 7th chord formulas
- Fretboard Logic - Patterns I & III major 7 arpeggios, open major, minor, and dominant 7 chord shapes
- Technique - 1-2-3-4 sequence exercise
- Rhythm Guitar - Introduction to Reggae
- Money Makers - Money Maker licks in Pattern III major
- Improvisation - Chord-tone soloing
- Practice - Continue practice routine development

UNIT 2 — 33
- Theory - Harmonizing the major scale with 7th chords
- Fretboard Logic - Patterns I and III dominant 7 arpeggios, using open 7th chords in progressions
- Technique - 1-2-3-1 sequence exercise
- Rhythm Guitar - Reggae Rhythm Guitar
- Money Makers - Double-stop bends, double-stop hammer-ons
- Improvisation - Soloing with Dominant 7 arpeggios
- Practice - Continue practice routine development

UNIT 3 — 65
- Theory - Chord families with 7th chords in major keys, analyzing chord progressions with 7th chords
- Fretboard Logic - Patterns II and IV minor 7 arpeggios, Patterns II and IV major 7 barre chords
- Technique - 1-3-2-1 sequence exercise
- Rhythm Guitar - Reggae rhythm guitar
- Money Makers - Pattern III money makers over a progression in D
- Improvisation - Using Patterns IV and II minor 7 arpeggios over a progression in A minor
- Practice - Continue practice routine development

UNIT 4   95

- Theory - Analyzing chord progressions in major keys
- Fretboard Logic - Patterns II and IV minor and minor 7(♭5) arpeggios, Patterns II and IV major and dominant 7 barre chords
- Technique - 1-2-3 triplet sequence exercise
- Rhythm Guitar - Reggae rhythm guitar
- Money Makers - Pattern III money makers over a progression in A
- Improvisation - Using Patterns IV and II minor 7(♭5) arpeggios in a progression in D minor
- Practice - Continue practice routine development

UNIT 5   121

- Theory - Harmonizing the natural minor scale with 7th chords
- Fretboard Logic - Patterns II, IV, and V major 7th arpeggios, Patterns II and IV minor 7th barre chords
- Technique - Diatonic 3rds sequence exercise
- Rhythm Guitar - Reggae rhythm guitar
- Money Makers - Pattern III money makers over a progression in A
- Improvisation - Soloing with chord tones in F
- Practice - Continue practice routine development

UNIT 6   149

- Theory - Harmonic analysis in minor key progressions with 7th chords, chord families with 7th chords in minor keys
- Fretboard Logic - Patterns II, IV, and V dominant 7 arpeggios, Patterns IV and II minor 7(♭5) barre chords
- Technique - Diatonic 4ths sequence exercise
- Rhythm Guitar - Introduction to Country rhythm guitar
- Money Makers - Licks in Pattern IV minor pentatonic
- Improvisation - Soloing with chord tones in G minor
- Practice - Continue practice routine development

UNIT 7   179

- Theory - Analyzing minor chord progressions with 7th chords
- Fretboard Logic - Patterns I, III, and V minor 7 arpeggios, Patterns II and IV 7th chord shapes, using movable 7th chords in progressions
- Technique - Diatonic 5ths sequence exercise
- Rhythm Guitar - 3/4 time in Country rhythm guitar
- Money Makers - Pattern V minor pentatonic licks
- Improvisation - Chord tone soloing in D major
- Practice - Continue practice routine development

Fretboard Biology   *Level 3: Table of Contents*

UNIT 8 — 203

- Theory - Introduction to Blues harmony
- Fretboard Logic - Patterns I, III, and V minor 7(♭5) arpeggios, progressions using movable 7th chord shapes
- Technique - Diatonic 6ths sequence exercise
- Rhythm Guitar - Basic embellishments
- Money Makers - Pattern I minor pentatonic licks
- Improvisation - Chord tone soloing in D minor
- Practice - Continue practice routine development

UNIT 9 — 225

- Theory - Constructing the Blues Scale
- Fretboard Logic - Pattern I major in-position arpeggios, Patterns I, III, and V dominant 7 chords
- Technique - Diatonic 7ths sequence exercise
- Rhythm Guitar - Imitating steel guitar
- Money Makers - Pattern II minor pentatonic licks
- Improvisation - Using Pattern I in-position arpeggios in F major
- Practice - Continue practice routine development

UNIT 10 — 249

- Theory - Level 3 Summary
- Fretboard Logic - Pattern II minor in-position arpeggios, Patterns I, III, and V minor 7(♭5) chords
- Technique - Technique summary
- Rhythm Guitar - Country rhythm guitar
- Money Makers - Pattern III minor pentatonic licks
- Improvisation - Using Pattern II in-position arpeggios in E minor
- Practice - Continue practice routine development

APPENDICES — 271

- Appendix 1 - Theory exercise answer keys
- Appendix 2 - Octave Shape Family Trees
- Appendix 3 - Chord chart
- Appendix 4 - In-Position Arpeggios

LEVEL 3 INTRODUCTION

Fretboard Biology Level 3 builds on the Levels 1 and 2 material. If you haven't completed those Levels, go back and at the very least make sure you are confident in all the material. In Level 3 you will continue the study of Theory, Fretboard Logic, Technique, Rhythm Guitar, Improvisation, and practice techniques.

What's in Level 3

- In the Theory Modules you will learn about recognizing and building 7th chords. Next, you will learn to harmonize the major and natural minor scales with 7th chords. With your knowledge of the harmonized scales, you will learn harmonic analysis in progression with 7th chords. You will also learn about Blues harmony and melody.
- In the Fretboard Logic Modules you will learn major 7, dominant 7, minor 7 and minor 7(♭5) arpeggios and how they fit into the "Family Tree" of the fretboard. The Family Tree keeps all the Fretboard Logic information organized. In addition, you will learn to organize arpeggios "in position", so they are readily accessible to you in any key.
- You will learn five Patterns each of movable major 7, dominant 7, minor 7 and minor 7(♭5) chords and how they fit within the family tree.
- In the Technique Modules you will learn a variety of chops-building scale and interval sequences.
- In the Improvisation Modules you will learn how to solo in various progressions that use 7th chords while, as always, striving for good story telling through motif development and the use of the elements of contrast.
- In the Rhythm Guitar Modules you will study two styles: Reggae and Country.
- There is a new sequence of Modules called "Money Makers" in Level 3. This series focuses on must-know "low-hanging fruit" guitar vocabulary.
- As always, there is continued guidance on building effective practice routines.

This is a progressive course. Each Module in each Level builds on the information from the previous one. You'll get the most out of the program by staying with the sequence.

Let's get started.

UNIT 1

Learning Modules

> **Theory** - 7th Chord Formulas

> **Fretboard Logic** - Patterns I & III Major 7 Arpeggios, Open Major, Minor, and Dominant 7 Chord Shapes

> **Technique** - 1-2-3-4 Sequence Exercise

> **Rhythm Guitar** - Introduction to Reggae

> **Money Makers** - Money Maker Licks in Pattern III Major

> **Improvisation** - Chord-Tone Soloing

> **Practice** - Continue Practice Routine Development

THEORY

Introduction to 7th Chords

In this Unit you will learn how to build 7th chords using the same process used when building triads. If you remember from Level 2, to build a triad, you placed a note a 3rd above the root and a 5th above the root. The process is the same when building 7th chords, but in addition to a 3rd and 5th, there is also a 7th placed above the root.

Triads and 7th Chords

The 7th chord is made up of three notes above the root: All 7th chords contain a root, a 3rd, a 5th, and a 7th. There are four 7th chord types found in diatonic, major, and natural minor harmony, and the familiar term, "quality", is used to identify them.

The four qualities are: major 7, dominant 7, minor 7, and minor 7(♭5). There are other 7th chord types that will be introduced later.

Qualities of 7th Chords

Major 7   *Dominant 7*   *Minor 7*   *Minor 7(♭5)*

You will notice terms in Theory that have different meanings in different contexts:

- A major 7 is an interval but the term "major 7" is also used to name a 7th chord quality.
- A minor 7 is an interval but the term "minor 7" is also used to name a 7th chord quality.

7th Chord Formulas

Here are the interval formulas for the first four 7th chord types:

Major 7

The major 7 chord contains a ma3, P5, and ma7

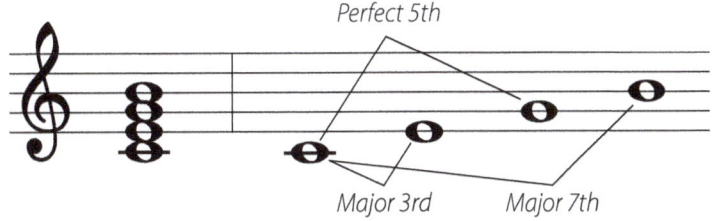

Dominant 7

The dominant 7 chord contains a ma3, P5, and mi7

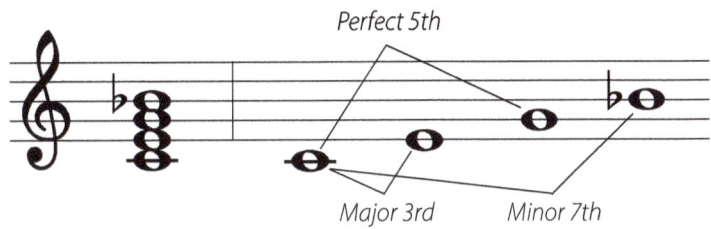

Minor 7

The minor 7 chord contains a mi3, P5, and mi7

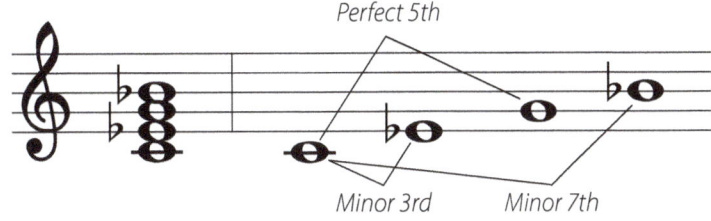

Minor 7(♭5)

The minor 7(♭5) chord contains a mi3, D5, and mi7

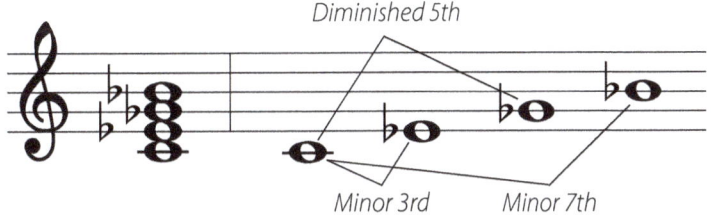

Here is another way to think about 7th chords:

- The major 7 chord is a major triad with a ma7
- The dominant 7 chord is a major triad with a mi7
- The minor 7 chord is a minor triad with a mi7
- The minor 7(♭5) chord is a diminished triad with a mi7

Qualities of 7th Chords

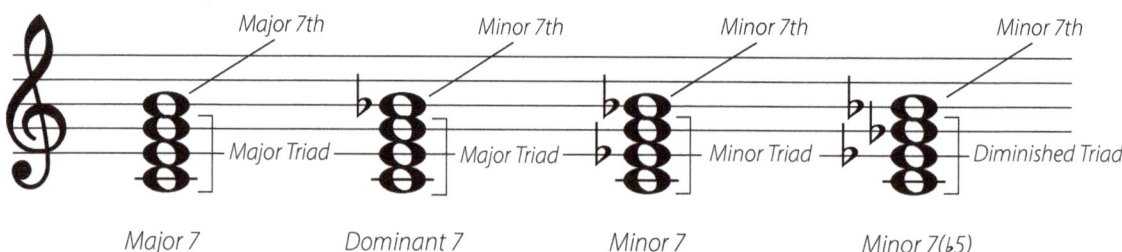

Remember that with key signatures, intervals, and triads you need to know the information from two different perspectives. When you see key signatures, intervals, and triads on the page, you need to recognize what they are and be able to name them properly. You also need to know them the opposite way: you need to be able to write them on the staff.

It is the same for 7th chords. You need to know them from two perspectives: First, when you see a 7th chord written on the staff, you need to be able to identify and label it properly. This is called "analyzing the 7th chord". Second, when you are writing music, you need to be able to build and write the 7th chord on the staff.

Analyzing 7th Chords

To analyze and label an existing 7th chord, determine the qualities of the 3rd, 5th, and 7th. Then compare the intervals with the four quality formulas.

Here are a few examples:

The dominant 7 chord has a major 3rd, perfect 5th and minor 7th.

The minor 7 chord has a minor 3rd, perfect 5th and minor 7th.

Building 7th Chords

To build a 7th chord, follow the interval formula for the desired chord quality and build the appropriate quality 3rd, 5th, and 7th intervals above the root.

Here are a few examples:

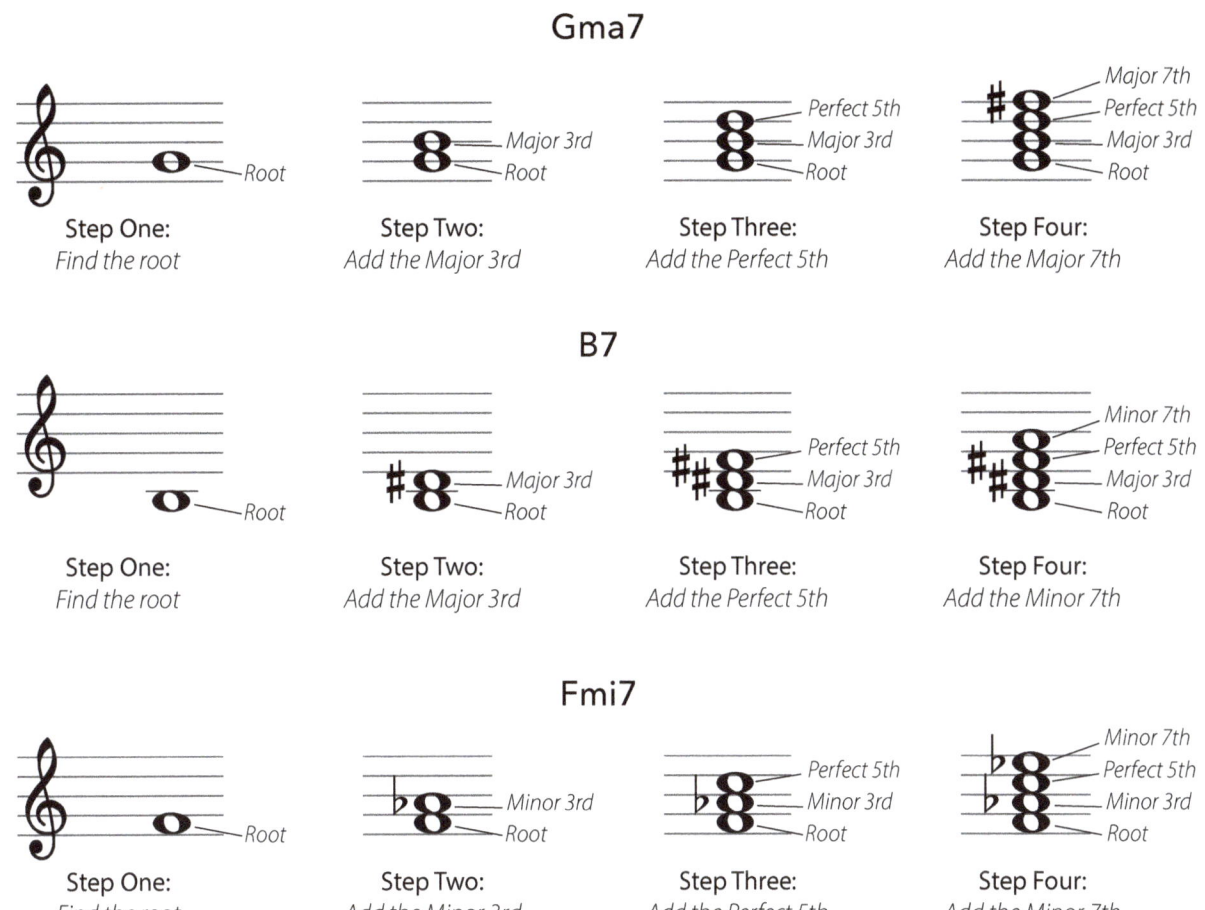

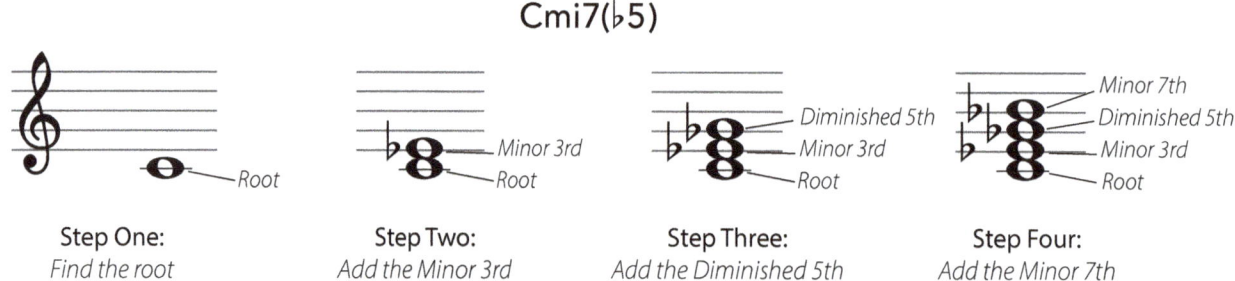

Labeling 7th Chords

It is important to label 7th chords clearly. To start, review how triads are labeled:

- The major triad is labeled with just the letter – no need to write ma or maj or major – just use the letter of the root, as in "C".
- The minor triad is labeled with the letter of the root plus mi – don't write min or minor – just "Cmi".
- The augmented triad is labeled with a + sign – don't write "aug" or "augmented" – just "C+".
- The diminished triad is labeled with a "°" – don't write dim or diminished – just "C°".

There are other ways to label triads but the way they are shown here is universally understood and will always work.

Major 7 Chords

Major 7 chords are best labeled with the letter name (like "C") followed by "ma7" (i.e., Cma7). Writing out the word "major" or "maj" is unnecessary. Using a triangle or upper case M can be misleading. Different regions of the country and world interpret the triangle or a single upper case "M" differently. Some notation software uses a capital "M". When writing by hand, this can be misinterpreted because of the variations in different handwriting styles ,and as a result the wrong chord could be played. So when writing by hand, use "ma7".

Dominant 7 Chords

Dominant 7th chords are best labeled with the letter name (like "C") followed by "7" (i.e., C7). Writing out the word "dominant" or "dom" is unnecessary. Using a triangle or other symbols can be misleading. Some notation software uses "dom", but when writing by hand just use "7". It is universally understood.

Minor 7 Chords

Minor 7th chords are best labeled with the letter name (like "C") followed by "mi7" (i.e., Cmi7). Writing out the word "minor" or "min" is unnecessary. Some notation software uses a lower case "m", but when writing by hand use "mi7". Use of an upper case "M" or lower case "m" is unclear and could confuse the reader. Using a dash as in " C-7 "is also common and universally accepted as an efficient and clear way to notate C minor 7th.

Minor 7(♭5) Chords

Minor 7(♭5) chords are best labeled with the letter name (like "C") followed by "mi7(♭5)" (i.e., Cmi7(♭5)). Writing out the word "minor" or "min" is unnecessary. Often a diagonal "slash" across the diminished circle is used 'ø', and this is acceptable. The min7(♭5) chord is often referred to as "half diminished".

FRETBOARD LOGIC

In the Level 3 Fretboard Logic Modules you will learn 7th arpeggios. This is important knowledge for integrating chord tones into your solos. Chord tone soloing is the next big topic in the Improvisation Modules. Later in this Level you will learn how to organize arpeggios "in position" as a part of the Octave Shape system. This will help you access chord tones more efficiently when soloing. The benefits of organizing arpeggios in position will be obvious and is a crucial step to maturing as a soloist. Also in Level 3 you will learn open and movable 7th chord shapes.

Arpeggios

The 7th chord arpeggio is built by adding a 7th to a triad arpeggio. In the same way that pentatonic shells are used to build other scales, 7th arpeggios are built using triad arpeggios as a foundation. In this Module you will learn the Patterns I and III major 7 arpeggios.

Let's start with a Pattern I major triad arpeggio. Next, add a major 7th everywhere possible within the octave shape to build a Pattern I major 7 arpeggio.

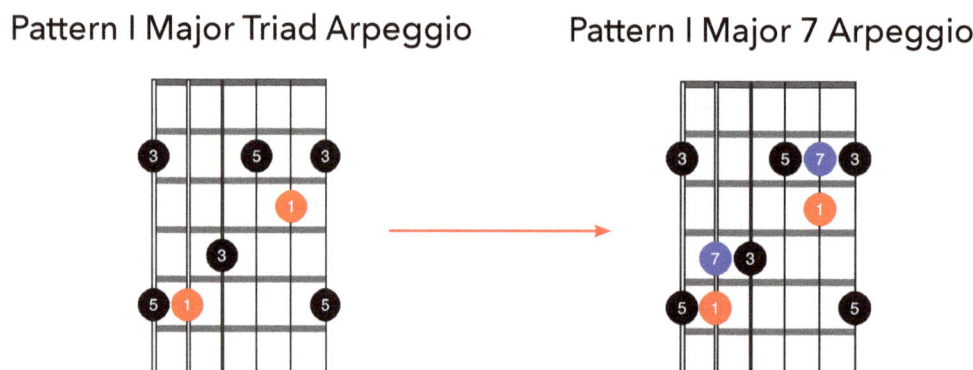

Practice this Pattern I major 7 arpeggio with alternate picking starting and ending on the lowest root in the Pattern.

Next, let's look at the Pattern III major triad arpeggio. Like in the previous example, add a major 7th everywhere possible within the octave shape to build a Pattern III major 7 arpeggio.

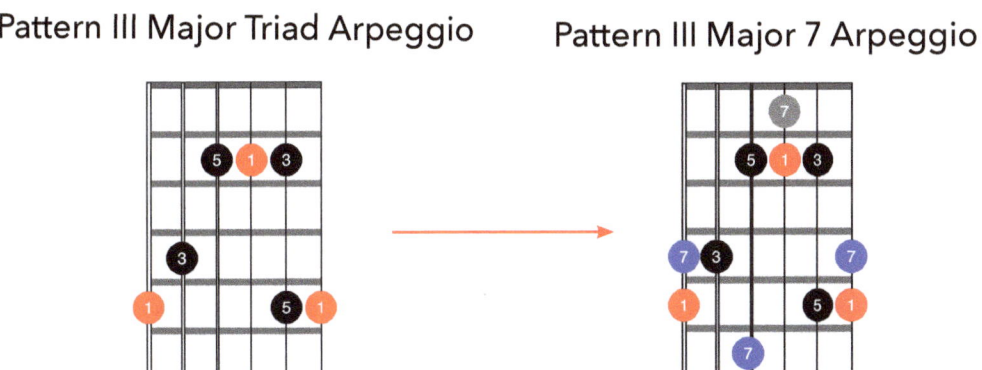

Pattern III Major Triad Arpeggio → Pattern III Major 7 Arpeggio

Again, practice this Pattern III major 7 arpeggio with alternate picking starting and ending on the root.

Chords

The Fretboard Logic Modules follow a basic theme: start with a simple structure from which more complex structures can be built. Many scales are built from pentatonic shells. Many arpeggios are built from triad shapes and the same is true with chords. In Level 1 you learned the common open-string triad chord voicings. In this Unit you will use them to build open-string 7th chord voicings.

Open A Major 7 and Dominant 7 Chords

The first chord is an open A voicing with the chord tones labeled. Replace the root on the 3rd string with a major 7th to create an open Ama7 chord as shown in the center. Replace the root on the 3rd string with a minor 7th to create an open A7 chord as shown on the right.

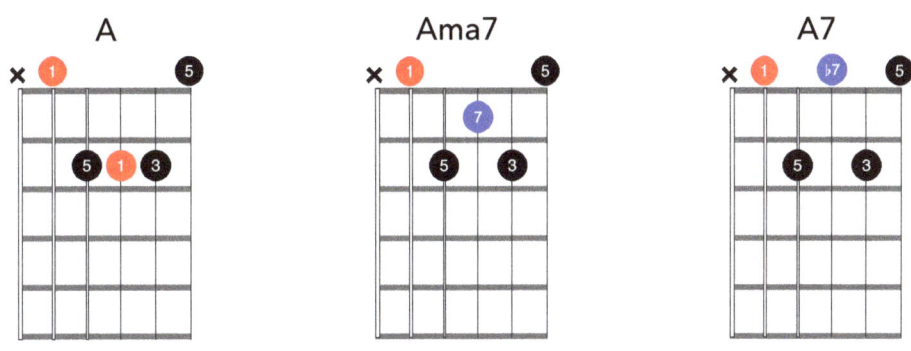

Open C Major 7 and Dominant 7 Chords

The first chord is an open C voicing with the chord tones labeled. Replace the root on the 2nd string with a major 7th to create an open Cma7 chord. Replace the 5th on the 3rd string with a minor 7th to create an open C7 chord.

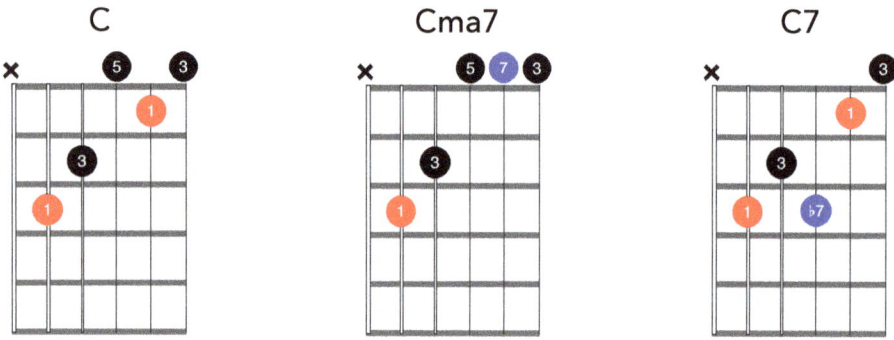

Open D Major 7 and Dominant 7 Chords

The first chord is an open D voicing with the chord tones labeled. Replace the root on the 2nd string with a major 7th to play an open Dma7 chord. Replace the root on the 2nd string with a minor 7th to create an open D7 chord.

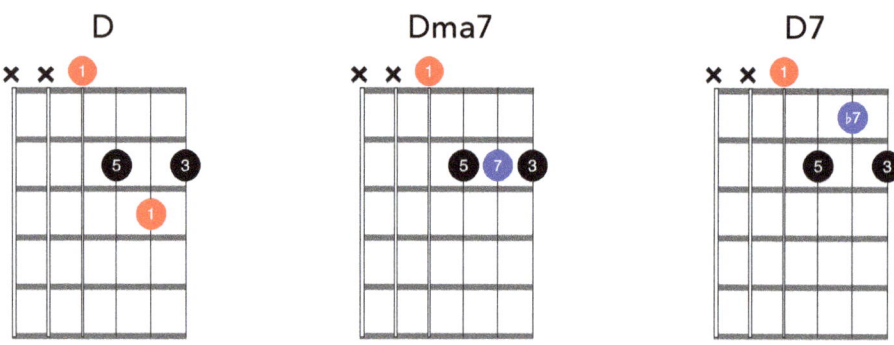

Open E Major 7 and Dominant 7 Chords

The first chord is an open E voicing with the chord tones labeled. Replace the root on the 4th string with a major 7th to create an open Ema7 chord. Replace the root on the 5th string with a minor 7th to create an open E7 chord. You can also play a minor 7th on the 2nd string at the 3rd fret. It is OK to play one or the other or both.

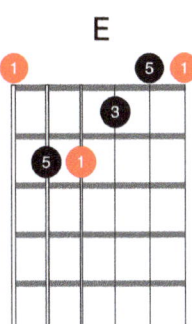
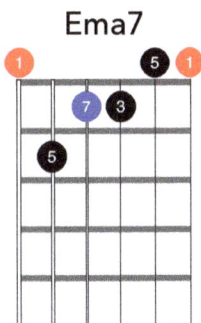
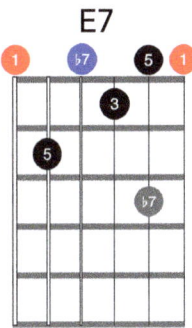

Open F Major 7 and Dominant 7 Chords

The first chord is an open F voicing with the chord tones labeled. Replace the root on the 1st string with a major 7th to create an open Fma7 chord. Replace the 5th on the 2nd string with a minor 7th to create an open F7 chord.

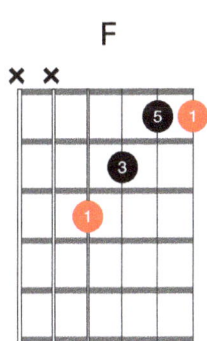
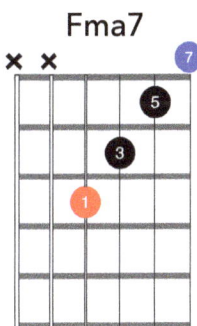
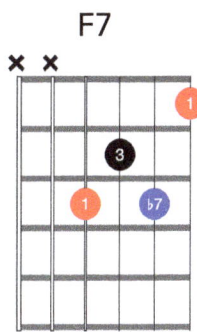

Open G Major 7 and Dominant 7 Chords

The first chord is an open G voicing with the chord tones labeled. Replace the root on the 1st string with a major 7th to play an open Gma7 chord. The 5th string is often muted with the fleshy part of the 2nd finger. Replace the root on the 1st string with a minor 7th to create an open G7 chord.

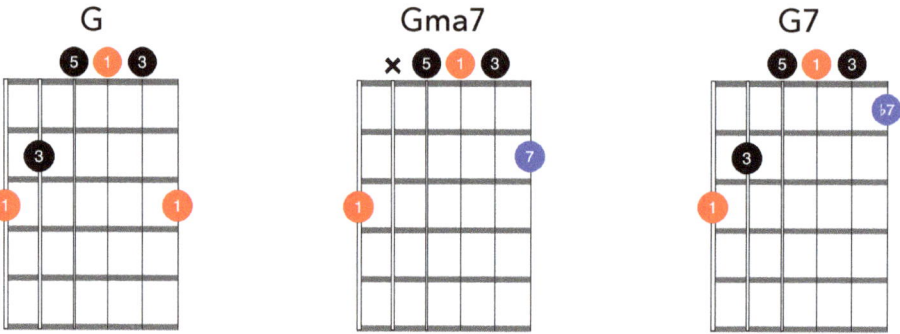

Open A Minor 7 Chords

The first chord is an open Ami voicing with the chord tones labeled. Replace the root on the 3rd string with a minor 7th to create an open Ami7 chord.

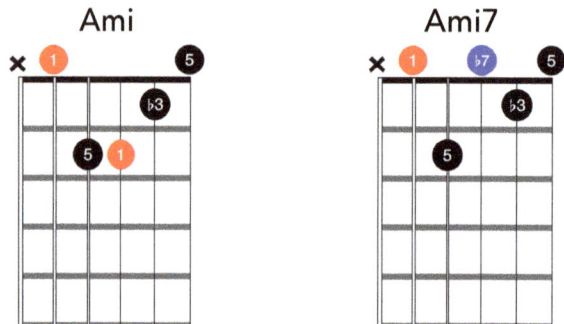

Open D Minor 7 Chords

The first chord is an open Dmi voicing with the chord tones labeled. Replace the root on the 2nd string with a minor 7th to create an open Dmi7 chord.

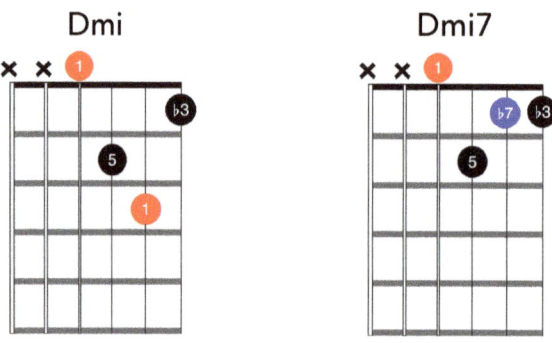

Open E Minor 7 Chords

The first chord is an open Emi voicing with the chord tones labeled. Replace the root on the 4th string with a minor 7th to create an open Emi7 chord. You can also play a minor 7th on the 2nd string at the 3rd fret. It is okay to play one or the other or both.

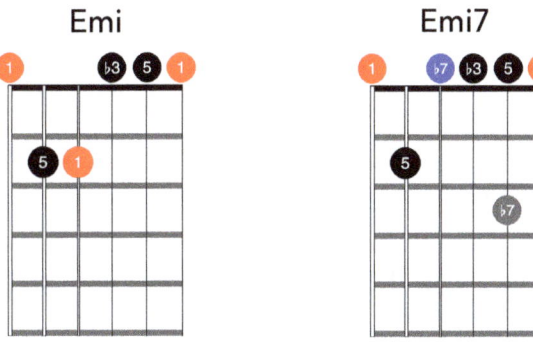

Open B7 Chord

Notice there aren't open string voicings for some chords – like chords with a B root or any chord whose root has a flat or sharp. They just aren't practical to play. But there is, oddly enough, a convenient and usable open string voicing for B7. Here it is:

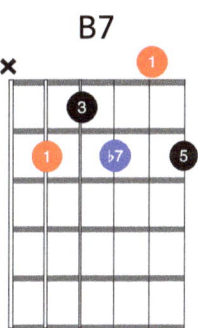

Although it is important to learn and memorize these open 7th voicings, it is more important to understand the logic of how each of them are built. Remember these basic guidelines:

- In a major 7 voicing, one of the roots in a major chord is replaced by a major 7th.
- In a dominant 7 voicing, one of the roots in a major chord is replaced by a minor 7th (or ♭7th).
- In a minor 7 voicing, one of the roots in a minor chord is replaced by a minor 7th (sometimes called ♭7th).

Be sure you understand the concept behind the construction of these three 7th chords. In the next Module, we will look at how these 7th chord voicings are used in progressions.

TECHNIQUE

Athletes spend a lot of time in the gym doing exercises to build their strength and agility even though the exercises aren't directly related to what they do in their sport. For example, no professional athlete actually does bench presses out on the field or court, but exercises like the bench press improve performance because they help make the athlete stronger and more flexible.

There is a parallel for musicians. After all, musicians are doing athletic things with their hands and fingers, so it only makes sense to work at the physical part of playing the instrument by doing exercises. These exercises, like bench presses, are not what you actually play when performing. But they will help improve your performance by increasing your accuracy, timing, speed, and endurance.

Sequence Exercises

In the Technique Modules of Level 3 you will learn a series of dexterity exercises to improve your picking and fretting hand coordination. The first exercise you will learn is a simple scale sequence. This exercise can be done with almost any scale in any pattern, but first, use the pattern IV major scale in the key of A. This is the easiest place to see and learn this sequence.

Pattern IV Major Scale

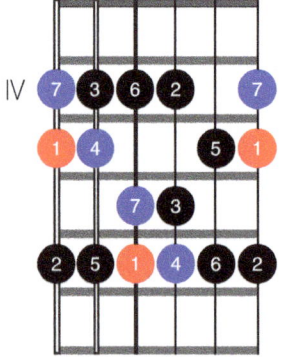

1-2-3-4 Sequence

This four-note exercise is called the "1-2-3-4 sequence". Learn it with an 8th-note subdivision. Play four notes in a row ascending starting on the tonic. Then play four notes in a row ascending starting on the 2nd scale degree. Next play four notes in a row ascending starting on the 3rd scale degree, and keep repeating this sequence up to the highest notes you can play in the scale pattern. Note that the numbers under each note identifies the scale degree.

Ascending, this sequence looks like this:

1-2-3-4 Sequence Exercise - Ascending

Descending, this sequence looks like this:

1-2-3-4 Sequence Exercise - Descending

Budget a few minutes to this each day. Practice this exercise very slowly and be consistent with alternate picking. When you feel like you're ready, set your metronome at slow tempo – perhaps 50 to 60 bpm – and play 8th notes. As it becomes easier, gradually increase the tempo. When you feel you're in control of the exercise, pick another major scale pattern and work it out there the same way, eventually in all five major scale patterns.

RHYTHM GUITAR

Reggae

The next series of five Modules will explore the style and typical rhythm guitar parts of the Reggae genre. The name Reggae was first used in Jamaica in the 60s and 70s. It is derived from a blend of the Ska and Rocksteady styles. While Ska, Rocksteady, and Reggae all share a common feature – playing the rhythm guitar parts on the upbeats rather than the downbeats – the biggest difference is the tempo. Ska is typically played at 90-132 beats per minute, Rocksteady is typically played around 80-100 beats per minute, and Reggae is usually played slower in the 60-80 beat per minute range.

Ska

The term "Ska" can mean the actual rhythm figure the guitar plays (the upbeats instead of playing on the beat), or it can also mean a style of dance or the style of Jamaican music that came before Reggae.

Reggae grooves are based on either straight or swinging 16th notes. There is no consensus about whether Reggae should be counted in half-time or in double-time. For consistency's sake, we will count in half-time throughout the Reggae Modules. As in any style, the guitar parts in Reggae interact with other instruments to create the overall matrix of the groove, so it is important to understand the roles of the drums, percussion, bass, and keyboards. Examine each of the instruments, starting with the drums.

Drums

The most common drum pattern is called the One Drop beat. The kick drum plays on beats two and four and there is no strong accent on beat one. There are a variety of high-hat and cross-stick patterns that fill out the core of the feel. Again, the subdivision is usually either straight or swung 16th notes. Other percussion instruments can add to the core groove in a variety of ways.

The other common bass drum pattern is the Stepper beat (or Steppers) which is also called a Straight-Four beat. This is where the bass drums plays four quarter notes per measure on the beat.

Bass

Reggae bass lines usually include the root at some point during the duration of a chord but not always on the first attack. Often the chord is outlined either fully or just partially using an arpeggio.

Organ

Organ is a common sound in Reggae and often plays what is called "the bubble". The bubble is a rhythm combining syncopated left hand patterns with off beats on the right hand. This interacts with the guitar, bass, and drum parts to create the complete groove. With the bubble, the right hand plays the off beats – the second 8th note of each beat – and the left hand plays the 16th note before and after. In order, it goes like this: the first 16th of a beat is a rest, the second 16th is the left hand, the third 16th (the "and") is the right hand, and the fourth 16th note is the left hand again.

Organ Bubble Hand Movement

Guitar

In Reggae, Ska, or Rocksteady, the defining guitar part is played on electric guitar with a clean tone. Generally, the guitar plays a full pattern II or IV barre chord or just their upper three or four strings. The attacks are on each 8th-note upbeat as opposed to playing on the beat.

In Reggae, the guitar parts are very repetitive and meant to be percussive. The parts are not complicated but finding the feel right is critical and comes from a lot of listening and playing with other musicians. While the term Ska refers to a style of Jamaican music, it also refers to actual rhythm pattern the guitar plays that is called the chop. Chop and Ska are synonymous in this case.

Progression in B Minor

Here is a two-bar progression in B minor with a straight-16th groove. This graphic shows the part called the Ska which is often doubled by piano and the right hand in the bubble played on the organ. Play the second 8th note of each beat – that's the "and" – with a downstroke.

Chop Part

Don't use open string voicings. It is best to use barre chords so you can control their duration by muting. You can mute by using partial pressure with your fretting hand and then releasing quickly to get a crisp "chop" sound; thus the descriptive term "chop". I suggest you experiment with different degrees of pressure in your fretting hand, from full pressure to full mute. With full mute, you have just enough contact with the strings so they don't ring.

Play this with the straight-16th groove backing track. I recommend you use the top four strings of a pattern IV Bmi barre chord and the top four strings of a pattern IV A major barre chord. Find a bright tone on your guitar; bright enough to cut but not be painful to the listener. Adjust your volume to be in the middle or slightly below the mix. The part will cut so you don't have to be too loud.

Here is a slight variation to this pattern you should know. Adding to what you just played, place another attack on the 16th note that immediately follows the chop using an upstroke, which is the fourth 16th note of the beat. Try to catch just the higher strings with the upstroke.

Chop Part (variation)

Here is another important variation. Adding to what you just played, place another attack on the second 16th note of the beat with an upstroke. Make a downstroke motion on the beat, missing the strings, and then catch the strings on the second 16th note with an upstroke. Then play the "and" – the third 16th note – with a downstroke, and then the fourth 16th note with an upstroke. This is called the "mento rhythm".

Mento Rhythm

Again, experiment with the pressure you apply with your fretting hand.

MONEY MAKERS

In the Fretboard Biology program, Money Makers are short licks, fills, and musical ideas that every guitar player should know. Think of Money Makers as need-to-know vocabulary. The ideas you will learn in the Money Maker Modules relate to soloing and improvisation, so perhaps you can think of this as an extra series of Improvisation Modules. Consider the information in these Modules as essential for the working guitarist. The ideas you learn can be learned quickly and immediately added to your vocabulary.

Before we get started, let's take a look at a term that will be used throughout the Money Maker modules in this unit: Double Stop.

Double Stop

A Double Stop - two notes played at the same time.

Pattern III Major Money Makers

To begin, review the Pattern III major pentatonic shell, which is the home of many "major sounding" Money Makers. You already know you can build on the pentatonic shell to create a major scale, so in addition, over the next few Modules, we'll explore many of the common licks that live inside the Pattern III Octave Shape.

Pattern III C Major Pentatonic Scale

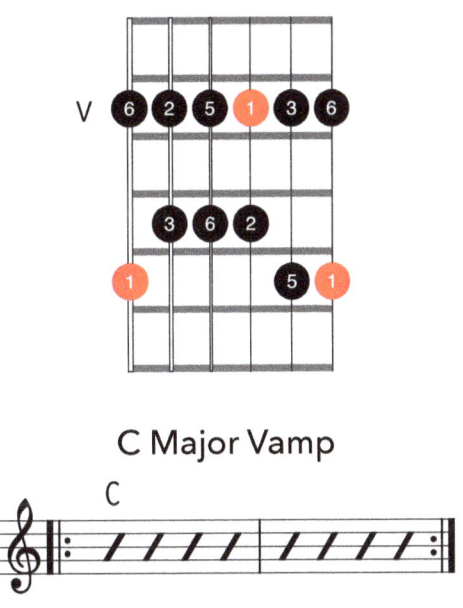

C Major Vamp

These examples will be shown in the key of C major, demonstrated on a static C major chord and played in the vicinity of the Pattern III pentatonic shell in 5th position.

Double Stops: Strings 3 and 2

This part uses some of the 3rd shapes from the major scale as double stops on the 3rd and 2nd strings.

1. With your 1st finger, play a double stop at the 5th fret, C on the 3rd string, and E on the 2nd string. That is a major 3rd shape. You remember when we talked about interval shapes and how important they are. It's time to use that knowledge.

2. Next, play D on the 3rd string 7th fret with your 3rd finger as well as F on the 2nd string at the 6th fret. That is a minor 3rd shape.

3. Next, move that shape up a whole step. Play E on the 3rd string 9th fret with your 3rd finger as well as G on the 2nd string at the 8th fret. That also a minor 3rd shape.

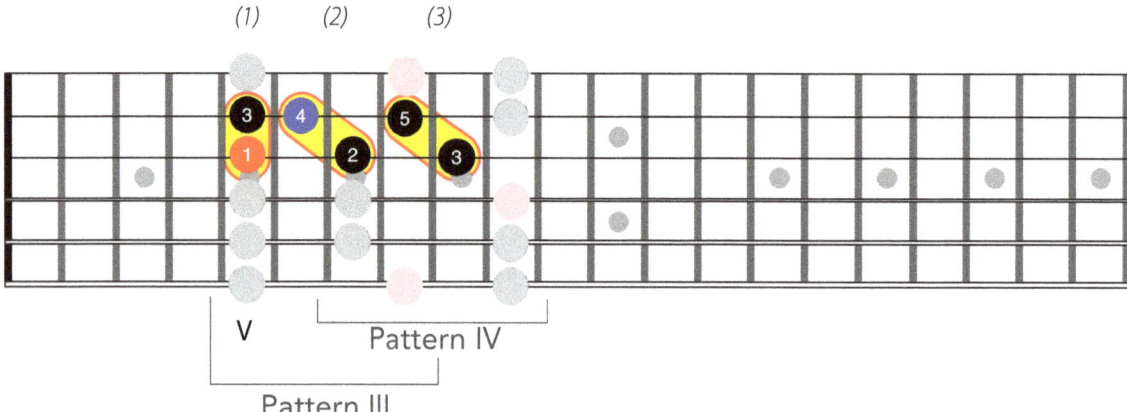

Move through these shapes in order, ascending and descending. You can make a lot of music with this simple idea moving it up and down over a C chord. You can pick every note, hammer-on and slide, or reverse slide and pull-off.

The C and E at the 5th fret are the root and 3rd of the C chord. The E and G are the 3rd and 5th of the C chord. So you are actually playing chord tones. You use the D and F double stop to connect the two.

Double Stops: Strings 4 and 3

Here are more ideas within the Pattern III Octave Shape.

1. With your 1st finger play a double stop at the 5th fret, this time G on the 4th string and C on the 3rd string. That is a perfect 4th shape.

2. Immediately hammer-on the 4th string at the 7th fret with your 3rd finger playing A, and play C on the 3rd string, too. That is a minor 3rd shape.

3. Repeat the perfect 4th shape: G on the 4th string and C on the 3rd string.

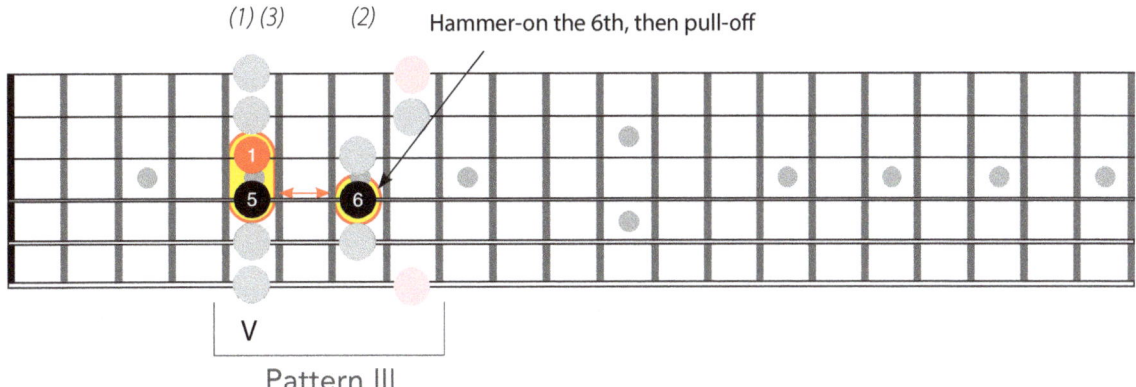

Pattern III

4. To complete this idea, add one more part. With your 1st finger play another double stop at the 5th fret, this time D on the 5th string and G on the 4th string. That is a perfect 4th shape.

5. But immediately hammer-on the 5th string at the 7th fret with your 3rd finger playing E, and play G, too. That is a minor 3rd shape.

6. Then repeat the perfect 4th shape with D on the 5th string and G on the 4th string.

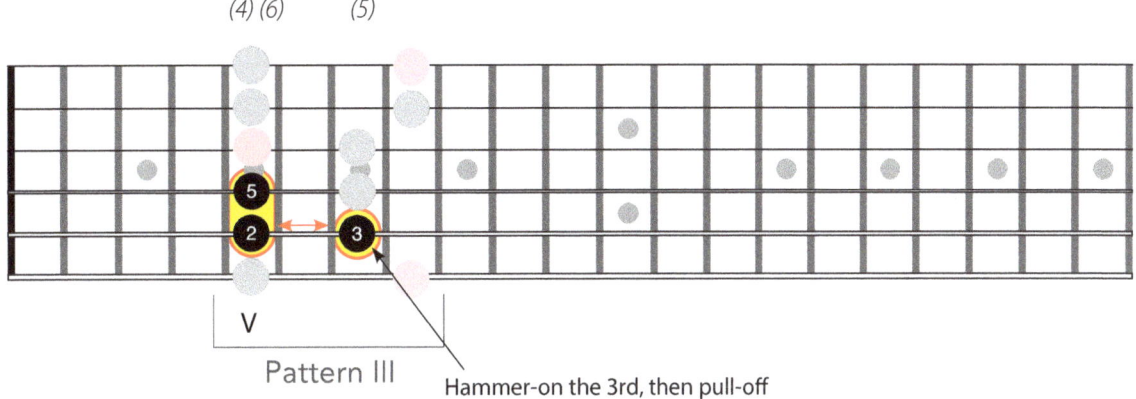

Pattern III

7. Lastly, finish the passage on the tonic, C. There are two choices for this. You can drop your 4th finger on C at the 8th fret of the 6th string, or slide out of position with your 1st finger and play C at the 3rd fret of the 5th string.

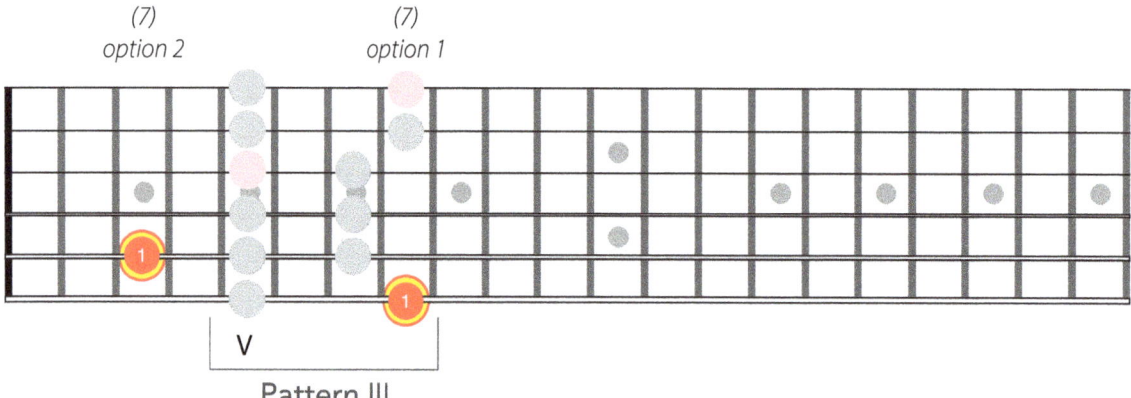

If you use the second option and play the low C on the 5th string, the 5th is available to you again on the 6th string at the 3rd fret. Then you can hammer-on the 6th at the 5th fret of the 6th string and repeat the root C on the 5th string.

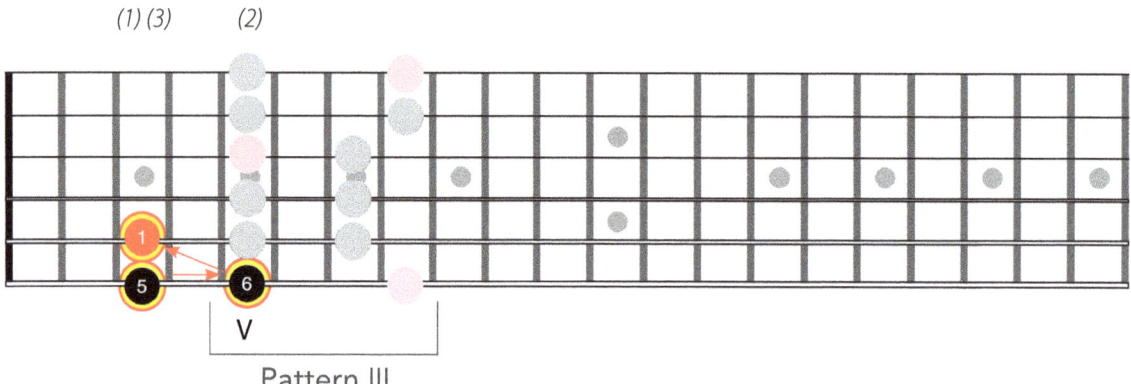

All of the Notes Used in This Example

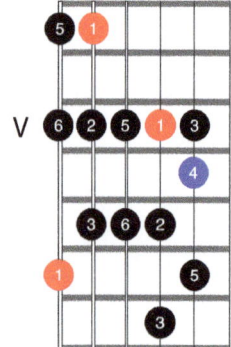

Fretboard Biology — Level 3 • Unit 1: Money Makers

This is a lot of fun and I hope you make a lot of music with this. There is a lot you can do with these short ideas and they can be used in so many styles. These ideas work well in Blues, Country, Classic Rock, Folk, Gospel, and even Jazz.

Pattern III Money Makers in D

Play some of these ideas with a different track in a different key. This also uses the pattern III shape but this example is in the key of D and instead of a static chord, this example has chord changes.

Pattern III D Major Pentatonic Scale

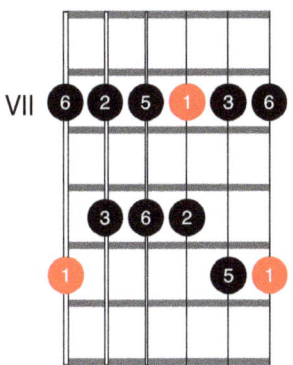

Progression in D Major

There are two examples of how you can include these money makers with a progression on the following pages.

Level 3 Unit 1 • Money Maker Demo 1

Level 3 Unit 1 • Money Maker Demo 2

IMPROVISATION

At the end of Level 2 you learned about using arpeggios to integrate chord tones into your solos. Throughout Level 3 you will be working on this subject using a couple of 7th chord arpeggios. At the end of the Level, you will learn an organizational system to advance your skills using chord tones to new heights.

Chord-Tone Soloing

The concept of chord-tone soloing is actually pretty simple. It is the idea that melodic lines should reflect the chord changes over which the solo is played. The musical device used to play chord tones is the arpeggio. Throughout the Fretboard Logic Modules in Level 3, you will learn all of the 7th chord arpeggios and immediately put them to work in the Improvisation Modules.

You just learned the Patterns I and III major 7 arpeggios in Fretboard Logic. You will use them here.

Pattern III Cma7 Arpeggio

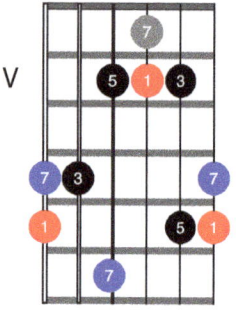

Pattern I Fma7 Arpeggio

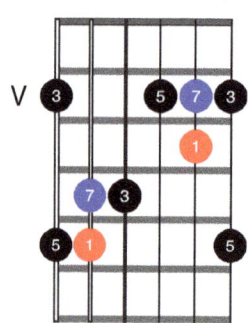

Here's a simple two-chord progression: Cma7 to Fma7. It is in the key of C.

Progression in C Major

If you were to play a key-center solo over this, you would just pick notes to play from the C scale. That might be less than satisfying to the listener and you because it's a little vague. I suggest you play a key-center solo over the track first.

Progression in C Major

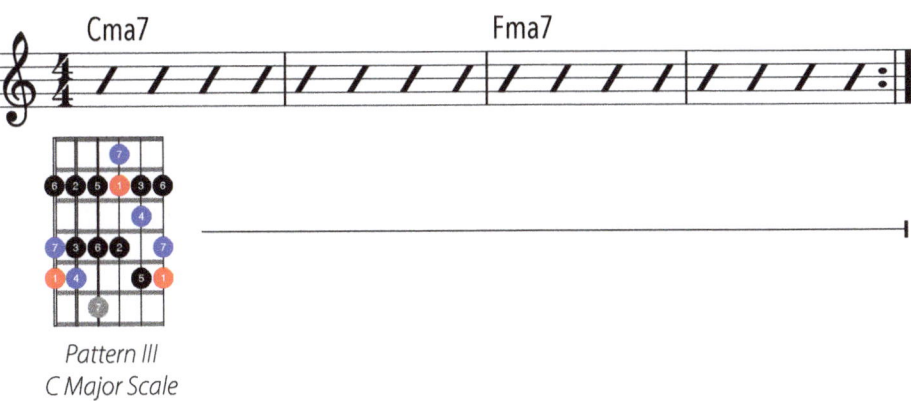

Now use the chord-tone approach. Over the Cma7, use the Pattern III Cma7 arpeggio. It fits perfectly because it contains the same notes as the chord. Next, on the Fma7, play the Pattern I Fma7 arpeggio. This fits perfectly, too, because it contains the same notes as the chord.

Progression in C Major

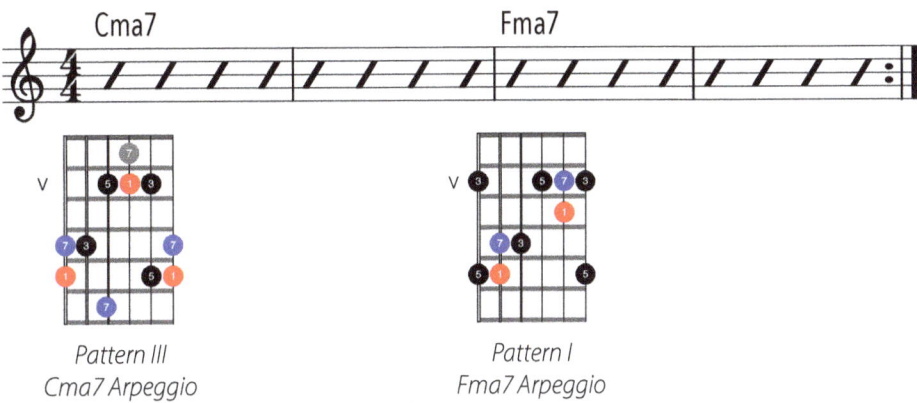

Chord-tone soloing does not mean that you play chord tones only. That is not the point. The goal is to incorporate chord tones in your melodic lines. Think of the arpeggios as a frame on which you build your lines. Chord tones can be connected with scale tones and chromatic tones. Sometimes improvisers will approach chord tones from a half step below or above.

As you begin working with chord tones, it is smart to play only the arpeggios over the chords as an exercise so you have a clear understanding of where they are on the fretboard. Think of them as notes you want to target – they are sometimes called "target notes". Devoting time to using chord tones only is an effective way to learn. Take another segment of your practice and create short motifs that blend chord tones and scale tones.

Take your time learning this. It is a whole different way to think about soloing – very different than just wandering through the scale. Throughout this Level you will gradually lead to using arpeggios "in position".

Level 3 Unit 1 • Improv Demo

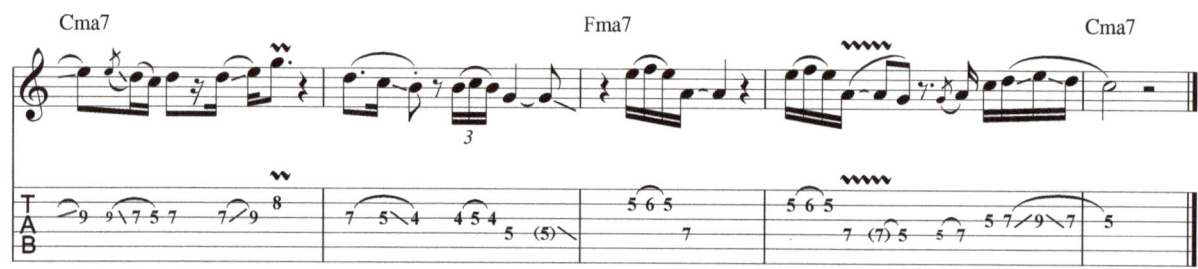

©2020 Fretboard Biology • fretboardbiology.com

PRACTICE

Theory

- ❏ Go to the tabs below the Theory video on the website and complete the quiz.
- ❏ Spend time memorizing the 7th chord formulas, as well as analyzing and building 7th chords.

Fretboard Logic

- ❏ Learn the pattern I and Pattern III major 7 arpeggios.
- ❏ Learn the chord voicings for the major 7, minor 7, and dominant 7 open chords.

Technique

- ❏ Practice playing the 1-2-3-4 sequence in the Pattern IV A major scale in fourth position.

Rhythm Guitar

- ❏ Learn the basics of Reggae rhythm and the role the rhythm guitar plays.

Money Makers

- ❏ Practice the Pattern III money maker licks using the tracks in the keys of C and D.

Improvisation

- ❏ Focus on chord-tone soloing using the Pattern III Cma7 and Pattern I Fma7 arpeggios over the progression provided.

UNIT 2

Learning Modules

> **Theory** - Harmonizing the Major Scale with 7th Chords
> **Fretboard Logic** - Patterns I and III Dominant 7 Arpeggios, Using Open 7th Chords in Progressions
> **Technique** - 1-2-3-1 Sequence Exercise
> **Rhythm Guitar** - Reggae Rhythm Guitar
> **Money Makers** - Double-Stop Bends, Double-Stop Hammer-Ons
> **Improvisation** - Soloing with Dominant 7 Arpeggios
> **Practice** - Continue Practice Routine Development

THEORY

In Level 2 you learned to harmonize the major and natural minor scales with triads. In the last Theory Module you learned how to build four types of 7th chords: major 7, dominant 7, minor 7 and minor 7(♭5). It is also essential to know how to harmonize the major and natural minor scales with 7th chords. In this Unit you will learn how 7th chords function together within major diatonic harmony. This understanding provides the knowledge required to arrange and create solid chord parts, solo, and improvise.

Harmonizing the Major Scale with 7th Chords

Recall from Level 2 that harmonizing a scale means to build chords on each scale degree. With 7th chords, like with triads, a chord built on the 1st scale degree is called the I chord. A chord built on the 2nd scale degree is called the II chord, and so on through the VII chord.

To harmonize a seven-note scale with 7th chords, start on the 1st scale degree and find the diatonic notes from the scale a 3rd, a 5th, and a 7th higher. These four notes create a 7th chord. Its quality is determined by the qualities of the 3rd, 5th, and 7th. When this process is repeated on the 2nd through 7th scale degrees, the result is the "harmonized scale".

Here is the C major scale with the scale degrees numbered one through seven plus the octave.

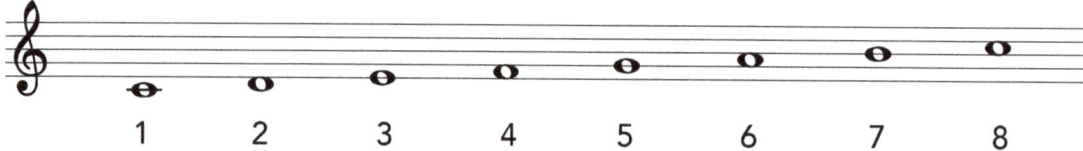

The I Chord

Start with the 1st scale degree, C.

Find a note a 3rd above C, and it has to be from the key, which is C. That note is E, the 3rd of the 7th chord. Next, find a note a 5th above C from the C scale. That note is G and it is the 5th of the 7th chord. Then find a note a 7th above C from the C scale. That note is B, the 7th of the 7th chord.

Next, determine the quality of the 7th chord. Analyze the intervals and compare these three intervals to the 7th chord interval formulas. E is a major 3rd above C, G is a perfect 5th above C, and B is a major 7th above C.

The 7th chord with a major 3rd, perfect 5th, and major 7th is a major 7 chord.

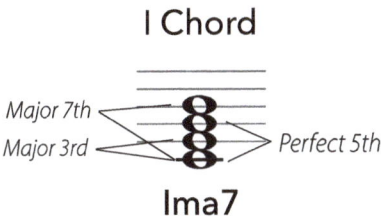

Conclusion: The I chord is major 7.

The II Chord

Next take the 2nd scale degree, D. Repeat the process of building a 7th chord from this note using notes from the C scale.

Find a note a 3rd above D: F. Next, find a note a 5th above D: A. Next, find a note a 7th above D: C.

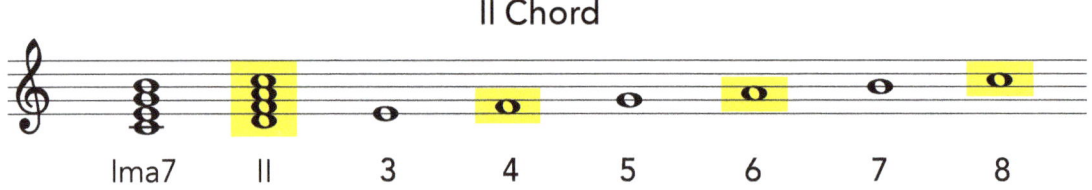

Analyze the intervals and compare them to the 7th chord interval formulas. F is a minor 3rd above D, A is a perfect 5th above D, and C is a minor 7th above D.

The 7th chord with a minor 3rd, perfect 5th, and minor 7th is a minor 7 chord.

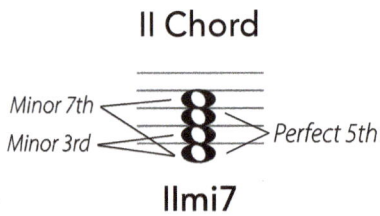

Conclusion: The II chord is minor 7.

The III Chord

Next, build a 7th chord on the 3rd scale degree, E.

Find a note a 3rd above E from the key of C: G. Next, find a note a 5th above E: B. Next, find a note a 7th above E from C scale: D.

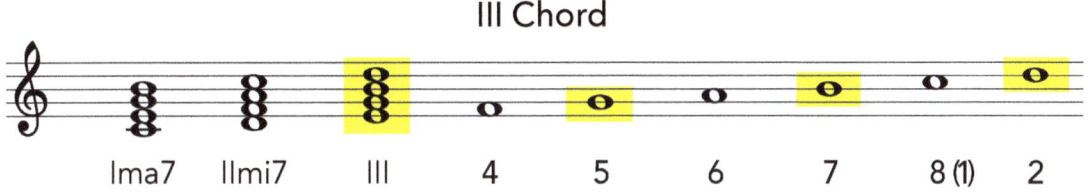

Analyze the intervals and then compare them to the 7th chord interval formulas. G is a minor 3rd above E, B is a perfect 5th above E, and D is a minor 7th above E.

The 7th chord with a minor 3rd, perfect 5th, and minor 7th is a minor 7 chord.

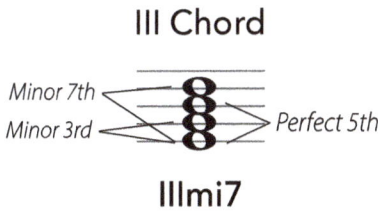

Conclusion: The III chord is minor 7.

The IV Chord

Build on the 4th scale degree, F.

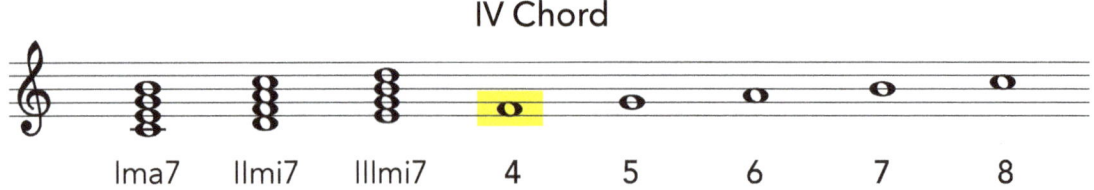

Find a note a 3rd above F: A. Next, find a note a 5th above F: C. Next, find a note a 7th above F: E.

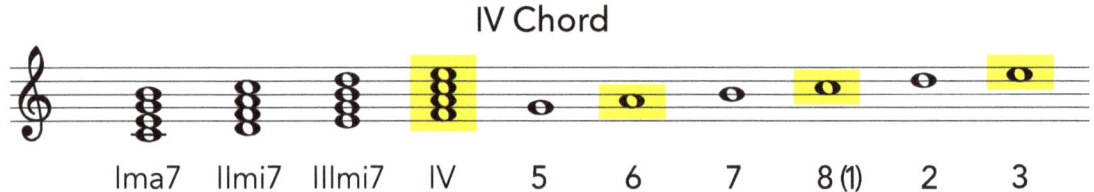

Analyze the intervals and then compare them to the 7th chord interval formulas. A is a major 3rd above F, C is a perfect 5th above F, and E is a major 7th above F.

The 7th chord with a major 3rd, perfect 5th, and major 7th is a major 7 chord.

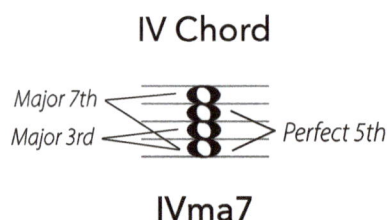

Conclusion: The IV chord is major 7.

The V Chord

Build a 7th chord on the 5th scale degree, G.

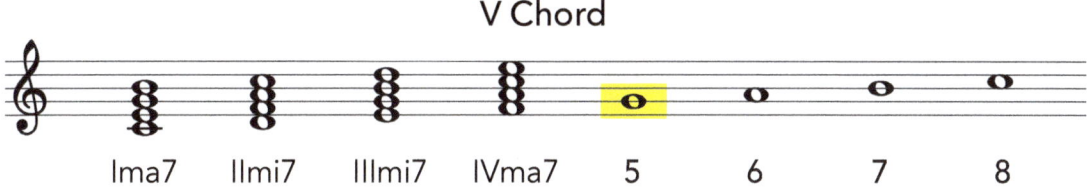

Find a note a 3rd above G: B. Next, find a note a 5th above G: D. Next, find a note a 7th above G: F.

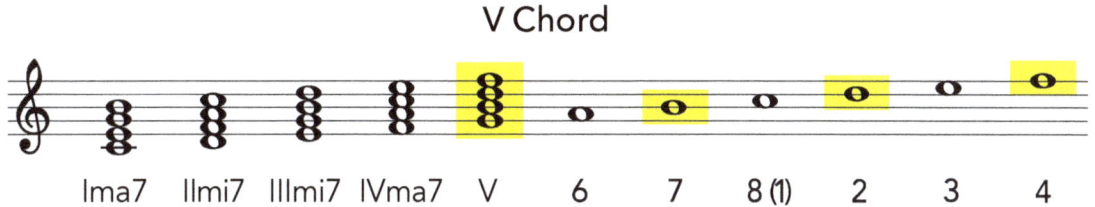

Analyze the intervals and compere them to the 7th interval formulas. B is a major 3rd above G, D is a perfect 5th above G, and F is a minor 7th above G.

The 7th chord with a major 3rd, perfect 5th, and minor 7th is a dominant 7 chord.

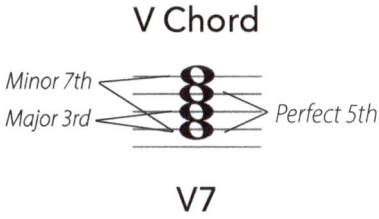

Conclusion: The V chord is dominant 7.

The VI Chord

Build a 7th chord on the 6th scale degree, A.

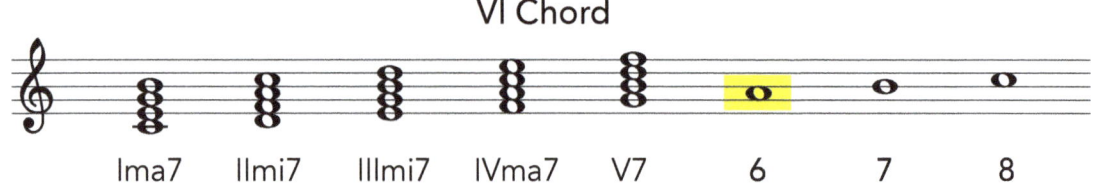

Find a note a 3rd above A: C. Find a note a 5th above A: E. Find a note a 7th above A: G.

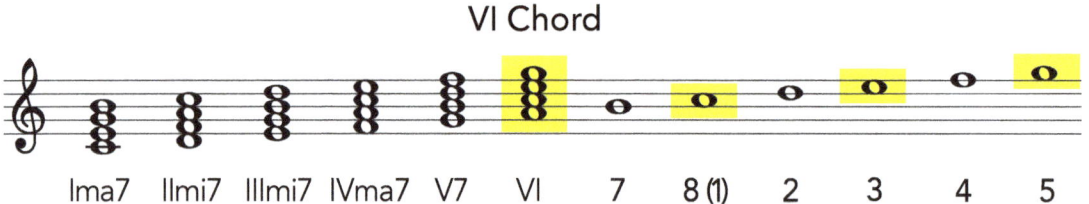

Analyze the intervals and compare them to the 7th chord interval formulas. C is a minor 3rd above A, E is a perfect 5th above A, and G is a minor 7th above A.

The 7th chord with a minor 3rd, perfect 5th, and minor 7th is a minor 7 chord.

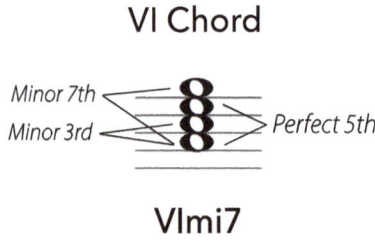

Conclusion: The VI chord is minor 7.

The VII Chord

Build a 7th chord on the 7th scale degree, B.

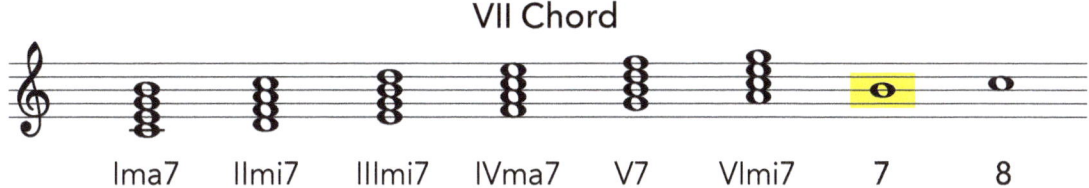

Find a note a 3rd above B from the key of C: D. Next, find a note a 5th above B: F. Next, find a note a 7th above B: A.

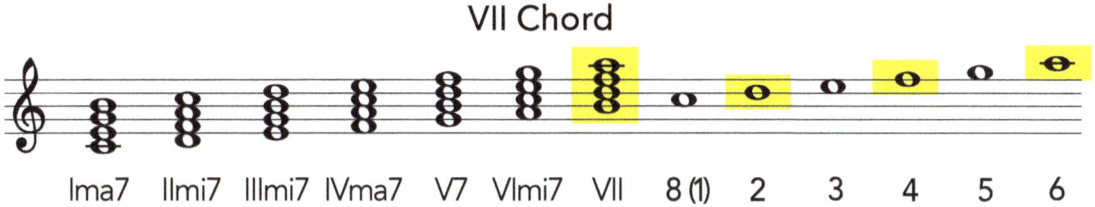

Analyze the intervals and compare them to the 7th interval formulas. D is a minor 3rd above B, F is a diminished 5th above B, and A is a minor 7th above B.

A 7th chord with a minor 3rd, diminished 5th, and minor 7th is a minor 7(♭5) chord.

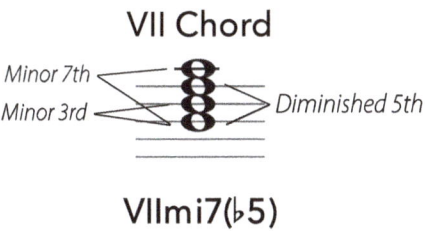

VIImi7(♭5)

Conclusion: The VII chord is minor7(♭5).

The Harmonized C Major Scale with 7th Chords

Chords are notated with Roman numerals. When numbering chords, also write an abbreviation for the chord quality, as is done with intervals and triads:

- ma7 for major 7 chords
- 7 for dominant 7 chords
- mi7 for minor 7 chords
- mi7(♭5) for minor7(♭5) chords (or half diminished).

The Harmonized C Major Scale with 7th Chords

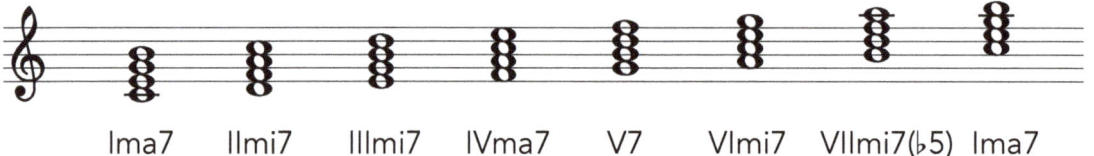

Ima7   IImi7   IIImi7   IVma7   V7   VImi7   VIImi7(♭5)   Ima7

In the key of C major, the chord symbols are written as follows:

- I chord is Cma7
- II is Dmi7
- III in Emi7
- IV is Fma7
- V is G7
- VI is Ami7
- VII is Bmi7(♭5)

These chords are diatonic to the key of C major. So if we repeat this process with the major scale on any other tonic, the result will be the same: the I chord will always be major 7, the II chord will always be minor 7, the III chord will always be minor 7, the IV chord will always be major 7, the V chord will always be dominant 7, the VI chord will always be minor 7, and the VII chord will always be minor 7(♭5).

Memorize it – no way around it. Here's a little trick that might help:

- I and IV are major 7
- V is dominant
- VII is minor 7(♭5)
- The rest are minor 7 – that is II, III, and VI.

Harmonic Analysis with 7th Chords

Next, you will learn about harmonic analysis for progressions with 7th chords. This is a critical skill used for understanding what to play when improvising, playing chords, or arranging. To do this you need to know what the chords are in any and every key. In other words, you should be able to answer questions like: What is the IV chord in G? What is the VI chord in A♭?

Because key signatures determine the notes of every key and because the qualities of the chords built on each scale degree is the same in all keys, any chord (I through VII) in any major key can be identified easily. Likewise, analysis of any diatonic chord progression is possible.

I suggest that you quiz yourself on the chords in every key. Be able to answer questions like:

- What is the II chord in E?
- What is the V chord in B♭?
- What is the VII chord in A?
- What is IV chord in D♭?
- What is the III chord in F#?
- What is the VI chord in G?

Do not skimp on practicing this skill. It is important. There is an exercise on the Fretboard Biology website to help you drill these until you can recite them quickly.

FRETBOARD LOGIC

Arpeggios

In Unit 1 you learned the Pattern I and III major 7 arpeggios. In this Unit you will learn the Patterns I and III dominant 7 arpeggios. The dominant 7 arpeggio is built by adding a 7th to a triad.

Here is a Pattern I major triad arpeggio. Add a minor 7th everywhere possible within the octave shape to build a Pattern I dominant 7 arpeggio.

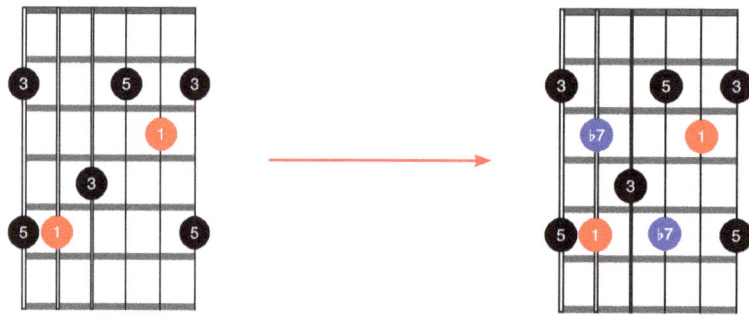

Next, look at a Pattern III major triad arpeggio. Add a minor 7th everywhere possible within the octave shape to build a Pattern III dominant 7 arpeggio. Practice this with alternate picking starting and ending on the root.

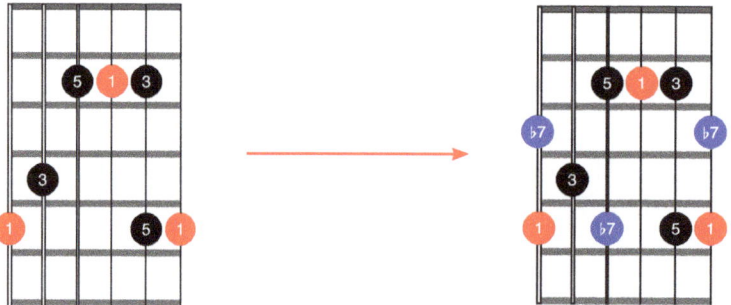

Chords

In the last Fretboard Logic Module you learned open string 7th chord voicings by building from the triad voicings. Practice those voicings using these progressions with a metronome.

Progression in A Major

Progression in C Major

Progression in D Major

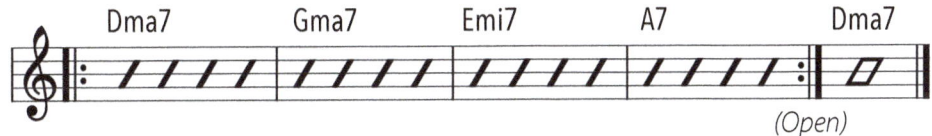

Progression in F Major

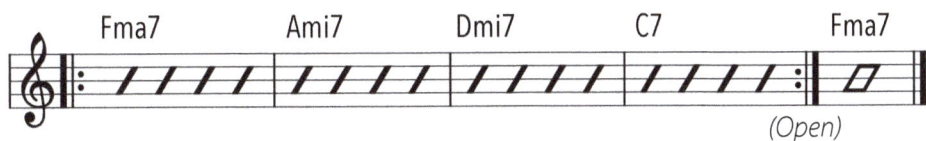

Progression in E Major

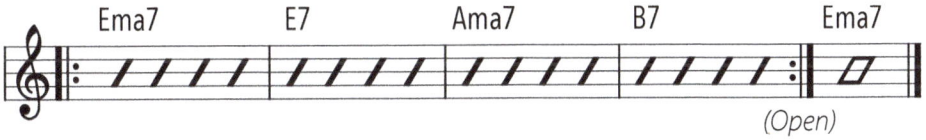

Progression in G Major

Progression in F Major

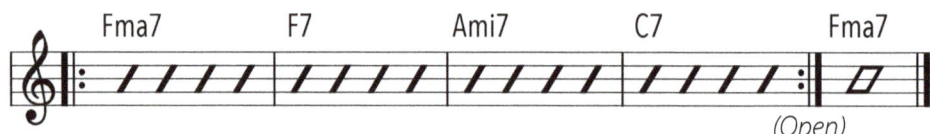

(Open)

Progression in A Minor

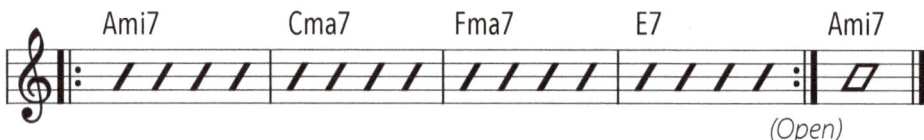

(Open)

Progression in G Minor

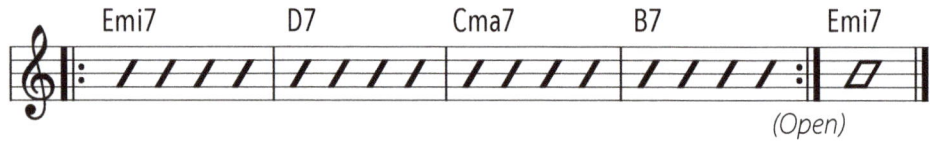

(Open)

Practice each of these progressions until you feel confident. Most guitarists underestimate the amount of practice time needed to play open string chords well. Don't skimp.

Fretboard Biology — Level 3 • Unit 2: Technique

TECHNIQUE

Here is a new scale sequence for your Technique workout. This exercise, like all you will learn in Level 3, can be played in almost any scale in any pattern. Again, start with the Pattern IV major scale in the key of A in fourth position. This exercise is a four-note sequence called the "1-2-3-1 sequence" and is written with 8th notes.

1-2-3-1 Sequence

Play three notes in a row ascending starting on the tonic and ending on the tonic. Then play three notes in a row ascending starting on the second degree and end back on the second scale degree. Next, play three notes in a row ascending starting on the third scale degree and end back on the third scale degree. Continue this to the highest notes you can play in the scale pattern.

Ascending this sequence will look like this.

1-2-3-1 Sequence Exercise - Ascending

Continue on with this pattern until you reach the highest note available in the pattern. Again, note that the numbers under each note identifies the note's scale degree.

Descending, this sequence looks like this:

1-2-3-1 Sequence Exercise - Descending

Add this to your practice routine and budget a few minutes to it each day. Work on this exercise slowly and be consistent with alternate picking. When you feel you are ready, set your metronome at slow tempo – perhaps 50 to 60 bpm. As it becomes easier, gradually increase the tempo. When you feel you are in control of the exercise, pick another major scale pattern and learn it, eventually in all five major scale patterns.

RHYTHM GUITAR

Reggae grooves are normally based on either a straight-16th or a swung 16th-note subdivision. The last Rhythm Guitar Module's example had a straight 16th-note groove. In this Module you will work with the same kind of rhythm guitar patterns but this time the 16th notes will be swung.

Progression in A Major

Here is a two-bar progression in A major with a swung-16th groove. Like the last example, play the second 8th note of each beat – that is the "and" – with a downstroke. Don't use open string voicings. It's best to use barre chords so you can control their duration by muting.

Chop Part

Use the top four strings of a pattern IV barre chord for all the chords: A, D and E. Your tone should be bright enough to cut but not painful. Adjust your volume to be in the middle or slightly below the mix. The part will cut so you don't have to be too loud.

Add the same variation to this pattern that was added in the last Rhythm Guitar Module but here with the swung-16th groove. Add another attack with an upstroke on the 16th note that immediately follows the chop – that is the fourth 16th note of the beat. Catch the upper strings with the upstroke.

Chop Part (variation)

Next, add the third variation you learned last Rhythm Guitar Module but this time with the swung-16th groove. Add another attack on the second 16th note of the beat with an upstroke. Make a downstroke motion on the beat but miss the strings; catch the strings on the second 16th note with an upstroke. Play the "and" – the third 16th note – with a downstroke and then the fourth 16th note with an upstroke. This is the mento rhythm again.

Mento Rhythm

Keep experimenting with the amount of pressure you apply with your fretting hand.

MONEY MAKERS

This Module adds new ideas around the Pattern III major pentatonic shell area, so you will use the Pattern III shape as sort of a home base. The money makers you learn in this and following Money Makers Module are all inside or adjacent to the Pattern III octave shape. These examples are in the key of C major and will be presented on a static C major chord, again, around Pattern III in 5th position.

Pattern III C Major Pentatonic Scale

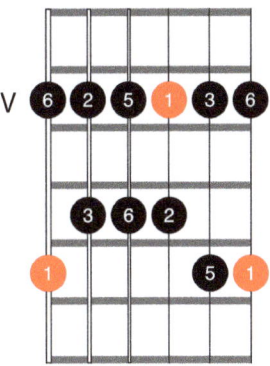

Double Stops: Strings 3 and 2

Here is a move similar to the one you learned in the last Money Makers module, except this time using a bend.

1. Place your 2nd finger at the 7th fret of the 3rd string – that is D. Place your 3rd finger at the 8th fret of the 2nd string – that is G.

2. This a 4th but you are going to change that quickly by bending the 3rd string. Bend the 3rd string up a whole step with a push bend to E.

3. Release the bend to your starting position and then resolve down to C at the 5th fret of the 3rd string and an E at the 5th fret of the 2nd string.

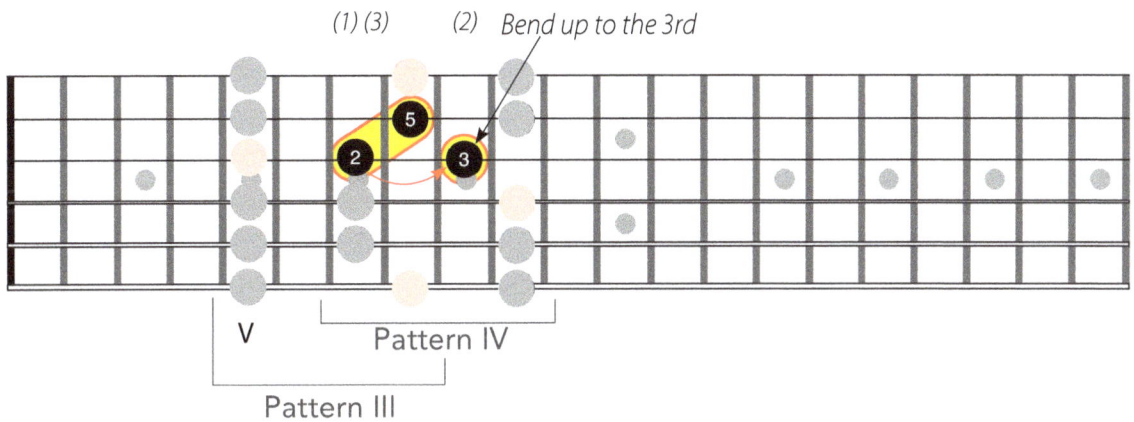

Double Stops: Strings 2 and 1

Here is a hammer-on lick on strings 2 and 1. This will feel familiar to you.

1. With your 1st finger play a double stop at the 8th fret, G (the 5th) on the 2nd string, and C (the root) on the 1st string. That is a perfect 4th shape.

2. Immediately hammer-on the 2nd string at the 10th fret with your 3rd finger playing A, and play the C, too. That's a minor 3rd shape. A is the 6th.

3. Then repeat the perfect 4th shape of G on the 2nd string and C on the 1st string.

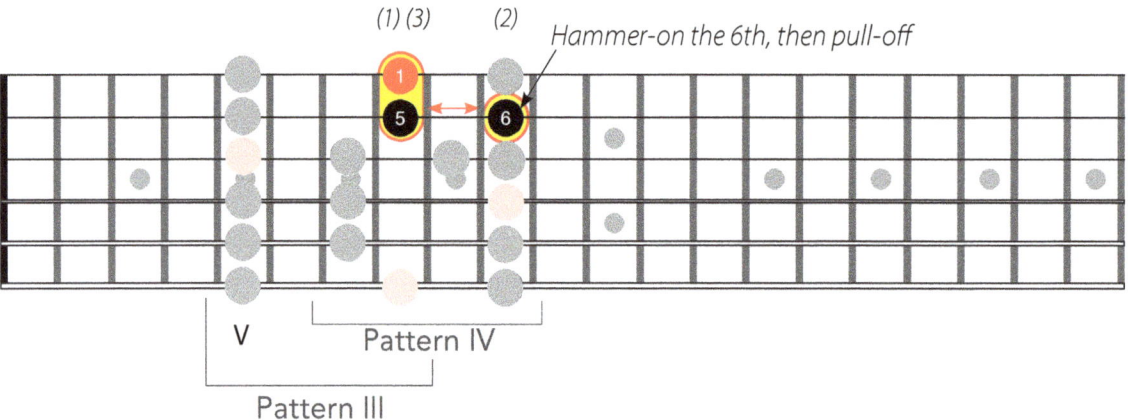

Here's a variation of that lick:

1. With your 1st finger play a double stop at the 8th fret, G (the 5th) on the 2nd string, and C (the root) on the 1st string.

2. But immediately slide both notes up to the 10th fret with your 1st finger playing A (the 6th) on the 2nd string and also D (the 9th) on the 1st string.

3. Then immediately slide your finger back to G and C in 8th position.

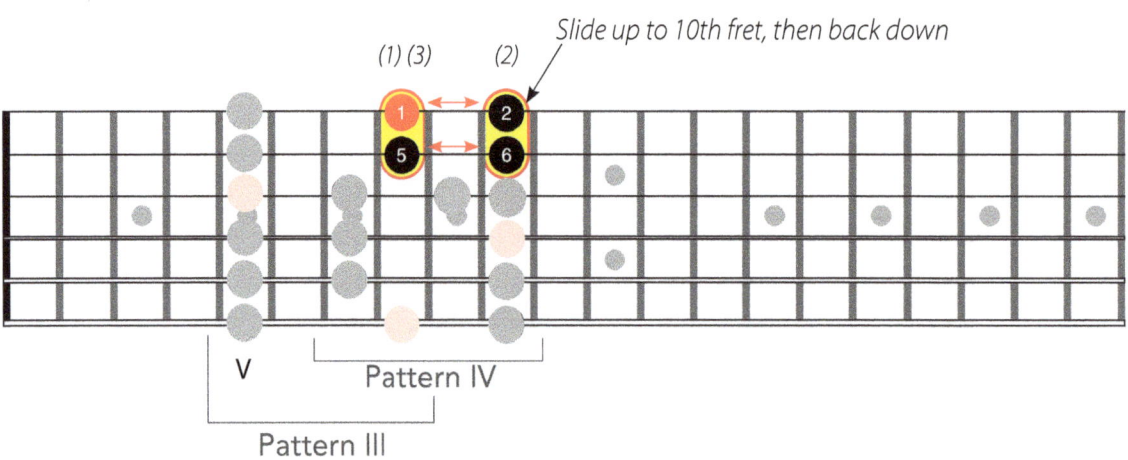

Here is another Pattern III gem:

1. Place your 4th finger on C (the root) at the 8th fret of the 1st string. Place your 1st finger on E (the 3rd) at the 5th fret of the 2nd string.
2. This is a minor 6th shape. C is the root of the C chord and E is the major 3rd. Holding your 4th finger in place, slide into E with your 1st finger from a half step below.
3. Next, while holding C with your 4th finger, put your 2nd finger on F (the 4th) at the 6th fret. Play the two strings together.
4. After playing F, return to E and, if you like, finish with C at the 5th fret of the G string.

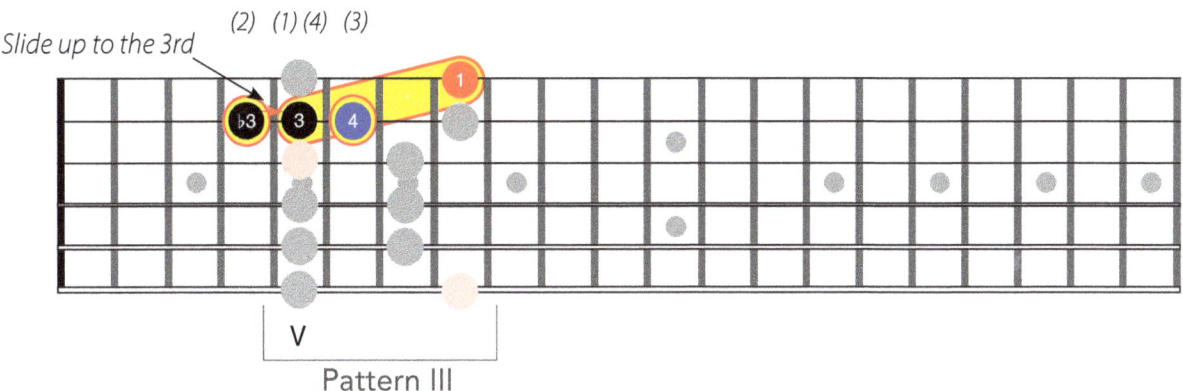

C Major R&B Vamp

Try these ideas over a static R&B vamp in the key of C. Then play these new ideas with the other track that is in the key of D. Keep using the money makers inside the Pattern III shape.

Progression in D Major

Remember: these ideas are transposable to all major keys. So let's put some of these money makers together in a D major progression.

I hope you're having fun with the money makers. Remember that these ideas work well in Blues, Country, Classic Rock, Folk, Gospel, and even Jazz.

Level 3 Unit 2 • Money Maker Demo 1

Track: 3-019

Level 3 Unit 2 • Money Maker Demo 2

Level 3 Unit 2 • Money Maker Demo 3

Level 3 Unit 2 • Money Maker Demo 4

Level 3 Unit 2 • Money Maker Demo 5

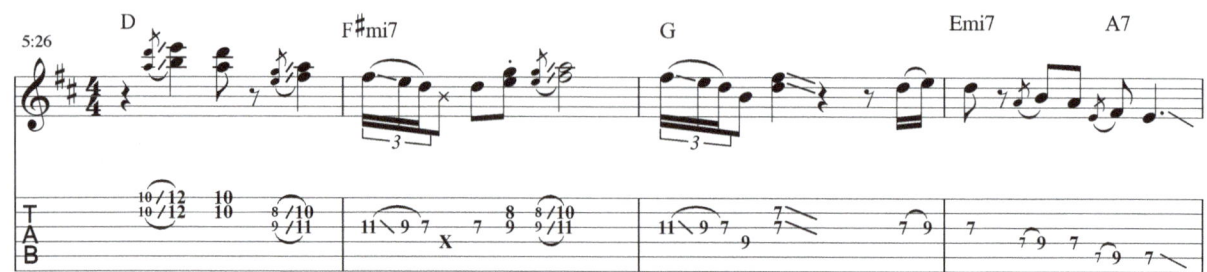

IMPROVISATION

In the last Improvisation module you started working with chord tone soloing and used a two-chord progression using the Patterns I and III major 7 arpeggios. The concept of chord tone soloing is pretty simple. Executing, however, is quite another thing and requires determined practice over an extended period of time. But it is possible to use the concept at a basic level almost immediately if you single out some arpeggio notes as target notes. As you increase your knowledge of arpeggios, you will get better and better at making musical sense with them.

You just learned the Patterns I and III dominant 7 arpeggios in Fretboard Logic and you will use them here.

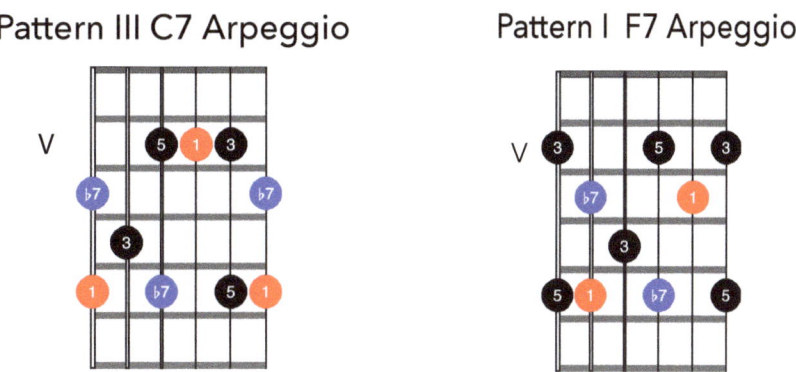

Here is a simple two-chord progression: C7 to F7.

Progression in C Major

This progression is in the key of C and if you were to play a key-center solo over this, you would use the C major pentatonic scale as your source of notes. That would work but would be less than satisfying to the listener because it is vague.

Progression in C Major

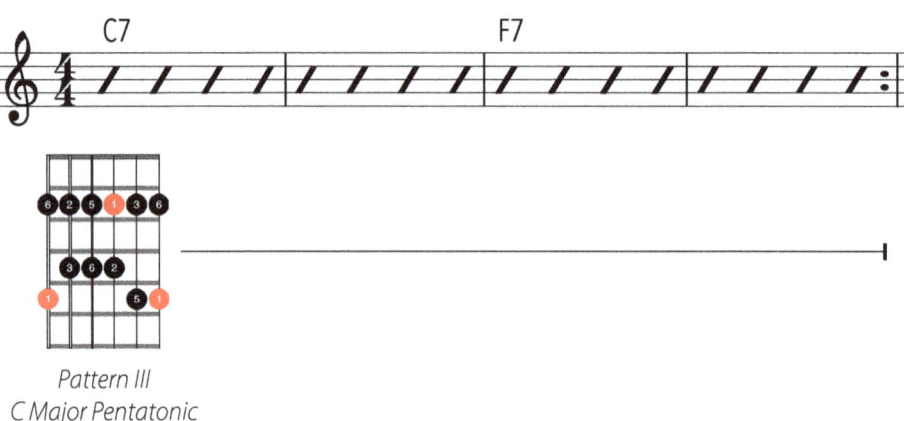

Next use the chord-tone approach. Over the C7, use the newly-learned Pattern III C7 arpeggio. It fits perfectly because it uses the notes played in the chord. Next, over the F7, play the Pattern I F7 arpeggio. This fits perfectly, too, because it uses the notes of the chord.

Progression in C Major

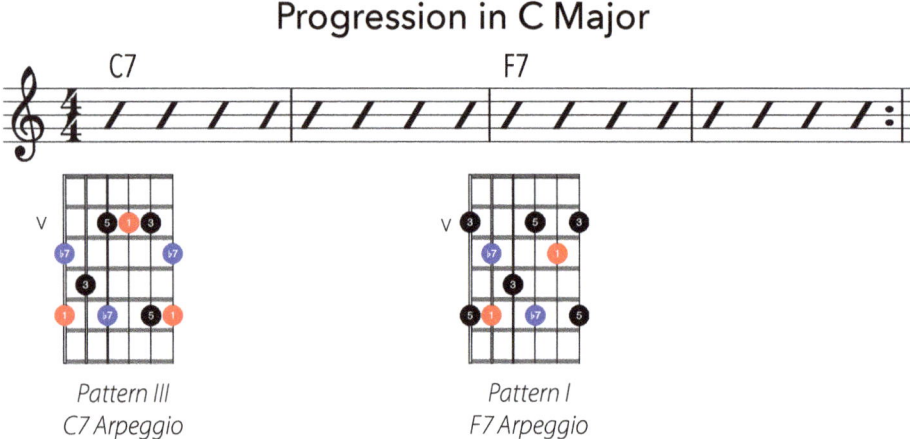

Remember that chord-tone soloing doesn't mean using only chord tones. The goal is to incorporate chord tones in your melodic lines. Think of the arpeggios as a frame on which you can build your lines. Chord tones can be connected with scale tones of even chromatic tones.

When learning to use chord tones, it is a good idea to play just arpeggios over the chords as an exercise to train yourself on where they are on the fretboard. They are the target notes and the best way to learn them is to spend time playing strictly chord tones.

Take another segment of your practice and create short motifs that blend chord tones and scale tones. Keep at this. It's a new way for you to think while soloing and will pay big dividends.

Fretboard Biology — Level 3 • Unit 2: Improvisation

Level 3 Unit 2 • Improv Demo

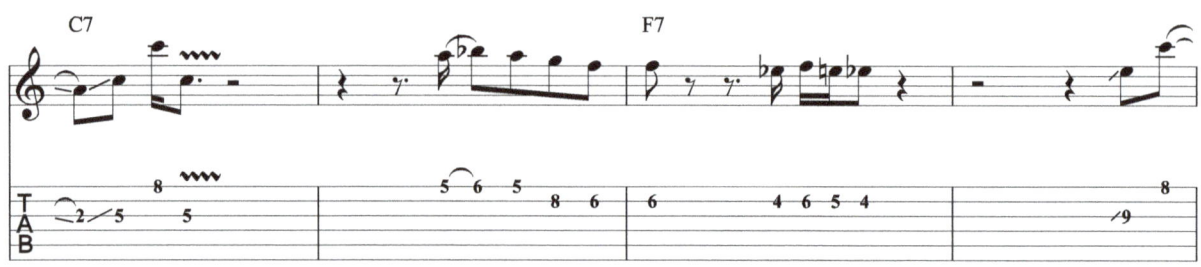
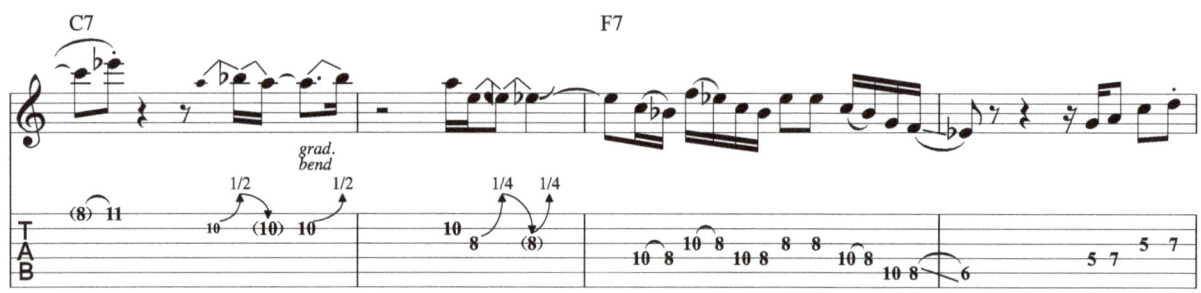
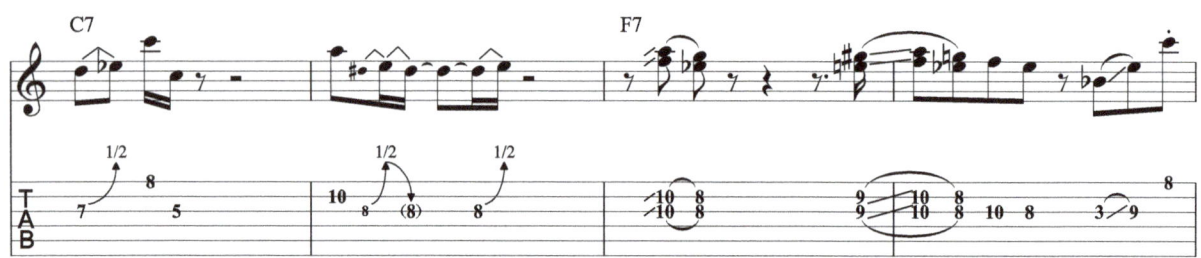
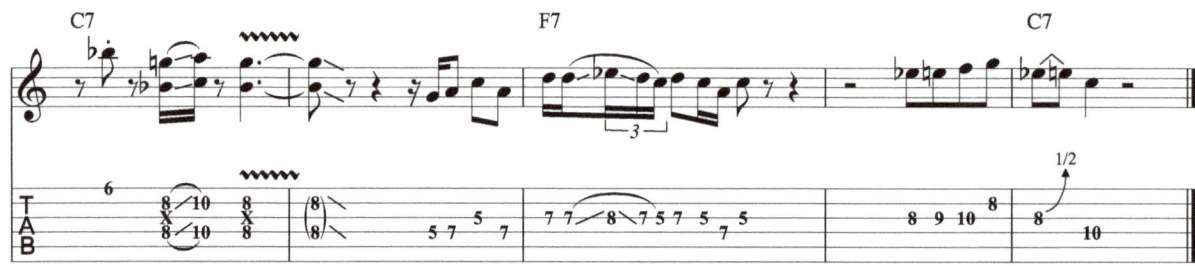

PRACTICE

Theory

- ☐ Go to the tabs below the Theory video on the website and complete the quiz.
- ☐ Memorize the harmonized major scale with 7th chords.

Fretboard Logic

- ☐ Learn the Patterns I and III dominant 7 arpeggios.
- ☐ Practice the chord progressions using open voice 7th chords.

Technique

- ☐ Practice playing the 1-2-3-1 sequence using strict alternate picking.

Rhythm Guitar

- ☐ Practice the examples with the swung 16th-note Reggae progression provided.

Money Makers

- ☐ Practice the double-stop bends and hammer-ons presented in the module.

Improvisation

- ☐ Focus on chord-tone soloing over the progression provided using the Pattern III C7 and Pattern I F7 arpeggios.

UNIT 3

Learning Modules

> **Theory** - Chord Families with 7th Chords in Major Keys, Analyzing Chord Progressions with 7th Chords

> **Fretboard Logic** - Patterns II and IV Minor 7 Arpeggios, Patterns II and IV Major 7 Barre Chords

> **Technique** - 1-3-2-1 Sequence Exercise

> **Rhythm Guitar** - Reggae Rhythm Guitar

> **Money Makers** - Pattern III Money Makers Over a Progression in D

> **Improvisation** - Using Patterns IV and II Minor 7 Arpeggios over a Progression in A Minor

> **Practice** - Continue Practice Routine Development

THEORY

In this Unit you will learn about harmonic analysis in major keys in progressions with 7th chords. It is common on gigs or sessions to see crude chord charts with no key signature. You will find yourself in situations where the chord charts are not necessarily done with perfection in mind because someone hurriedly sketched out the changes for the rehearsal or gig. You need to have another way to know at a glance what key the song is in and how the chords in the progression function within the key.

Chord Families

Knowing the "function" of a chord means that you know the number of each chord and therefore the chord family to which each one belongs: tonic, subdominant, or dominant. With that, you know the emotional tendency of each chord: home, moving away from home, or moving toward home.

You learned about chord families when you harmonized the major scale in triads. There are three families:

- **Tonic Family:** Ima, IIImi, and VImi. These chords make you feel at home or rest.
- **Subdominant Family:** IVma and IImi. These chords make you feel like you're moving away from the tonic.
- **Dominant Family:** Vma and VII°. These chords pull you back toward home (the tonic).

7th chords fit into the same families:

- The Tonic family consists of Ima7, IIImi7, and VImi7
- The Subdominant family consists of IVma7 and IImi7
- The Dominant family consists of V7 and VIImi7(♭5)

7th Chord Families in Major

FAMILY	MEMBERS	EMOTIONAL EFFECT
Tonic	Ima7, IIImi7, VImi7	At home, resolved
Subdominant	IVma7, IImi7	Moving away from tonic
Dominant	V7, VIImi7(♭5)	Moving toward tonic

Analyzing Chord Progressions

In an earlier Unit you learned a basic method for harmonic analysis in progressions where all the chords are triads. Here's how that worked: You determined all of the keys to which each chord could belong and then looked for a single key common to all the chords. The same method works with 7th chord progressions, too.

Let's use the same method to analyze this progression in a major key.

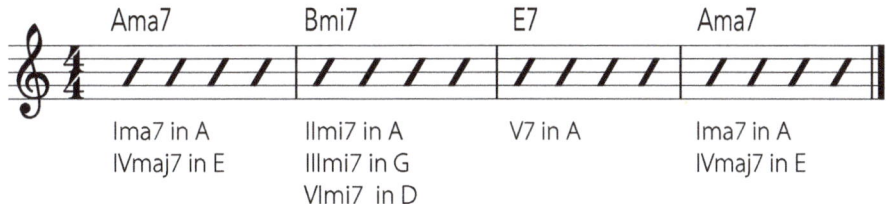

Ama7	Bmi7	E7	Ama7
Ima7 in A	IImi7 in A	V7 in A	Ima7 in A
IVmaj7 in E	IIImi7 in G		IVmaj7 in E
	VImi7 in D		

Is there one key to which all chords belong? Yes: A major.

Let's try another. Determine all of the keys to which each chord could belong:

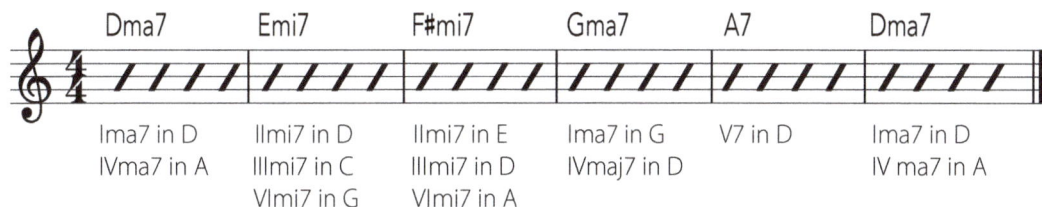

Dma7	Emi7	F#mi7	Gma7	A7	Dma7
Ima7 in D	IImi7 in D	IImi7 in E	Ima7 in G	V7 in D	Ima7 in D
IVma7 in A	IIImi7 in C	IIImi7 in D	IVmaj7 in D		IV ma7 in A
	VImi7 in G	VImi7 in A			

Is there one key to which all chords belong? Yes: D major.

Shortcuts to Finding the Key

This methodical approach works fine but it is very slow, so consider a different approach. There are other clues in both of these progressions that can speed up and simplify the process. The last chord of the progression is often the tonic chord, but that indicator is not 100% reliable.

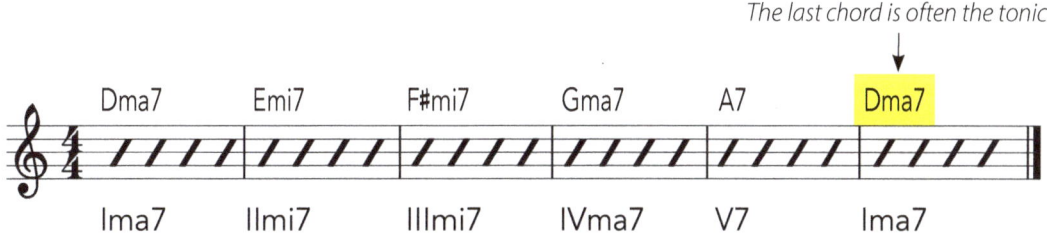

The last chord is often the tonic

Dma7	Emi7	F#mi7	Gma7	A7	Dma7
Ima7	IImi7	IIImi7	IVma7	V7	Ima7

Another clue is that the roots of the Emi7 and F#mi7 are a whole step apart. There is only one place in the harmonized major scale where two minor 7 chords are positioned one whole step apart: IImi7 and IIImi7. If Emi7 is II and F#mi7 is III, D must be I.

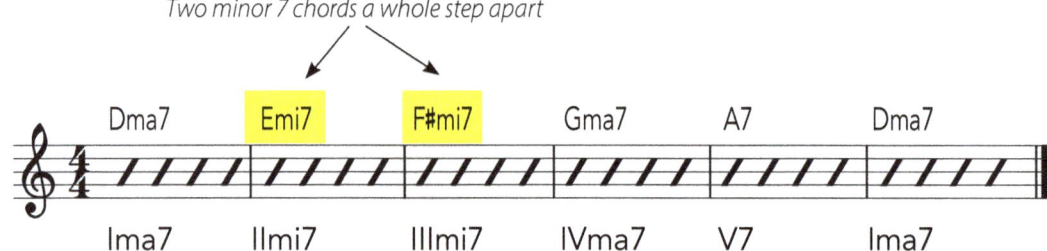

One of the most effective clues is the A7. There is only one dominant 7th chord in the harmonized major scale, the V7 chord. If A7 is V, D is I.

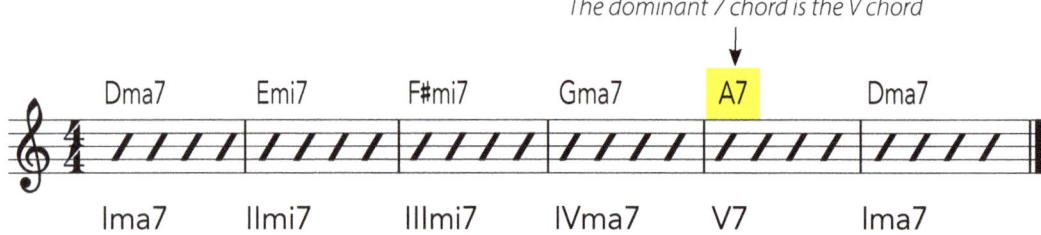

A dominant 7th chord is often an effective clue about the key.

A Quick Review

This is a good place to pause and review your progress with harmonic analysis thus far. You have learned a very thorough, deliberate, and slow method for harmonic analysis when analyzing major or minor progressions consisting of only triads. You also learned to use this same method for analyzing major key progressions made up of 7th chords.

You also learned a couple of shortcuts for identifying the key of a diatonic progression:

- Look at the last chord of the progression. This is often, but not always, the key.
- Look to see if there are two minor 7 chords are a whole step apart. The occurs between the 2nd and the 3rd scale degree of a key.
- A common clue for locating the key is the dominant 7. There is a high probability that a dominant 7th chord in a progression is the V7 because there is only one dominant 7th chord in the harmonized major scale (the V).

Instead of the slow and methodical way to analyze a progression, try using these clues in a few more examples. Look at this progression.

For the sake of analysis, focus on the A7 and assume it is the V7 in the key. A7 is V7 in D. This progression is in the key of D.

Progression in D Major

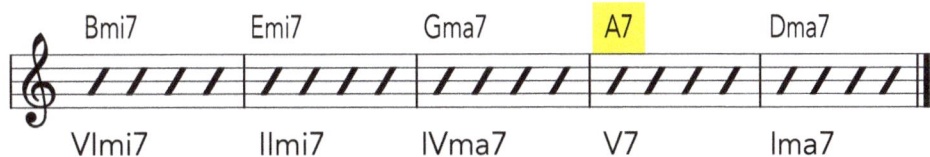

Let's look at another progression, and it has no dominant 7. Focus on the last chord as well as B♭mi7 and Cmi7, two minor 7 chords a whole step apart. That relationship happens in only one place in a major key: between II and III. If B♭mi7 is the II chord, then A♭ is the I chord.

Progression in B♭ Major

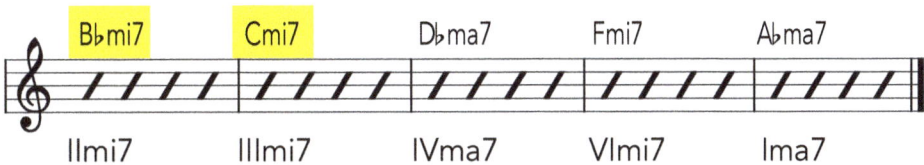

This next progression has a dominant 7 chord: D7. For the sake of analysis, we can assume it is V7. Therefore, D7 is V7 in the key of G.

Progression in G Major

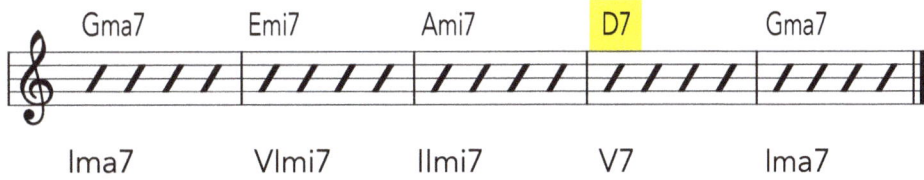

These methods and clues are great tools. Use them when analyzing the harmony of a song. There is still another way to instantly recognize and analyze chord progressions.

Common Chord Groups

Certain groups of chords tend to "hang out together". It's only logical that you see them together frequently because they are part of the same key and are used in combination over and over, in song after song. You get used to seeing them together. Songs tend to use chord progressions or parts of progressions that have been used many times before When you get used to analyzing progressions, you start to notice these "teams of chords" that are frequently used together.

Think of this analogy. Let's say you showed up to a new class and it was the first day. You are in a classroom with 30 other people and you don't know any of them; it's just a collection independent and unknown faces. But over the following weeks, small social groups begin to form and you get used to a certain group of three or four people who you see hanging together and perhaps another group of three or four and maybe a few pairs of people. After a few more weeks, these social groups become pretty well defined and the distinct people in that classroom become very familiar to you. It's no longer a large group of vague, non-descript faces; they now have an identity as do their small social groups.

Your brain begins to see chords of a key the same way. You see a group of chords together so much that there's no need for conscious analysis – you just know they belong together in a key. For example, when I see a progression like the one on the previous page – Gma7, Emi7, Ami7, D7, Gma7 – I know it's in the key of G without thinking because it is so common to see these exact chords together. In addition, the specific order of the chords (I, VI, II, V, I) is very common.

In fact, musicians routinely refer to common short chord progressions as entities unto themselves like: "I–IV–V", "II-V-I", "I-VI-IV-V-I", or "III-VI-II-V-I". These chord number sequences become actual names. A "II-V-I" is a "thing".

This will happen for you, too, if you start analyzing every song you play. There is a lot more harmonic analysis in this course but you should make it a habit in your process of learning songs. Every time you see a new song, analyze it.

There is another significant benefit from analyzing chord progressions. You will start to recognize how progressions sound. Much of the skill of "ear training" is really about recognizing melodies and chord progressions you have already heard. If you analyze a progression and know how it sounds, I guarantee that when you hear the same progression used in another song, you will recognize it and be able to identify the chords.

The ability to quickly analyze chord progression provides important benefits:

- Understanding the function indicates the "family" each chord belongs to and therefore its emotional tendency.
- Sometimes chords can be substituted for one another within a family. This offers options for reharmonization. This means we can substitute a chord from the same family as the chord originally written for variation.
- You can use the arpeggio of another chord within the family as a melodic device.

Harmonic analysis is the beginning of understanding of what is going on inside a song with respect to chord movement. Understanding the harmony of a song will open your mind to options you wouldn't know otherwise.

Practice analyzing all kinds of songs you already know. Take songs or parts of songs and see if you can figure out each chord's number – that is, its function – and that is the indicator of which chord family each one belongs.

Progression Analysis Exercise

The next few pages contain an exercise to help you develop your skills in quickly analyzing progressions. The example below will show you how to fill out the worksheet. Your goal is to identify three things: 1) the key of the progression, 2) the number of each chord in the progression, and 3) the family to which each chord belongs.

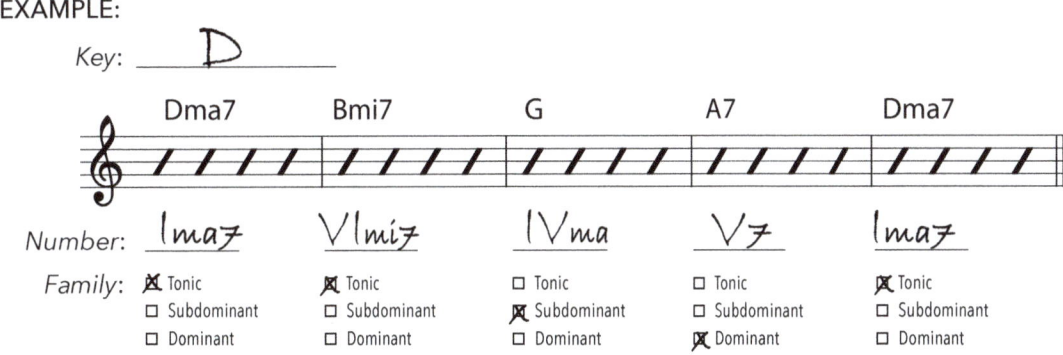

Once you complete the exercise, you can check the answer key in the Appendix of this book. If you struggle with this exercise, keep working at it until it becomes second-nature.

Good luck!

Progression Analysis Exercise

Answer key located on Page 272

Step One: Make a tentative determination of the key.
Step Two: Based on this, determine the number (function) of each chord.
Step Three: Confirm and label the key and function of each chord.

EXAMPLE:

Key: __D__

| Dma7 | Bmi7 | G | A7 | Dma7 |

Number: Ima7   VImi7   IVma   V7   Ima7

Family:
- ☒ Tonic / ☐ Subdominant / ☐ Dominant
- ☒ Tonic / ☐ Subdominant / ☐ Dominant
- ☐ Tonic / ☒ Subdominant / ☐ Dominant
- ☐ Tonic / ☐ Subdominant / ☒ Dominant
- ☒ Tonic / ☐ Subdominant / ☐ Dominant

Key: _____

| Cma7 | Dmi7 | G7 | Cma7 |

Number: _____ _____ _____ _____

Family:
- ☐ Tonic / ☐ Subdominant / ☐ Dominant
- ☐ Tonic / ☐ Subdominant / ☐ Dominant
- ☐ Tonic / ☐ Subdominant / ☐ Dominant
- ☐ Tonic / ☐ Subdominant / ☐ Dominant

Key: _____

| Dma7 | Bmi7 | Emi7 | A7 | Dma7 |

Number: _____ _____ _____ _____ _____

Family:
- ☐ Tonic / ☐ Subdominant / ☐ Dominant
- ☐ Tonic / ☐ Subdominant / ☐ Dominant
- ☐ Tonic / ☐ Subdominant / ☐ Dominant
- ☐ Tonic / ☐ Subdominant / ☐ Dominant
- ☐ Tonic / ☐ Subdominant / ☐ Dominant

©2021 Joe Elliott • FretboardBiology.com

Progression Analysis Exercise

Key: _____

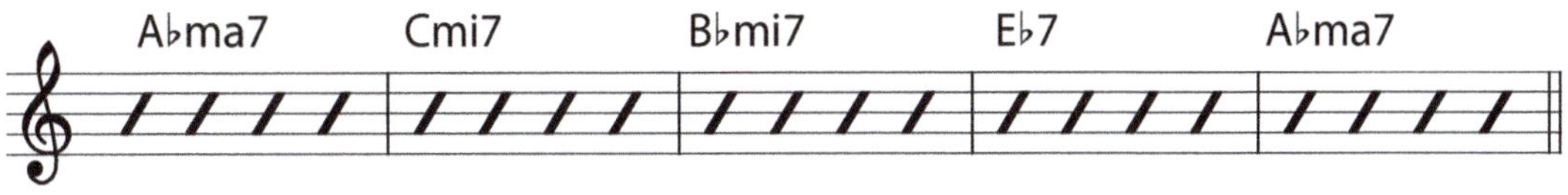

| Abma7 | Cmi7 | Bbmi7 | Eb7 | Abma7 |

Number: _____ _____ _____ _____ _____

Family:
- ☐ Tonic ☐ Tonic ☐ Tonic ☐ Tonic ☐ Tonic
- ☐ Subdominant ☐ Subdominant ☐ Subdominant ☐ Subdominant ☐ Subdominant
- ☐ Dominant ☐ Dominant ☐ Dominant ☐ Dominant ☐ Dominant

Key: _____

| Gma7 | Bmi7 | Cma7 | D7 | Gma7 |

Number: _____ _____ _____ _____ _____

Family:
- ☐ Tonic ☐ Tonic ☐ Tonic ☐ Tonic ☐ Tonic
- ☐ Subdominant ☐ Subdominant ☐ Subdominant ☐ Subdominant ☐ Subdominant
- ☐ Dominant ☐ Dominant ☐ Dominant ☐ Dominant ☐ Dominant

Key: _____

| Fma7 | Dmi7 | Gmi7 | C7 | Fma7 |

Number: _____ _____ _____ _____ _____

Family:
- ☐ Tonic ☐ Tonic ☐ Tonic ☐ Tonic ☐ Tonic
- ☐ Subdominant ☐ Subdominant ☐ Subdominant ☐ Subdominant ☐ Subdominant
- ☐ Dominant ☐ Dominant ☐ Dominant ☐ Dominant ☐ Dominant

Key: _____

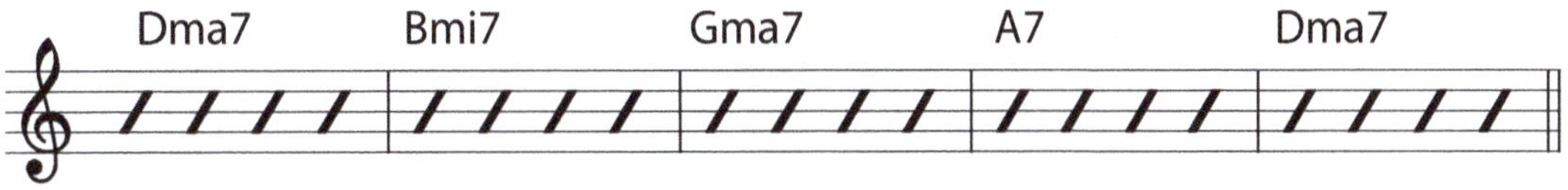

| Dma7 | Bmi7 | Gma7 | A7 | Dma7 |

Number: _____ _____ _____ _____ _____

Family:
- ☐ Tonic ☐ Tonic ☐ Tonic ☐ Tonic ☐ Tonic
- ☐ Subdominant ☐ Subdominant ☐ Subdominant ☐ Subdominant ☐ Subdominant
- ☐ Dominant ☐ Dominant ☐ Dominant ☐ Dominant ☐ Dominant

Progression Analysis Exercise

Key: _____

| D♭ma7 | Fmi7 | E♭mi7 | A♭7 | D♭ma7 |

Number: _____   _____   _____   _____   _____

Family:
- ☐ Tonic
- ☐ Subdominant
- ☐ Dominant

- ☐ Tonic
- ☐ Subdominant
- ☐ Dominant

- ☐ Tonic
- ☐ Subdominant
- ☐ Dominant

- ☐ Tonic
- ☐ Subdominant
- ☐ Dominant

- ☐ Tonic
- ☐ Subdominant
- ☐ Dominant

Key: _____

| Bma7 | Ema7 | C#mi7 | F#7 | Bma7 |

Number: _____   _____   _____   _____   _____

Family:
- ☐ Tonic
- ☐ Subdominant
- ☐ Dominant

- ☐ Tonic
- ☐ Subdominant
- ☐ Dominant

- ☐ Tonic
- ☐ Subdominant
- ☐ Dominant

- ☐ Tonic
- ☐ Subdominant
- ☐ Dominant

- ☐ Tonic
- ☐ Subdominant
- ☐ Dominant

Key: _____

| G#mi7 | A#mi7 | D#mi7 | C#7 | F#ma7 |

Number: _____   _____   _____   _____   _____

Family:
- ☐ Tonic
- ☐ Subdominant
- ☐ Dominant

- ☐ Tonic
- ☐ Subdominant
- ☐ Dominant

- ☐ Tonic
- ☐ Subdominant
- ☐ Dominant

- ☐ Tonic
- ☐ Subdominant
- ☐ Dominant

- ☐ Tonic
- ☐ Subdominant
- ☐ Dominant

Key: _____

| B♭mi7 | Cmi7 | D♭ma7 | E♭7 | A♭ma7 |

Number: _____   _____   _____   _____   _____

Family:
- ☐ Tonic
- ☐ Subdominant
- ☐ Dominant

- ☐ Tonic
- ☐ Subdominant
- ☐ Dominant

- ☐ Tonic
- ☐ Subdominant
- ☐ Dominant

- ☐ Tonic
- ☐ Subdominant
- ☐ Dominant

- ☐ Tonic
- ☐ Subdominant
- ☐ Dominant

©2021 Joe Elliott • FretboardBiology.com

FRETBOARD LOGIC

You have already learned two major 7th and two dominant 7th chord arpeggios. In this module you will learn the patterns II and IV minor 7th arpeggios.

Arpeggios

Minor 7th arpeggios are built by adding a minor 7th to a minor triad arpeggio. Let's start with a Pattern II minor triad arpeggio. Next, add a minor 7th everywhere possible within the octave shape to build a Pattern II minor 7 arpeggio. Practice this with alternate picking starting and ending on the root.

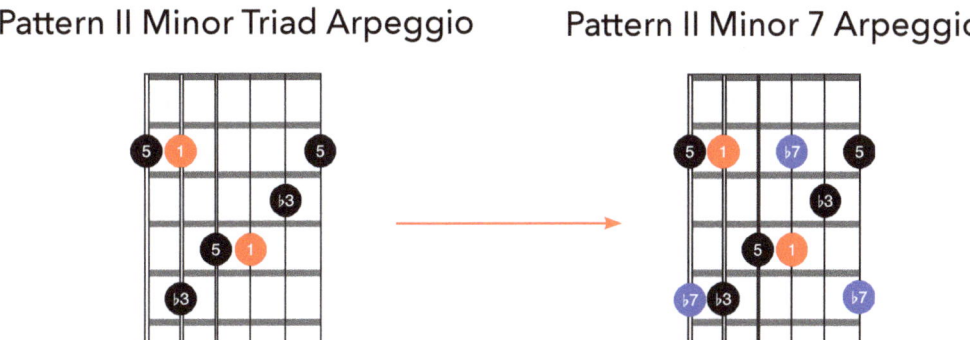

Now, start with a Pattern IV minor triad arpeggio and add a minor 7th everywhere possible within the octave shape to build a Pattern IV minor 7 arpeggio. Practice this with alternate picking starting and ending on the root.

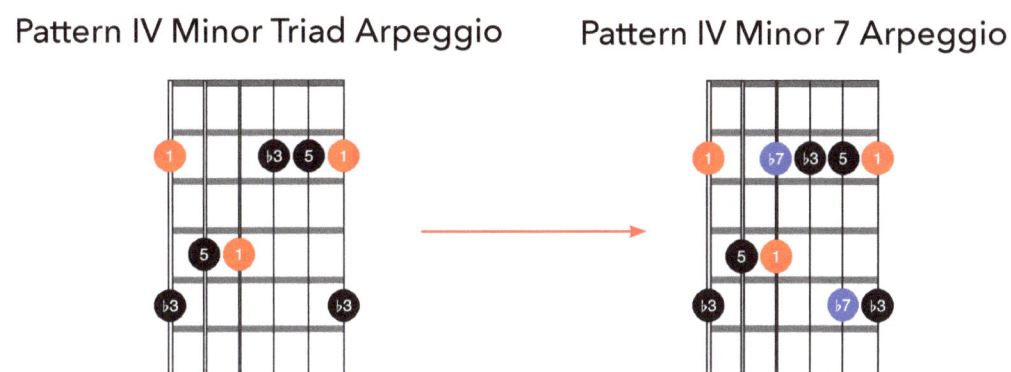

Chords

It is important to know 7th chord voicings for every root, in the same way you use barre chords for triads. You learned open-string 7th chord voicings by building from the triad voicings. Do the same with the common triad barre chords. Begin with the Patterns IV and II barre chords and build major 7 chords.

Here is a Pattern IV major barre chord with the chord tones labeled. To create a major 7 chord within this shape, replace the root on the 4th string with a major 7th. To make this practical to play, omit the 5th played on the 5th string and the root on the 1st string. Mute the 1st and 5th strings. The result is a Pattern IV ma7. It is movable anywhere on the fretboard.

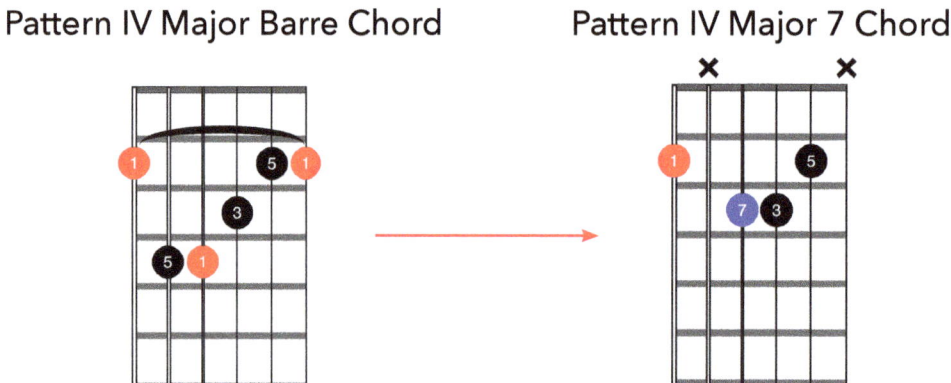

Do the same with the Pattern II major barre chord. Here is a Pattern II major barre chord with the chord tones labeled. To create a major 7 chord within this shape, replace the root on the 3rd string with a major 7th. The result is a Pattern II ma7. Don't play the 6th string. This chord shape is movable anywhere on the fretboard, too.

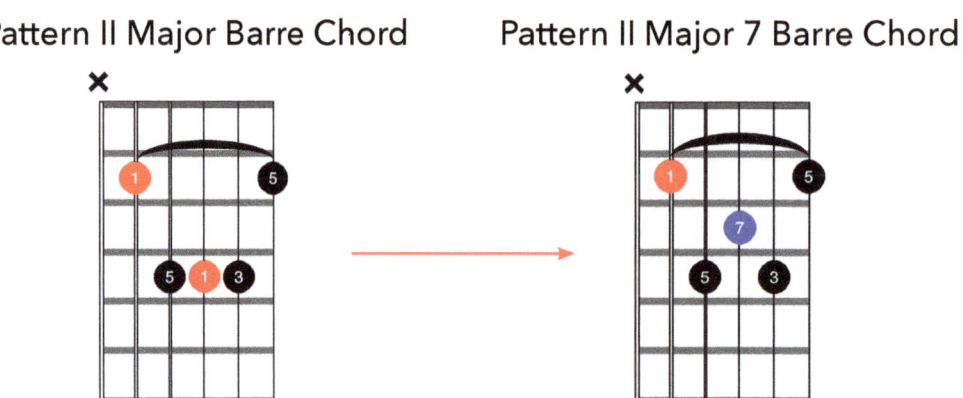

TECHNIQUE

By now you realize that it takes a lot of time to learn and practice the sequences presented in the Technique modules. You don't have to include all of these in your practice routine. Instead, I encourage you to sample each of the sequences introduced in Level 3 and add one or more to your routine. Or perhaps you could rotate them through your practice routine.

Some guitarists love to do these exercises and can spend hours and hours playing them. Other guitarists don't like doing them at all. My advice here is to remember that it's all about balance—balance between practicing Technique, Rhythm Guitar, and Improvisation. The percentage of practice time you budget for Technique exercises depends on your own goals, physical abilities, and development. Sequences can help you develop strength, coordination, and agility.

1-3-2-1 Sequence

Here is a new sequence and, like the others, it can be played in most scales. And as with the previous two sequences, learn it in the Pattern IV major scale in the key of A and with an 8th-note subdivision. This is called the "1-3-2-1" sequence. Ascending, this sequence looks like this:

1-3-2-1 Sequence Exercise - Ascending

Continue ascending with this pattern until you reach the highest note available in the pattern.

Descending, this sequence looks like this.

1-3-2-1 Sequence Exercise - Descending

Continue descending with this pattern until you reach the lowest note available in the pattern. Remember that the numbers below the staff represent the scale degree of each note.

Start slow and use alternate picking. Work up to using the metronome at a slow tempo. Add this to your practice routine and budget a few minutes to this each day. As it becomes easier, gradually increase the tempo. When you feel you are in control of the exercise, pick another major scale pattern and work it out there the same way, eventually in all five major scale patterns.

RHYTHM GUITAR

The examples in the first two Rhythm Guitar modules had one guitar part, but it is common for Reggae bands to have two or even three guitar players. This module teaches a part to play in addition to the chop. It is important to think about how multiple guitar parts interact in Reggae. Usually multiple parts stay out of each other's way. There are instances where doubling parts is a good idea, but for now, stay with the idea that a second guitar part should play where the first guitar part doesn't.

Progression in C Minor

Here's a two-bar progression in C minor. It has a straight 16th-note groove.

Progression in C Minor

Like in the first two examples, it needs the essential chop part played with the second 8th note of each beat with a downstroke.

Chop Part

The second part, however, is played on each beat, and the second 16th that follows with a wah pedal. The interaction between the two parts is really effective for filling out the groove.

Wah Pedal Part

Play the first chop part. Note that this blends with the organ bubble and piano on the off beats.

Next play the wah part on beats 1 and 3. When using a wah pedal for this part, move your foot with the beat: down on the beat and back on the off beats. I would suggest practicing the part in this Module with light fretting hand pressure. This is primarily a percussive "scratch" sound.

If you don't have a wah pedal you can still practice the part. With no wah, I suggest using a bright tone by using your bridge pick up or middle and bridge pickups. Stay a little below the mix with your volume.

Using a Wah Pedal

A wah pedal can be thought of as an extreme tone control, which radically changes your tone from super bright when the pedal is down (forward) to the high frequencies being cut when the pedal is up (back). Because of the accentuation of high frequencies when the pedal is in the down position, be mindful of how bright your tone is. With a wah pedal, you might want to experiment by using your neck pickup so your tone isn't so bright that it hurts your audience.

Wah technique is not as easy as it seems and there are so many expressive possibilities with the pedal that it deserves special attention. The part you learn in this Module is a good entry point into using a wah.

MONEY MAKERS

This module uses the same progression in D that was used in the previous Money Makers module and uses the Pattern III major pentatonic scale in D in 7th position.

Pattern III D Major Pentatonic Scale

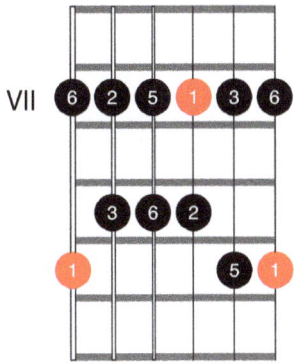

Progression in D Major

The goal in this Module is to play a few specific double-stop combinations over specific chords. This means you will use money makers to play chord tones. You will also learn some perfect 4th double stops to use on the 3rd and 2nd strings.

Double-Stops over the Ima Chord (D)

For the 1st chord, D, the following double stops are good places to start, end, or turn your phrase. To "turn your phrase" means that there are places in the pattern that, if you're ascending, you can turn around and descend; or the opposite, if you're descending, you can turn around and ascend.

Double Stops: Strings 2 and 1

1. With your 1st finger play a double stop at the 10th fret, A (the 5th) on the 2nd string, and D (the root) on the 1st string. That is a perfect 4th shape.

2. Immediately hammer-on the 2nd string at the 10th fret with your 3rd finger playing B, and play the D, too. That's a minor 3rd shape. B is the 6th.

3. Then repeat the perfect 4th shape of A on the 2nd string and D on the 1st string.

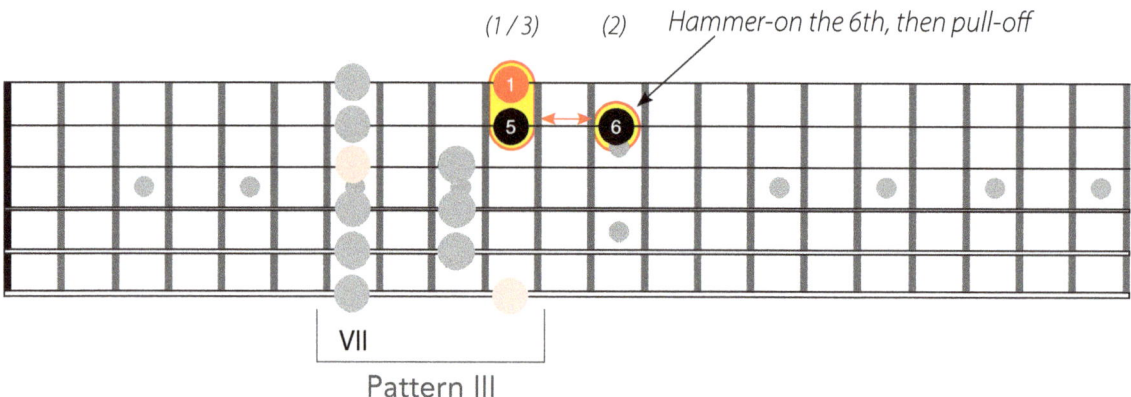

For the next double stop, slide into the 7th fret of the 2nd string with your 1st finger while playing the 10th fret on the 1st string with the 4th finger.

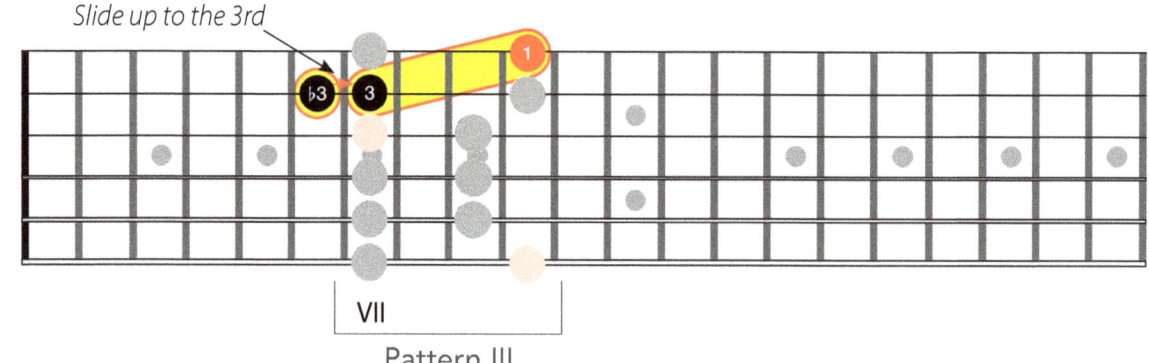

Double Stops: Strings 3 and 2

1. Play this double stop with your 3rd finger on the 3rd string at the 9th fret, and your 2nd finger on the 2nd string at the 8th fret.
2. Slide up to one step so that your 3rd finger is on the 11th fret, and your 2nd finger is on the 10th fret.
3. Next, play the D with your 1st finger on the 3rd and 2nd strings at the 7th fret.

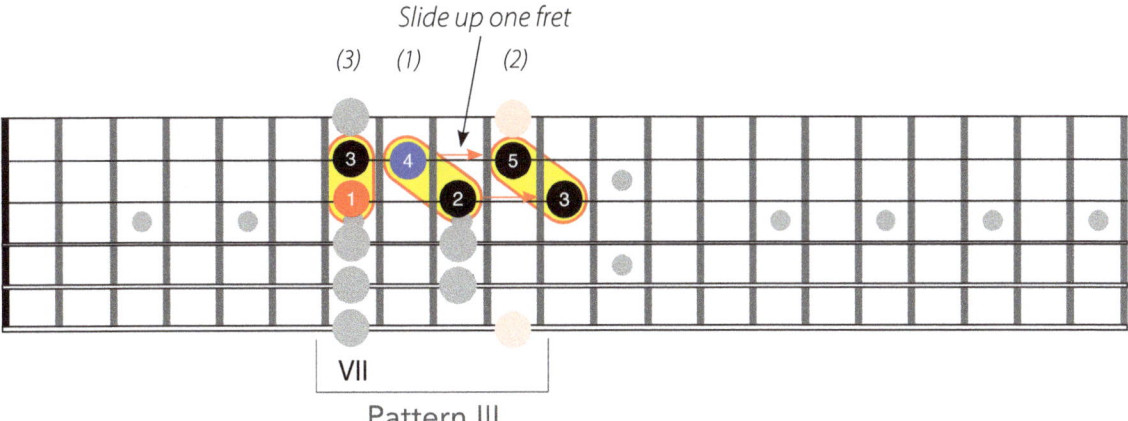

Pattern III

Double Stops: Strings 4 and 3

Strings 4 and 3 At the 7th fret for both the 4th and 3rd strings.

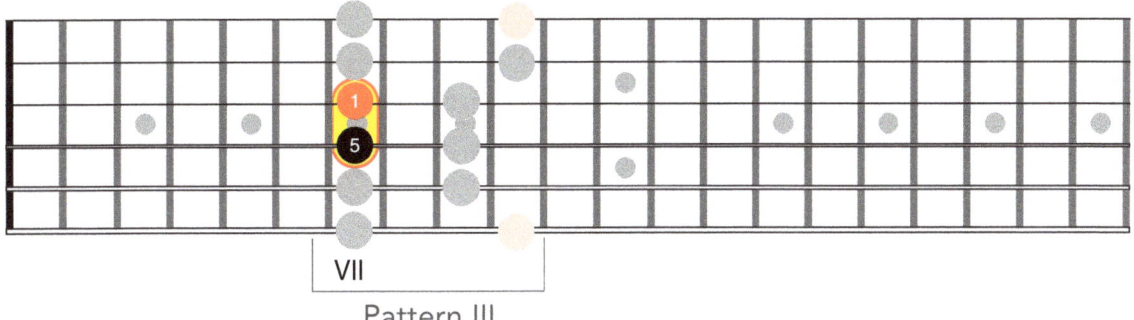

Pattern III

Double Stops: Strings 5 and 4

Strings 5 and 4 at the 9th fret for the 5th string and at the 7th fret for the 4th string.

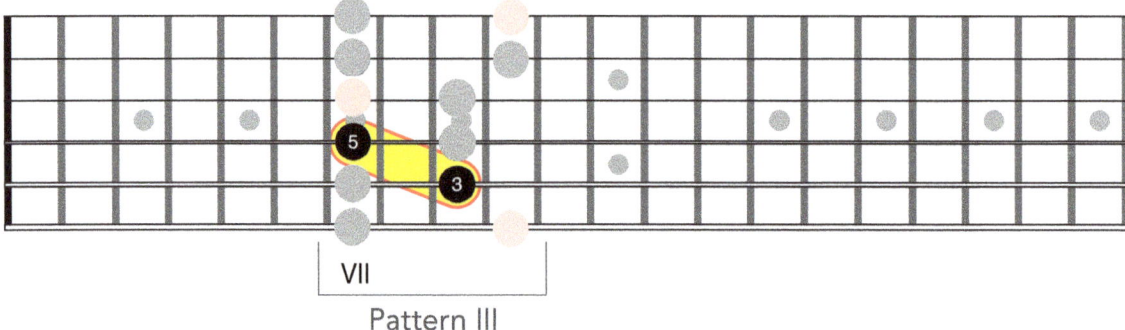

These Pattern III money makers work well on the I chord because they're chord tones. Lock this away for future reference. It is all transposable to any key.

Double Stops over the IIImi7 Chord (F#mi7)

For the 2nd chord in the progression, F#mi7, these double stops are good places to start, end, or turn the phrase. Remember, the numbers of the highlighted notes in these double stops are chord tones of the F#mi7 and don't refer to scale degrees of the Pattern III pentatonic shell.

Double Stops: Strings 3 and 2

Here are two double stops on strings 3 and 2 that you can use on the III chord.

1. At the 11th fret for the 3rd string and at the 10th fret for the 2nd string.

2. At the 6th fret for the 3rd string and at the 7th fret and 2nd string. This is a 4th shape.

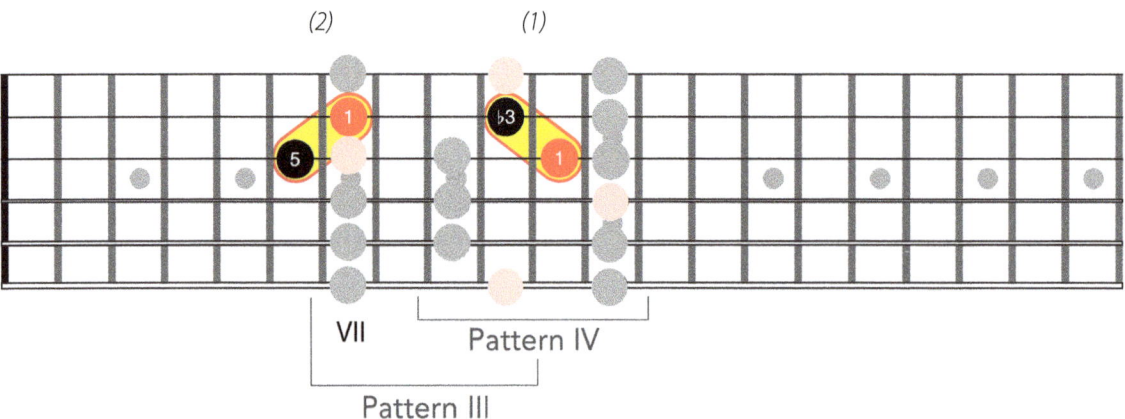

Double Stops: Strings 5 and 4

At the 9th fret for the 5th string and at the 7th fret for the 4th string.

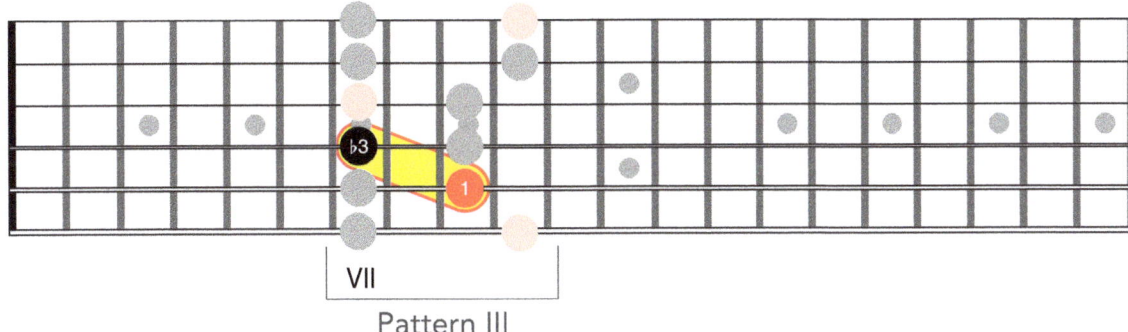

Pattern III

These money makers work well on the III chord because they use its chord tones. Log this away and remember this. It is transposable to any key.

Double Stops over the IVma Chord (G)

For the 3rd chord in the progression, G, these double stops are good places to start, end, or turn a phrase. Remember, the numbers of the highlighted notes in these double stops are chord tones of the G and don't refer to scale degrees of the Pattern III pentatonic shell. The tonic of the major scale is the 5th of the IV chord, G.

Double-Stops: Strings 2 and 1

At the 10th fret and with the 2nd string, hammer-on to the 12th fret.

Hammer-on the 3rd, then pull-off

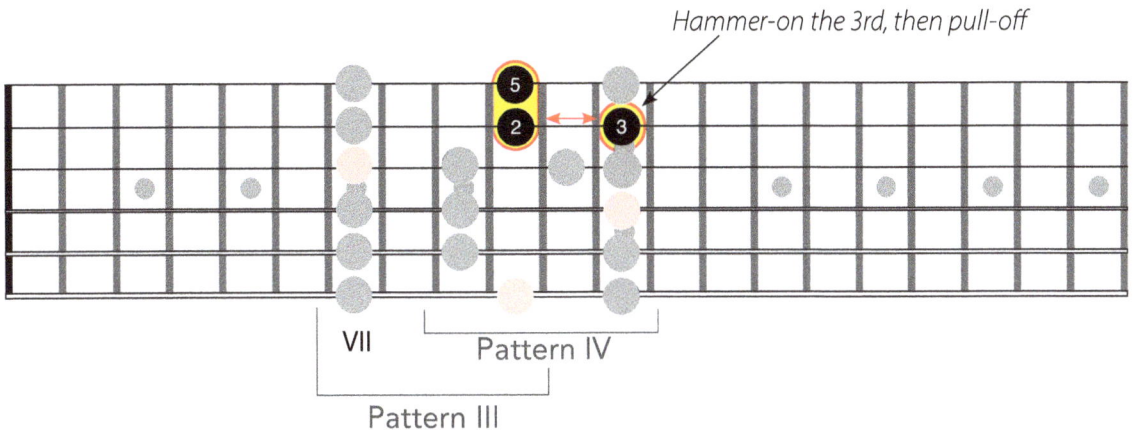

Pattern III / Pattern IV

Double Stops: Strings 3 and 2

At the 7th fret for the 3rd string and at the 8th fret for the 2nd string. This is a 4th shape.

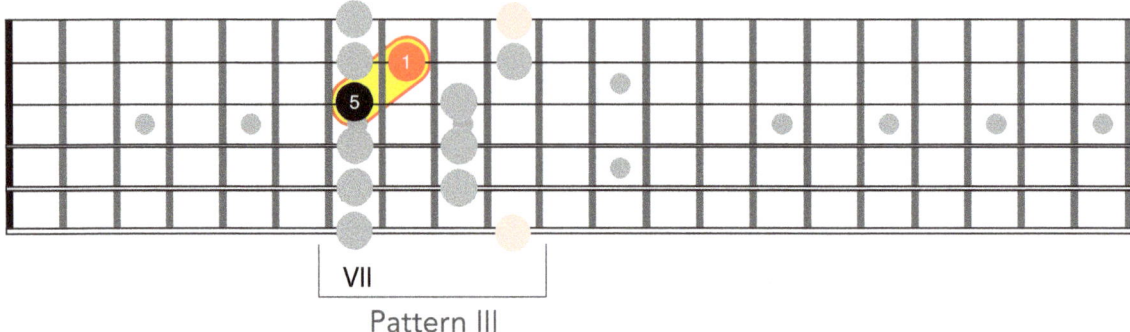

Double Stops: Strings 4 and 3

At the 9th fret for the 4th string and at the 7th fret for the 3rd string

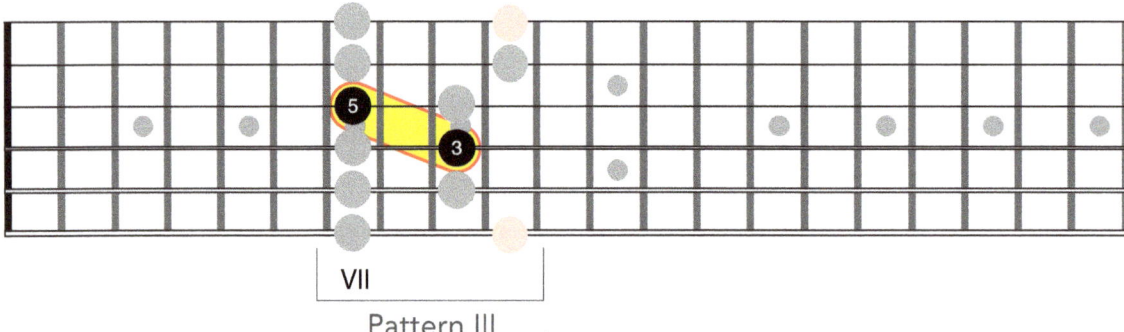

These Pattern III money makers work well on the IV chord because they're chord tones. Log this for future reference. It is transposable to any key.

Double Stops over the IImi7 Chord (Emi7)

For the 4th chord in the progression, Emi7, these double stops are good places to start, end, or turn the phrase. Remember, the numbers of the highlighted notes in these double stops are chord tones of the Emi7 and don't refer to scale degrees of the Pattern III pentatonic shell.

Double Stops: Strings 2 and 1

At the 10th fret and with the 2nd string, hammer-on to the 12th fret.

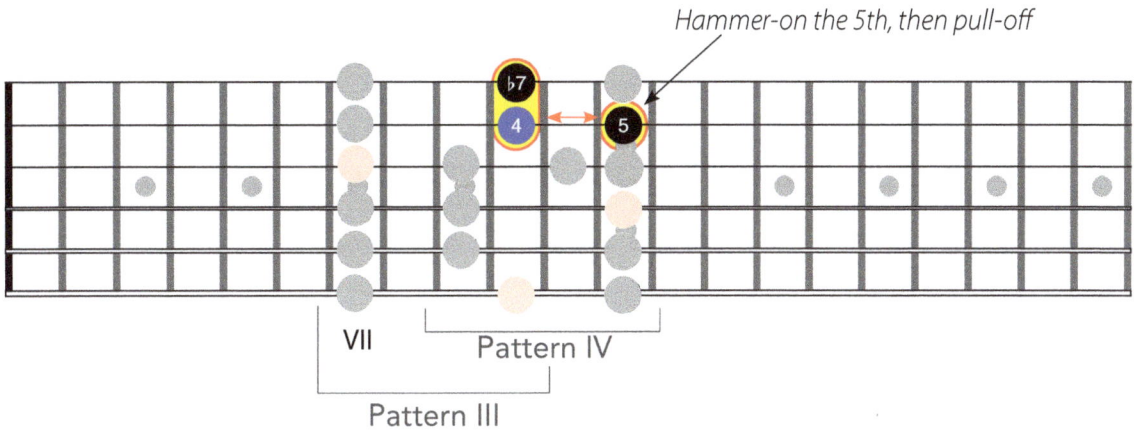

On the 2nd string slide into the 7th fret while playing the 10th fret on the 1st string with the 4th finger.

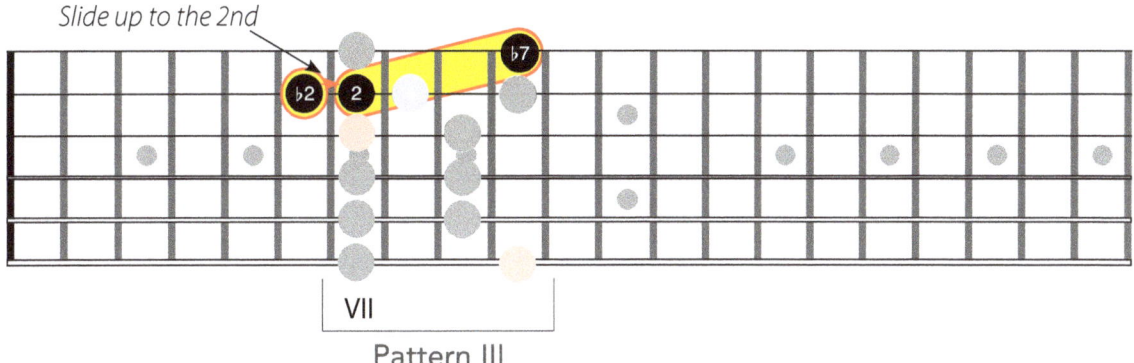

Double Stops: Strings 3 and 2

At the 7th fret for the 3rd string and at the 8th fret for the 2nd string. This is a 4th shape.

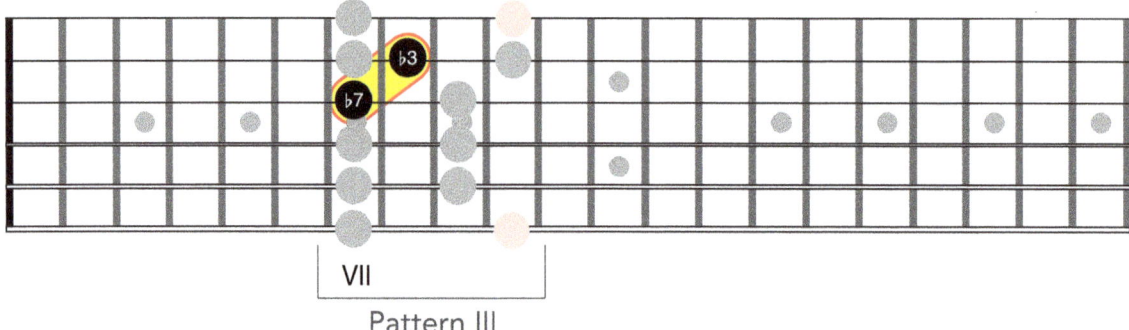

Pattern III

Double Stops: Strings 4 and 3

At the 9th fret for the 4th string and at the 7th fret for the 3rd string.

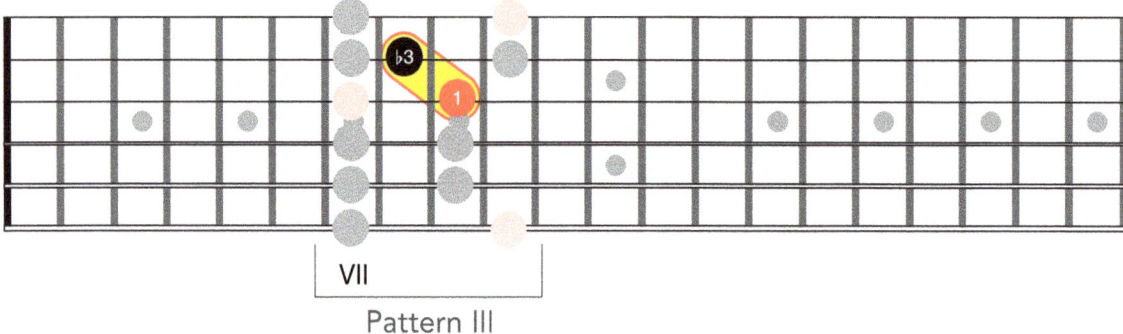

Pattern III

These Pattern III money makers work well on the II chord because they're chord tones. Lock this away for future reference. It is transposable to any key.

Double Stops over the A7 (V7) Chord

For the 5th chord, A7, these double stops are good places to start, end, or turn a phrase. Remember, the numbers of the highlighted notes in these double stops are chord tones of the A7 and don't refer to scale degrees of the Pattern III pentatonic shell.

Double Stops: Strings 3 and 2

At the 9th fret for the 3rd string and at the 10th fret and 2nd string. This, again, is a perfect 4th shape.

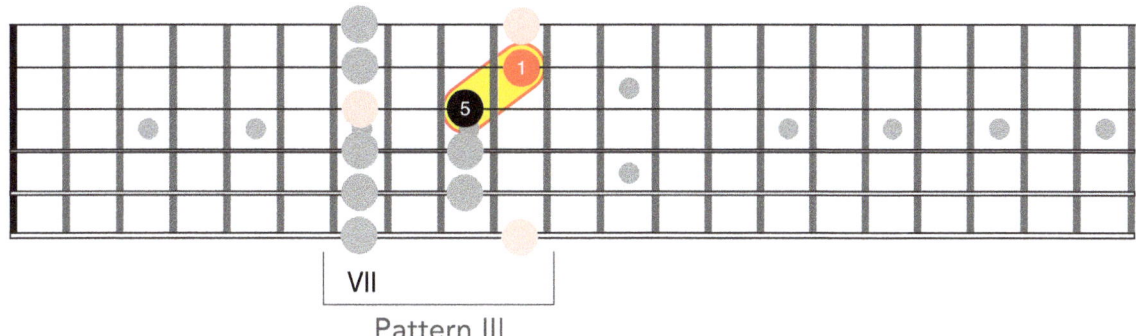

Pattern III

Double Stops: Strings 5 and 4

At the 7th fret for both the 5th and 4th strings.

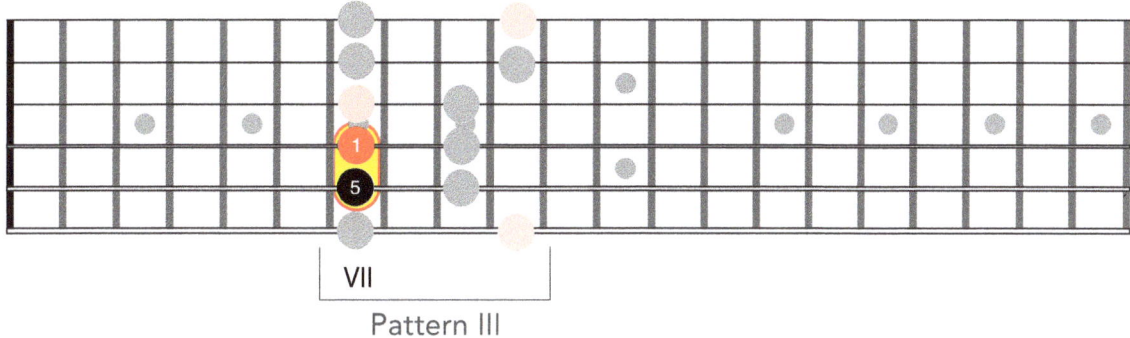

Pattern III

All of these ideas are transposable to all major keys.

Level 3 Unit 3 • Money Maker Demo

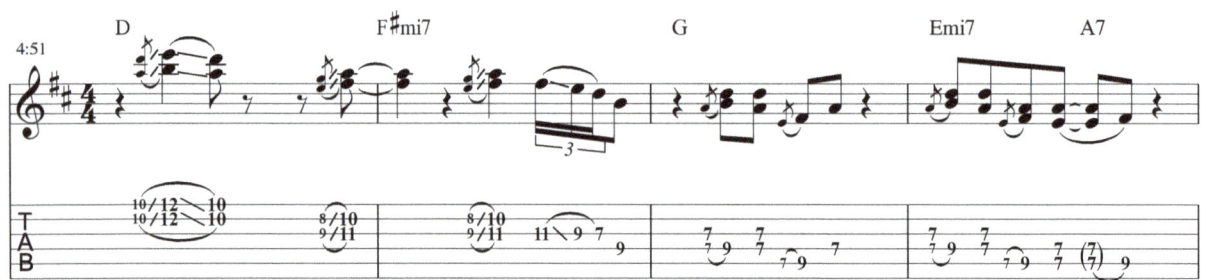

©2020 Fretboard Biology • fretboardbiology.com

Fretboard Biology Level 3 • Unit 3: Improvisation 91

IMPROVISATION

In the last two Improvisation modules you worked with chord tone soloing using major 7 and dominant 7 arpeggios. You just learned the Patterns II and IV minor 7 arpeggios in the Fretboard Logic module, and you will use them here.

Here's a simple two-chord progression: Ami7 to Dmi7 in the key of A minor. To play a key-center solo over this, the source of notes would be the A minor or A minor pentatonic scale. Play through it a few times using the key-center approach.

A Minor Progression

Now use the chord-tone approach. Over the Ami7, use the Pattern IV Ami7 arpeggio. It fits perfectly because the notes are the same as the notes in the chord. Next, over the Dmi7, play the Pattern II Dmi7 arpeggio. This fits perfectly, too, because you are playing the notes of the chord.

A Minor Progression

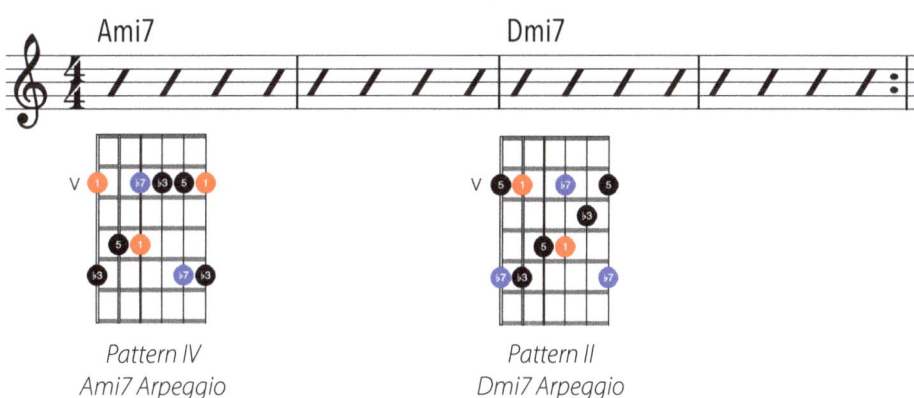

Pattern IV Ami7 Arpeggio   *Pattern II Dmi7 Arpeggio*

Like with the two previous progressions in Units 1 and 2, it is a good idea to play just the arpeggios at first to locate the shapes on the fretboard. Chord tones are target notes. Take another segment of your practice and create short motifs that blend chord tones with scale tones. Keep working on your chord tones!

Level 3 Unit 3 • Improv Demo

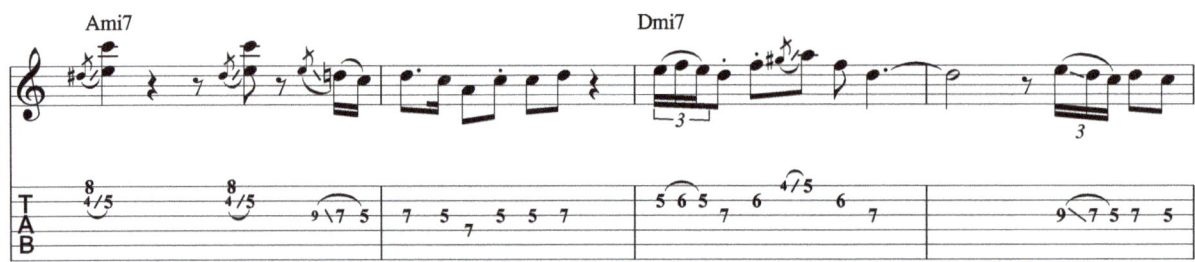

Fretboard Biology — Level 3 • Unit 3: Improvisation

PRACTICE

Theory

- ☐ Go to the tabs below the Theory video on the website and complete the quiz.
- ☐ Memorize chord families with 7th chords in major keys.
- ☐ Work through the Progression Analysis Exercise and check your work with the answer key in the Appendix.

Fretboard Logic

- ☐ Learn the Patterns II and IV minor 7 arpeggios and Patterns II and IV major 7 barre chords.

Technique

- ☐ Practice playing the 1-3-2-1 sequence using strict alternate picking.

Rhythm Guitar

- ☐ Practice the chop and wah pedal parts with a straight 16th-note Reggae groove.

Money Makers

- ☐ Practice the Pattern III major double-stop slides and hammer-ons presented in the Module.

Improvisation

- ☐ Focus on chord-tone soloing over the progression provided using the Pattern IV Ami7 and Pattern II D minor 7 arpeggios.

UNIT 4

Learning Modules

> **Theory** - Analyzing chord progressions in major keys

> **Fretboard Logic** - Patterns II and IV minor, and minor 7(♭5) arpeggios, Patterns II and IV major and dominant 7 barre chords

> **Technique** - 1-2-3 triplet sequence exercise

> **Rhythm Guitar** - Reggae rhythm guitar

> **Money Makers** - Pattern III Money Makers over a progression in A

> **Improvisation** - Using Patterns IV and II minor 7(♭5) arpeggios in a progression in D minor

> **Practice** - Continue practice routine development

THEORY

In the last Theory module you learned about harmonic analysis of chord progressions in major keys that have 7th chords. There are more examples to work through in this module. You will also determine the chord families to which each of these chords belong.

Progression 1

Here is the first progression:

One common indication of the key of a progression is the final chord, which is often the I chord. Consider this the first clue. Cma7 is the final chord. That implies C as the tonic.

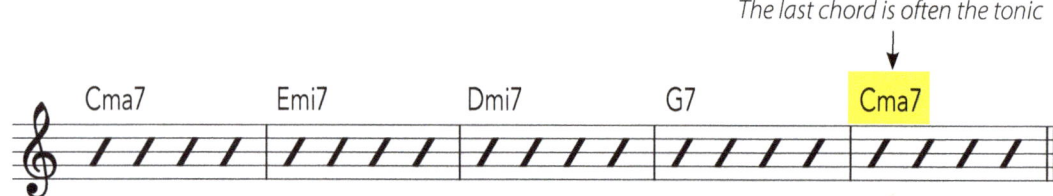

Another very common clue is a dominant 7 chord. In major diatonic harmony there is only one dominant 7 chord, the V7. This progression has G7. There is only one key in which G7 can be V7, and that is C.

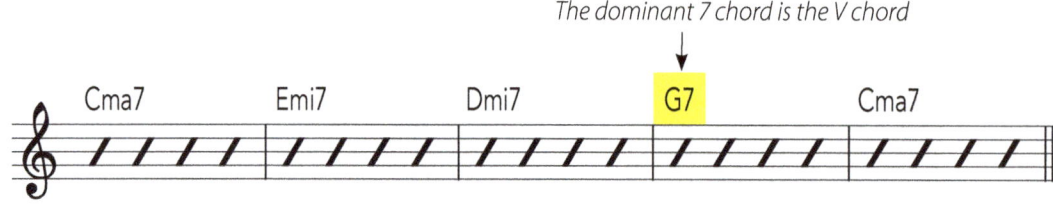

Another very common clue is where two minor 7 chords are a whole step apart. In major diatonic harmony there is only one place this occurs, between II minor 7 and III minor 7. Dmi7 and Emi7 are two minor 7 chords a whole step apart in the key of C.

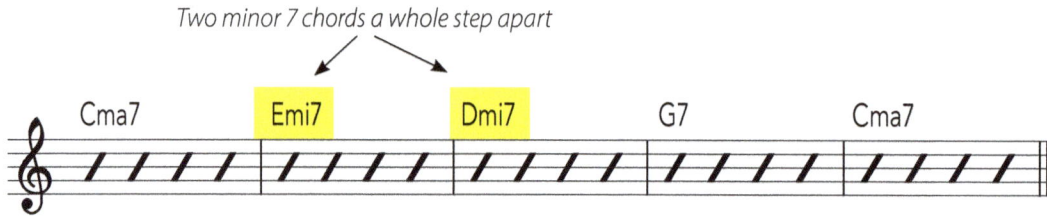

Because of these clues, start with the assumption that this progression is in the key of C. Here is the analysis:

- Cma7, the first chord, works as the I chord, Ima7.
- E is the 3rd scale degree in C and the III chord in a major key is minor 7. Therefore, Emi7 is IIImi7.
- D is the 2nd scale degree in C and the II chord in a major key is minor 7. Therefore, Dmi7 is IImi7.
- You have determined that G7 is V7 in the key of C.
- The last chord, Cma7, is Ima7.

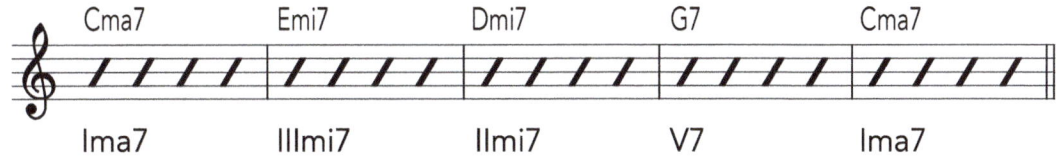

Progression 2

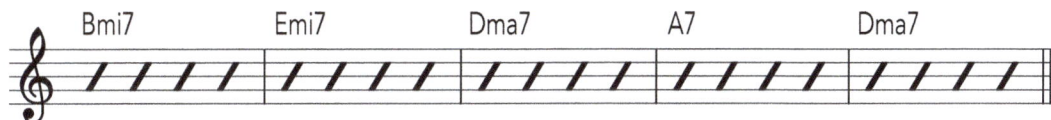

Look at the last chord, as it is often the I chord in the key. The last chord in this progression is Dma7. Start with the assumption Dma7 is the I chord and D is the tonic.

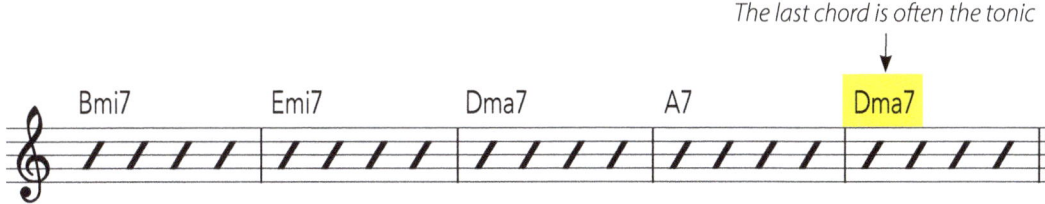

Another clue is a dominant 7 chord which is the V7 in a major key. This progression has A7. There is only one key where A7 can be V7, and that is D.

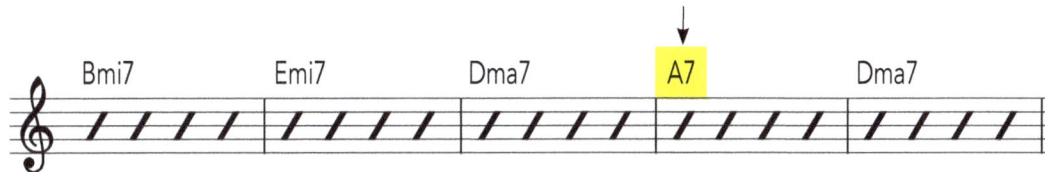

Because of these two clues, start with the assumption that this progression is in the key of D. Here is the analysis:

- B is the 6th scale degree in D and the VI chord in a major key is minor 7. Therefore, Bmi7 can be VImi7.
- E is the 2nd scale degree in D and the II chord in a major key is minor 7. Therefore, Emi7 can be IImi7.
- Dma7 is next and fits as the Ima7 in D.
- You have determined that A7 is V7 and the final chord, Dma7, is Ima7.

Key: D Major

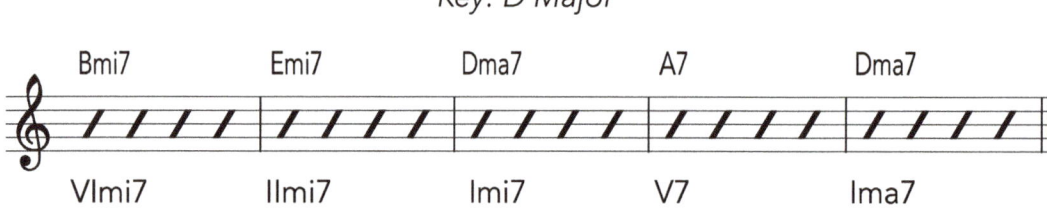

Progression 3

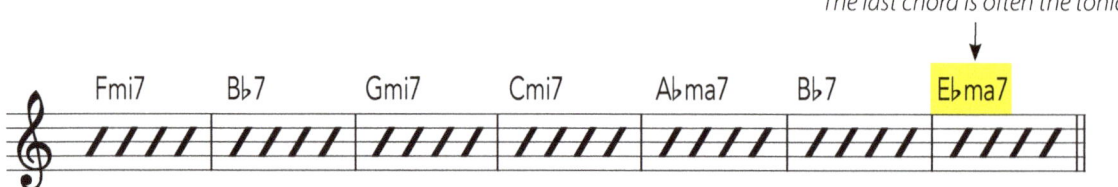

Because the last chord is E♭ma7, start with tentative the assumption that it is the I chord and the tonic is E♭.

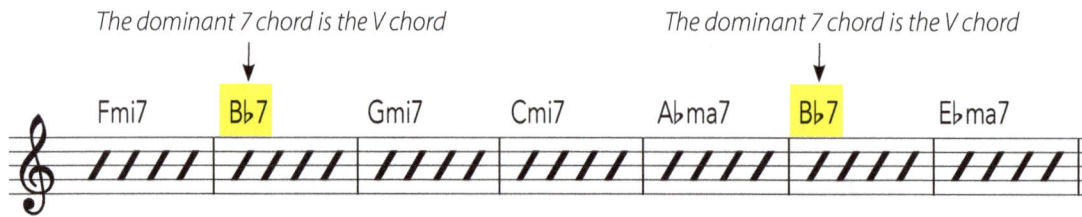

Another clue is the dominant 7 chord which is usually the V7 in a major key. This progression has B♭7. There is only one key where B♭7 can be V7, and that is E♭.

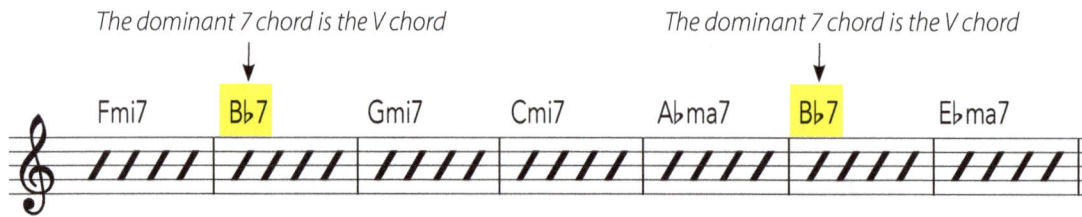

Fretboard Biology — Level 3 • Unit 4: Theory

There are two minor 7 chords a whole step apart, Fmi7 and Gmi7. In major diatonic harmony there is only one place this occurs, II minor 7 and III minor 7.

Two minor 7 chords a whole step apart

Fmi7 | B♭7 | Gmi7 | Cmi7 | A♭ma7 | B♭7 | E♭ma7

Because of these clues, start with the assumption that this progression is in the key of E♭. Here is the analysis:

- F is the 2nd scale degree in E♭ and the II chord in a major key is minor 7. Therefore, Fmi7 is IImi7.
- You have determined that B♭7 is V7 in E♭.
- G is the 3rd scale degree in E♭ and the III chord in a major key is minor 7. Therefore, Gmi7 is IIImi7.
- C is the 6th scale degree in E♭ and the VI chord in a major key is minor 7. Therefore, Cmi7 is VImi7.
- A♭ is the 4th scale degree in E♭ and the IV chord in a major key is major 7. Therefore, A♭ma7 is IVma7.
- You have determined that B♭7 is V7 and E♭ major 7 is Ima7.

Key: E♭ Major

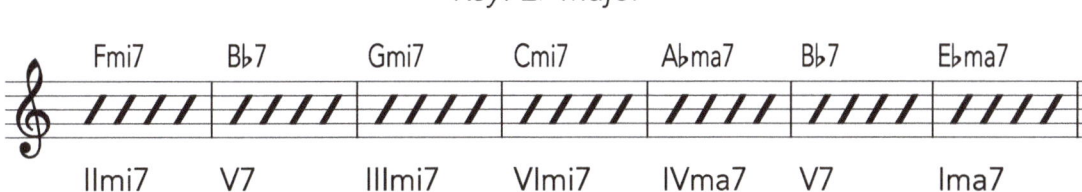

Fmi7 | B♭7 | Gmi7 | Cmi7 | A♭ma7 | B♭7 | E♭ma7
IImi7 | V7 | IIImi7 | VImi7 | IVma7 | V7 | Ima7

Progression 4

Ema7 | D#mi7 | G#mi7 | C#mi7 | F#7 | Bma7

Because the last chord is Bma7, think of it as Ima7 in the key of B to begin.

The last chord is often the tonic

| Ema7 | D#mi7 | G#mi7 | C#mi7 | F#7 | **Bma7** |

This progression has F#7 which is V7 in the key of B.

The dominant 7 chord is the V chord

| Ema7 | D#mi7 | G#mi7 | C#mi7 | **F#7** | Bma7 |

There are two minor 7 chords a whole step apart, C#mi7 and D#m7. They are IImi7 and IIImi7 in the key of B.

Two minor 7 chords a whole step apart

| Ema7 | **D#mi7** | G#mi7 | **C#mi7** | F#7 | Bma7 |

Because of these clues, start with the assumption that this progression is in the key of B. Here is the analysis:
- Ema7 is built on E, the 4th scale degree in B, and the IV chord is major 7.
- You determined that C#mi7 and D#m7, are IImi7 and IIImi7.
- G#mi7 is built on G#, the 6th scale degree in B and the VI chord is minor 7.
- You determined that F#7 is V7 in the key of B.

Key: B Major

| Ema7 | D#mi7 | G#mi7 | C#mi7 | F#7 | Bma7 |
| IVma7 | IIImi7 | VImi7 | IImi7 | V7 | Ima7 |

Progression 5

Notice that in this progression, the last chord is a dominant chord, which is often the V chord in a major key. So, the last chord is E♭7 which is probably not the I chord. Since this progression has E♭7, investigate the key in which it would be V7.

E♭7 is V7 in the key of A♭.

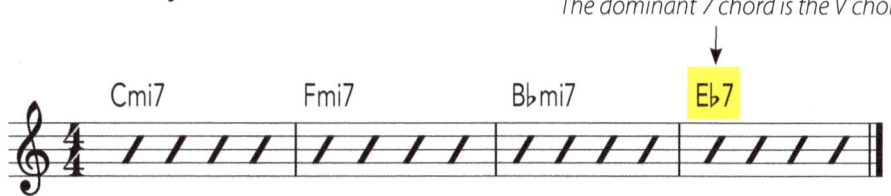

There are two minor 7 chords that are a whole step apart, B♭mi7 and Cmi7. They are IImi7 and IIImi7 in the key of A♭.

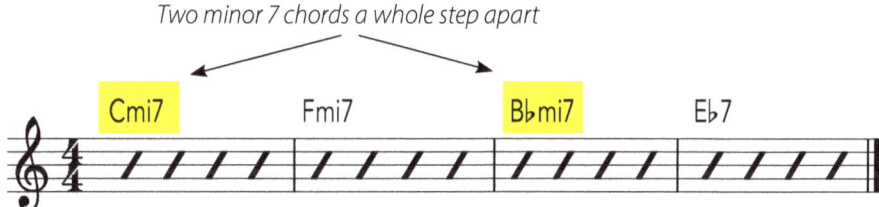

Because of these clues, start with the assumption that this progression is in the key of A♭. Here is the analysis:
- You determined that Cmi7 is IIImi7.
- Fmi7 is built on F, the 6th scale degree in A♭ and the VI chord is minor 7.
- You determined that B♭mi7 is IImi7.
- You determined that E♭7 is V7.

Key: A♭ Major

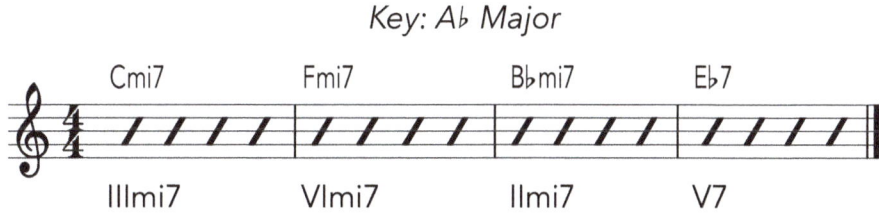

This progression is in the key of A♭ major but does not resolve to its tonic chord, A♭ma7. Is this possible? Absolutely.

Progression 6

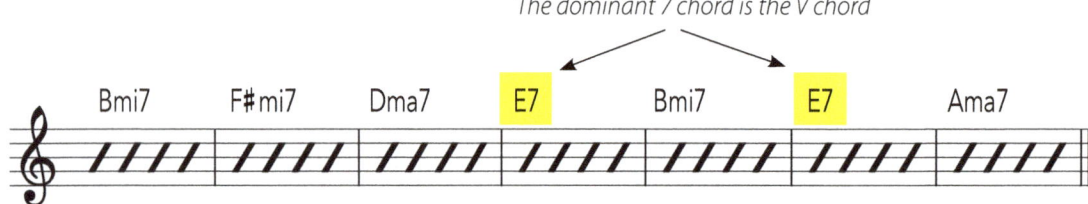

Because the last chord is Ama7, think of it as Ima7 and A as a the tonic.

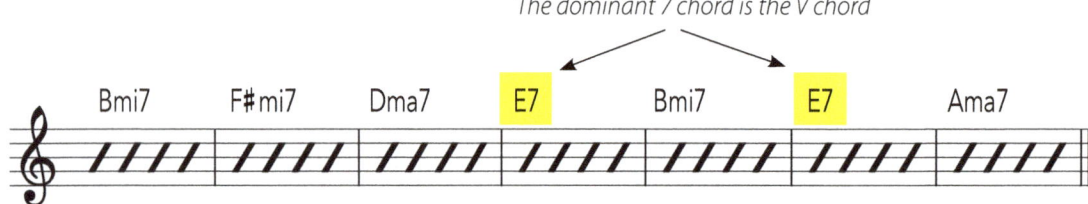

The last chord is often the tonic

This progression has E7, which is V7 in the key of A.

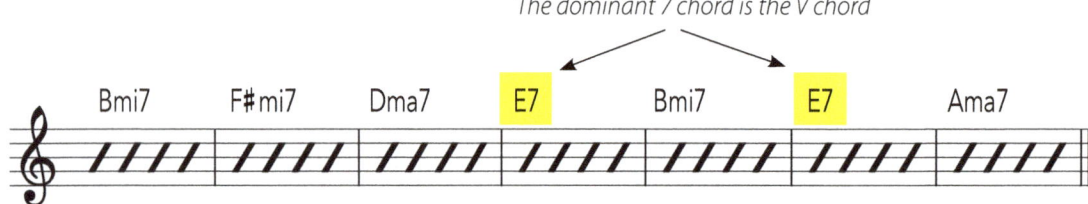

The dominant 7 chord is the V chord

Because of these clues, start with the assumption that this progression is in the key of A. Here is the analysis:

- Bmi7 is built on B, the 2nd scale degree in the key of A and the II chord is minor 7.
- F#mi7 is built on F#, the 6th scale degree in the key of A and the VI chord is minor 7.
- Dma7 is built on D, the 4th scale degree in A and the IV chord is major 7.
- You determined that E7 is V7 in the key of A.
- You determined that Bmi7 is IImi7 in the key of A.
- You determined that E7 is V7 in the key of A.
- A major 7 is Ima7.

Key: A Major

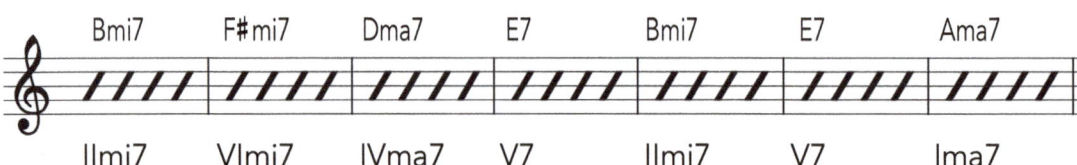

You now see how this is done. Get in the habit of analyzing every chord progression you see. For the time being there will be progressions that you won't understand because you have only learned analysis of progressions that use all diatonic chords.

As we progress through the Fretboard Biology Theory Modules, you will systematically be presented with methods of understanding the non-diatonic chords you will encounter. This is a gradual process that relies on your firm understanding of diatonic harmony. Make sure you are in command of diatonic harmony.

Progression Analysis Exercise

The next few pages contain an exercise to help you develop your skills in quickly analyzing progressions. The example will show you how to fill out this worksheet. Your goal is to identify two things: 1) the key of the progression and 2) the number of each chord in the progression.

EXAMPLE:

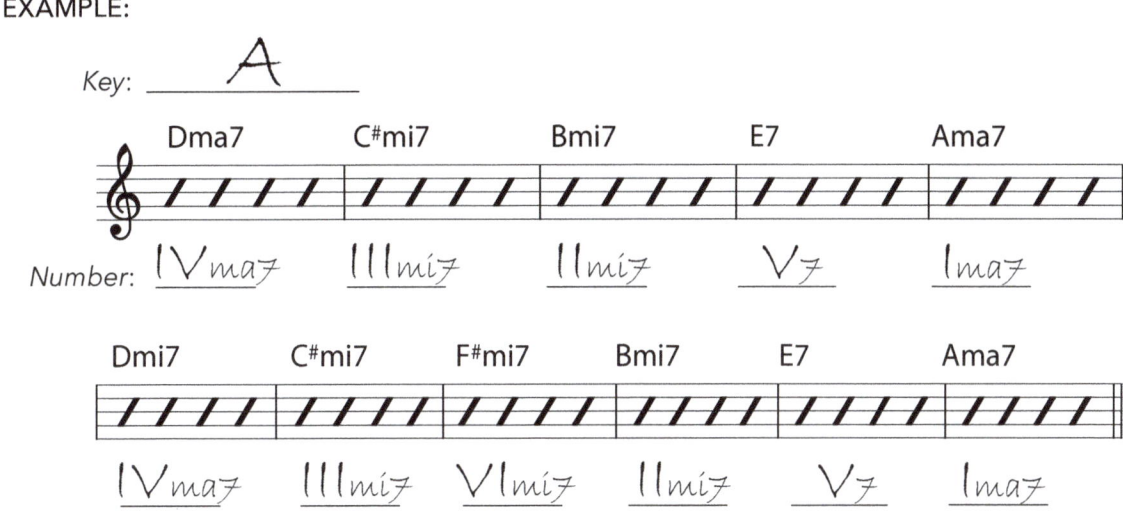

Once you complete the exercise, you can check the answer key in the Appendix of this book. If you struggle with this exercise, keep working at it until it becomes second-nature.

Good luck!

Progression Analysis Exercise

Answer key located on Page 275

Step One: Make a tentative determination of the key.
Step Two: Based on this, determine the number (function) of each chord.
Step Three: Confirm and label the key and function of each chord.

EXAMPLE:

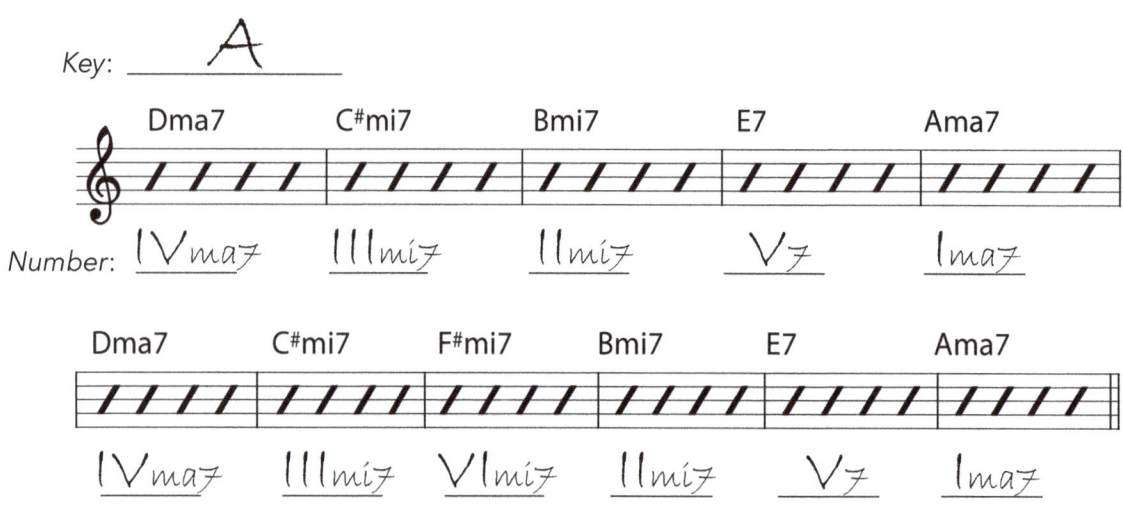

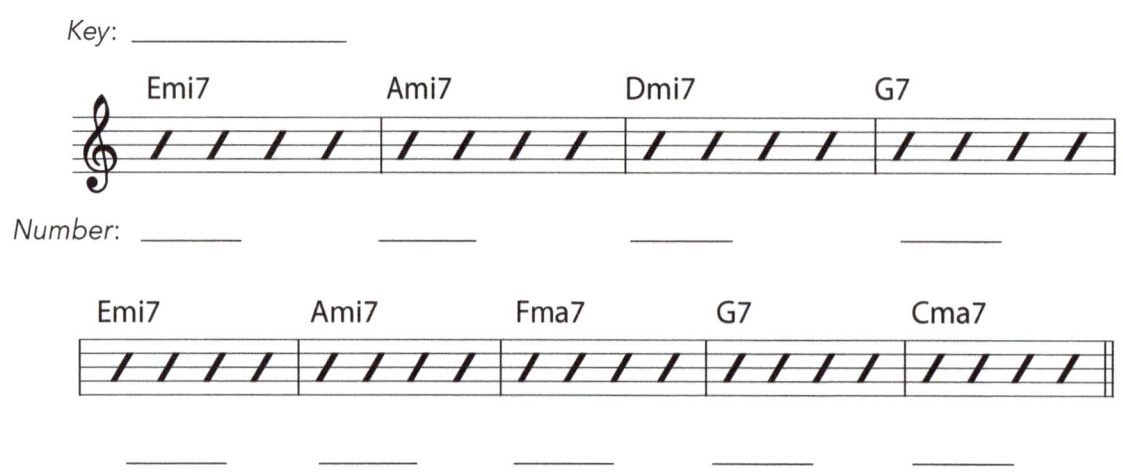

Progression Analysis Exercise

Key: _____

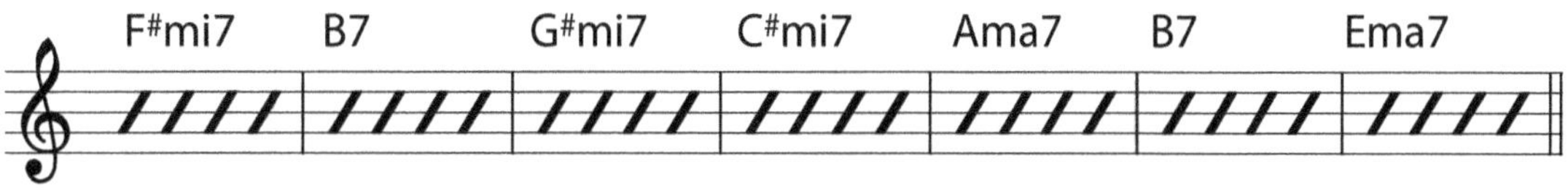

| F#mi7 | B7 | G#mi7 | C#mi7 | Ama7 | B7 | Ema7 |

Number: _____ _____ _____ _____ _____ _____ _____

Key: _____

| Dmi7 | Gmi7 | Cmi7 | Dmi7 | E♭ma7 |

Number: _____ _____ _____ _____ _____

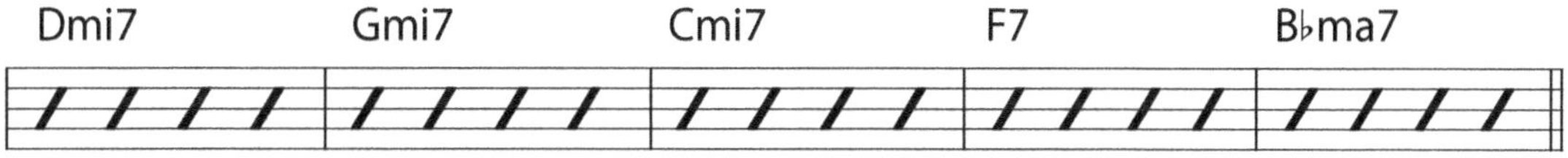

| Dmi7 | Gmi7 | Cmi7 | F7 | B♭ma7 |

_____ _____ _____ _____ _____

Key: _____

| Cma7 | Bmi7 | Ami7 | D7 | Gma7 |

Number: _____ _____ _____ _____ _____

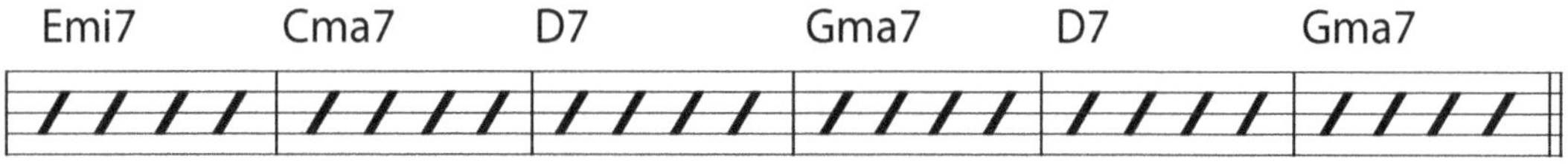

| Emi7 | Cma7 | D7 | Gma7 | D7 | Gma7 |

_____ _____ _____ _____ _____ _____

Progression Analysis Exercise

Key: _____

| A♭ma7 | D♭ma7 | B♭mi7 | E♭7 |

Number: _____   _____   _____   _____

| Cmi7 | Fmi7 | B♭mi7 | E♭7 |

_____   _____   _____   _____

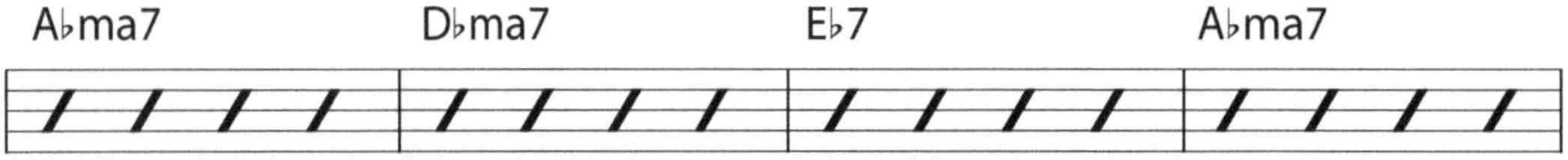

| A♭ma7 | D♭ma7 | E♭7 | A♭ma7 |

_____   _____   _____   _____

Key: _____

| Ami7 | Dmi7 | Gmi7 | C7 | Ami7 |

Number: _____   _____   _____   _____   _____

| Dmi7 | B♭ma7 | C7 | Gmi7 | C7 | Fma7 |

_____   _____   _____   _____   _____   _____

FRETBOARD LOGIC

You have learned two major 7, two dominant 7, and two minor 7 arpeggios. Next you will learn the Patterns II and IV minor 7(♭5) chord arpeggios.

Arpeggios

Minor 7(♭5) chords are built by adding a minor 7th to a diminished triad. They can also be derived from a minor triad arpeggio by flatting the 5th and adding a minor 7th.

First, on the Pattern II minor triad arpeggio, flat the 5th making it a diminished triad.

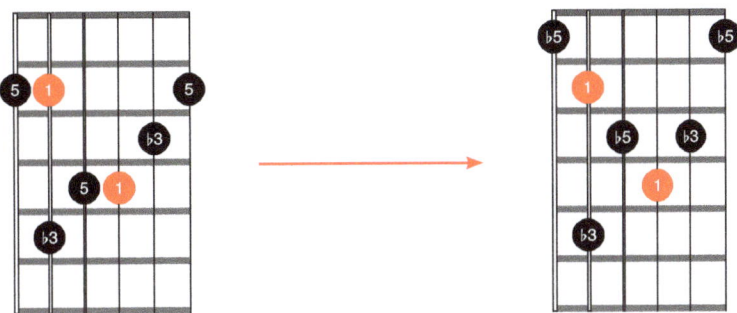

Pattern II Minor Triad Arpeggio   Pattern II Diminished Triad Arpeggio

Now add a minor 7th everywhere possible to the Pattern II diminished triad arpeggio to build the Pattern II minor 7(♭5) arpeggio.

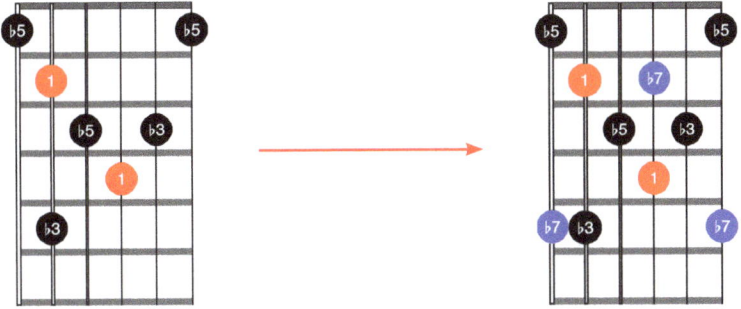

Pattern II Diminished Triad Arpeggio   Pattern II Minor 7(♭5) Arpeggio

Practice this with alternate picking starting and ending on the root.

Next, look at a Pattern IV minor triad arpeggio. Again, flat the 5th to create a Pattern IV diminished triad.

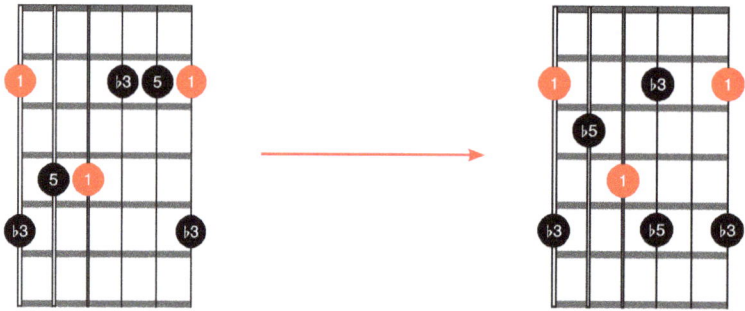

Next add a minor 7th everywhere possible within to build a Pattern IV minor 7(♭5) arpeggio.

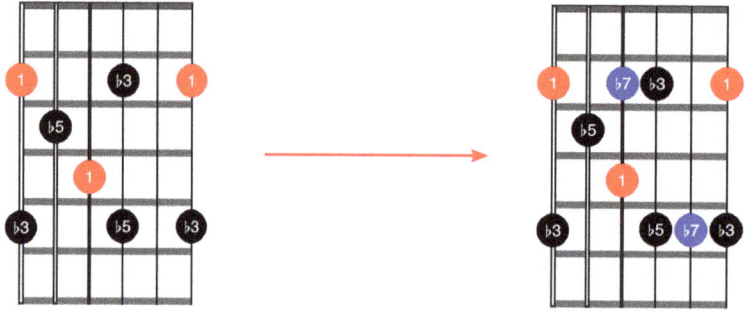

Practice this with alternate picking starting and ending on the root.

NOTE: Minor7(♭5) arpeggios are commonly played but diminished triad arpeggios are rarely played. They are included here for illustration purposes. I don't recommend putting time into practicing diminished triad arpeggios because the huge gap between the diminished 5th and the octave of the root makes them awkward to play. That being said, there are two different 7th chord arpeggios built on diminished triads: minor 7(♭5) and diminished 7. Minor 7(♭5) arpeggios are discussed here and diminished 7th arpeggios are discussed in a later Module.

Chords

Dominant 7 chords can be built from the Patterns IV and II barre chords. Here is a Pattern IV major barre chord with the chord tones labeled. Create a dominant 7 chord within this shape. Replace the root on the 4th string with a minor 7th. The result is a Pattern IV dominant 7 chord, and it's movable anywhere on the fretboard.

You can also add a minor 7th on the 2nd string (shown in gray).

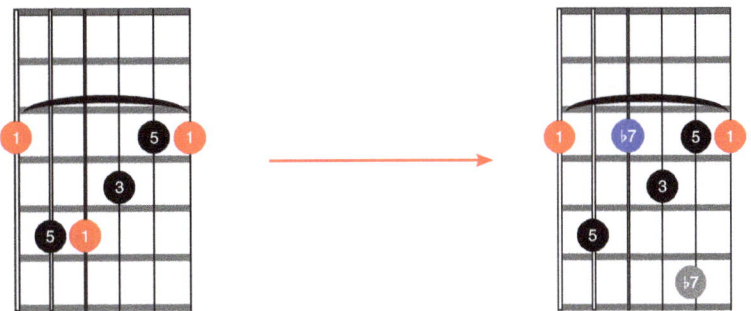

Here is a pattern II major barre chord with the chord tones labeled. Create a dominant 7th chord within this shape. Replace the root on the 3rd string with a minor 7th. The result is a Pattern II dominant 7 chord, and it's movable anywhere on the fretboard.

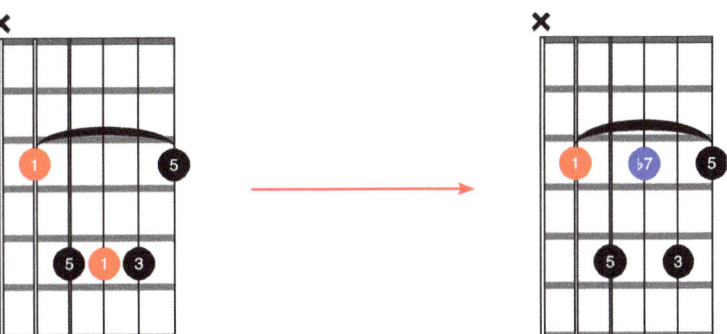

Be sure to check in on the Family Tree as you progress and see how the new information you learn fits in.

TECHNIQUE

In this module you will learn a scale sequence based on an 8th-note triplet subdivision. As with the others, learn it using the Pattern IV major scale in the key of A. It is a three-note sequence called it the "1-2-3 triplet sequence".

1-2-3 Triplet Sequence

Play three notes in a row ascending starting on the tonic. Next, play three notes in a row ascending starting on the 2nd scale degree. Next, play three notes in a row ascending starting on the 3rd scale degree and keep repeating this sequence up to the highest notes you can play in the scale pattern.

Ascending, this sequence looks like this.

1-2-3 Triplet Sequence Exercise - Ascending

Descending, this sequence looks like this.:

1-2-3 Triplet Sequence Exercise - Descending

Work on this exercise very slowly. Make sure you are consistent with alternate picking. When you feel like you are ready, set your metronome at slow tempo – perhaps 50 to 60 bpm.

RHYTHM GUITAR

In the last Rhythm Guitar module you learned parts that stay out of each other's way. In this module, you will learn another secondary guitar part that can be played along with the chop. In this example, the guitar part doubles the bass guitar part, but an octave higher. It's called a "stuck line".

Progression in A Major

Here is a two-bar progression in A major with a swung-16th groove.

A Major Progression

Like in the first three examples, it needs the essential chop part played with the second 8th note of each beat with a downstroke.

Chop Part

The second part doubles the bass guitar an octave higher. The stuck line brings the bass line more to the forefront as a counterpoint melody under the lead vocal melody.

Stuck Line

First, play the chop part, which will blend with the organ bubble and piano on the off beats.

Next play the stuck line. It should cut through the mix so use a moderately bright tone. Depending on your guitar, you might get the right tone by playing on your bridge pick up or middle and bridge pickups.

MONEY MAKERS

This module adds a couple of 6th interval double stop shapes to your Money Maker vocabulary. The progression for this example is in the key of A and has three chords: A, D, and E. The goal is to play some specific double stop combinations that fit over specific chords because they are chord tones. Here is the progression and analysis:

Shapes over the I major chord (A)

Over A, the I chord, the best two shapes are:

1. The 3rd, C#, 2nd finger at the 6th fret of the 3rd string. The root and tonic, A, 1st finger at the 5th fret of the 1st string.
2. The 5th of the A chord, E, 1st finger at the 2nd fret of the 4th string. The 3rd of the A chord, C#, also 1st finger at the 2nd fret of the 2nd string. Barre these notes.

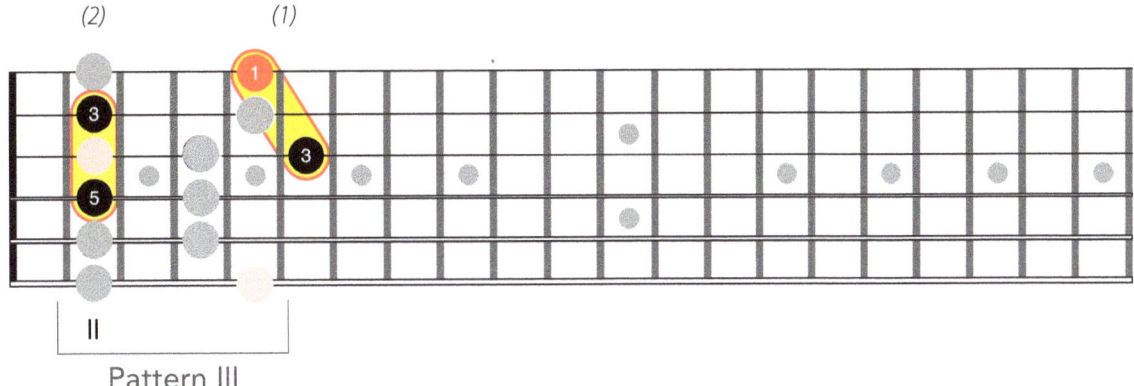

A is the I chord. These are I chord money makers based around Pattern III and are transposable to any key.

Shapes over the IVma Chord (D)

Over the chord IV chord, D, the best two shapes are:

1. The 5th of the D chord, A, 1st finger at the 2nd fret of the 3rd string. The 3rd of the D chord, F#, 1st finger at the 2nd fret of the 1st string. Barre these notes.

2. The 3rd of the D chord, F#, 3rd finger at the 4th fret of the 4th string. The root of the D chord, D, 2nd finger, 3rd fret, 2nd string.

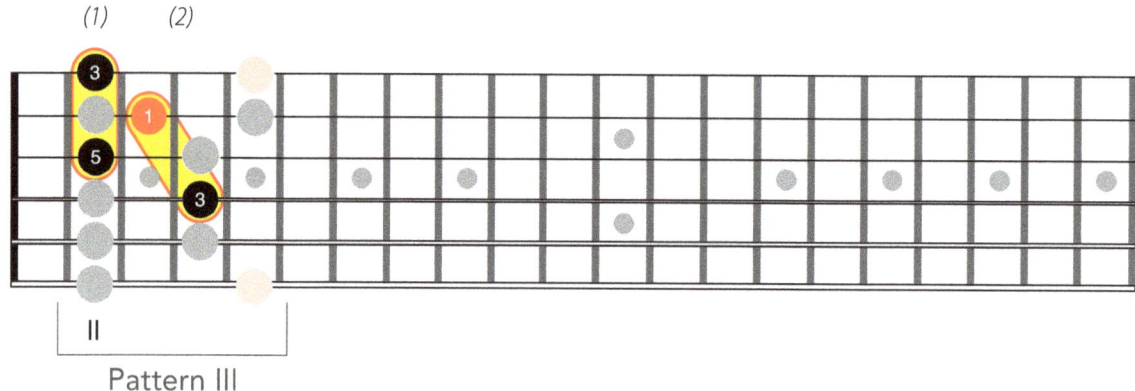

Pattern III

Notice how these are both pieces of a Pattern I D triad.

D Triad

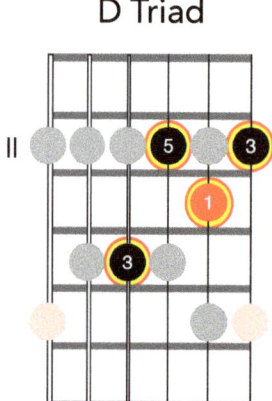

D is the IV chord. These are IV chord money makers with the Pattern III octave shape and transposable to any key.

Shapes over the Vma Chord (E)

Over the I chord E, the best two shapes are:

1. The 5th of the E chord, B, 1st finger at the 4th fret of the 3rd string. The 3rd of the E chord, G#, 1st finger at the 4th fret of the 1st string. Barre these two notes.
2. The 3rd of the E chord, G#, 3rd finger at the 6th fret of the 4th string. The root of the E chord, E, 2nd finger at the 5th fret of the 2nd string.

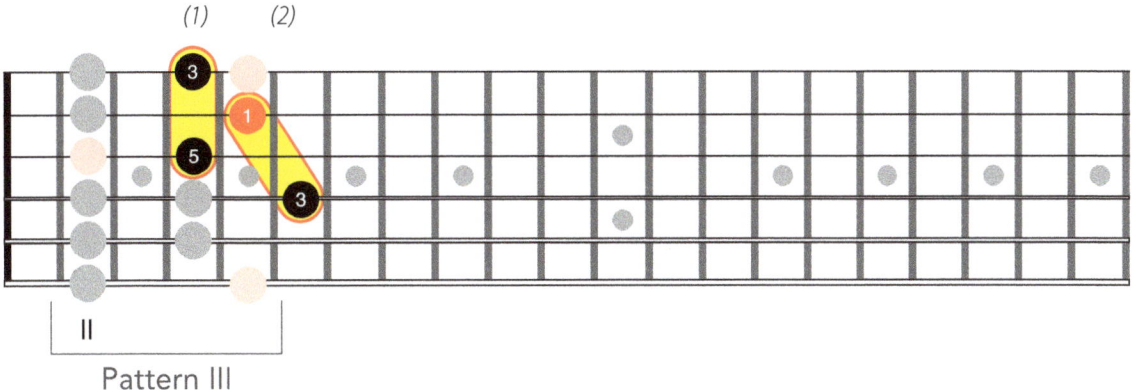

Pattern III

Again, notice how these are both pieces of a Pattern I E triad.

E Triad

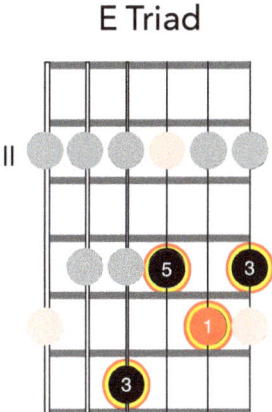

E is the V chord. These are V chord money makers when using Pattern III in any key. All of these ideas in this Module are transposable to all major keys.

Level 3 Unit 4 • Money Maker Demo

IMPROVISATION

You have used major 7, minor 7, and dominant 7 arpeggios so far to access chord tones. In the Fretboard Logic module, you just learned the Patterns II and IV minor 7(♭5). You'll put those to work in this module.

Minor7(♭5) chords have a very unstable sound because they are built from a diminished triad. Diminished triads are unstable because of the dissonant diminished 5th interval between the root and flatted 5th. Because of this instability, it does not make sense to vamp on a static minor7(♭5) chord. So instead, use a progression that moves between a minor7(♭5) and more stable sounding minor 7 chord.

Here is a simple two-chord progression: Emi7(♭5) to Dmi7. It is in the key of D minor and if you played a key-center solo over this, your sources of notes would be the D minor or D minor pentatonic scale. Like with the progressions in the earlier Units, that will be less than satisfying to the listener because it is a little vague.

But I suggest you first play a key-center solo over the track to get acquainted with the track and feel of the changes.

D Minor Progression

Next, use the chord-tone approach. On Emi7(♭5), use the Pattern II Emi7(♭5) arpeggio. It fits because the notes are the same as those in the chord. Next, over the Dmi7, play the Pattern II Dmi7 arpeggio. It fits because the notes are the same as those in the chord.

D Minor Progression

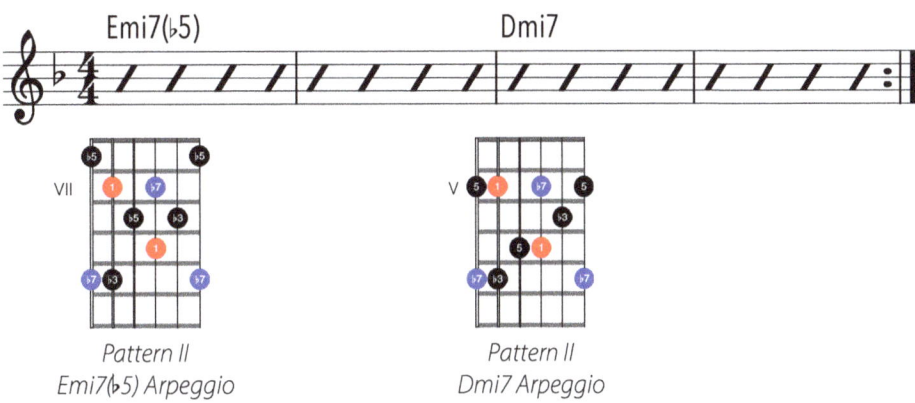

Pattern II Emi7(♭5) Arpeggio

Pattern II Dmi7 Arpeggio

Like with the previous progressions in Units 1, 2, and 3, practice playing only arpeggios for part of your practice. This will help you visualize the shapes on the fretboard.

Take another segment of your practice and create short motifs that blend chord tones and scale tones. Practice this in another position, too. On the Emi7(♭5), use the Pattern IV Emi7(♭5) arpeggio in 12th position. On the Dmi7, use the Pattern IV Dmi7 arpeggio in 10th position.

D Minor Progression

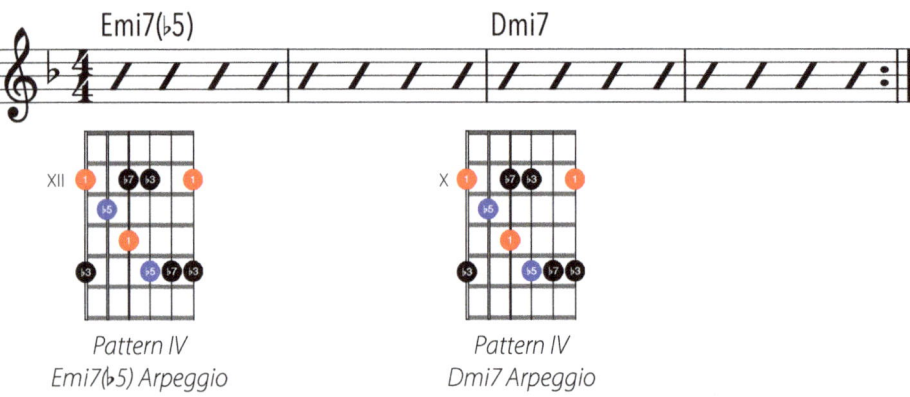

Practice this in another position, too. On the Emi7(♭5), use the Pattern IV Emi7(♭5) arpeggio in 12th position. On the Dmi7, use the Pattern IV Dmi7 arpeggio in 10th position. Keep working on your chord tones!

Level 3 Unit 4 • Improv Demo

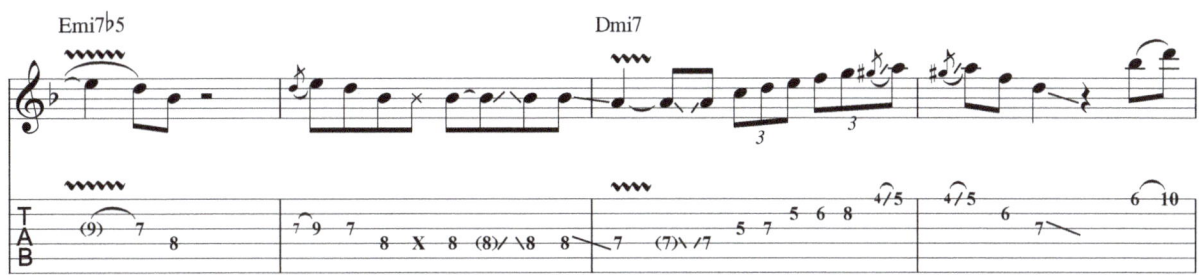

PRACTICE

Theory

- ☐ Go to the tabs below the Theory video on the website and complete the quiz.
- ☐ Work through the Progression Analysis Exercise and check your work with the answer key in the Appendix.

Fretboard Logic

- ☐ Learn the Patterns II and IV minor and minor 7(♭5) arpeggios.
- ☐ Learn and practice the Patterns II and IV major and dominant 7th barre chords.

Technique

- ☐ Learn the 1-2-3 triplet sequence using strict alternate picking.

Rhythm Guitar

- ☐ Practice the chop and stuck parts in Reggae rhythm guitar

Money Makers

- ☐ Practice the Pattern III money maker shapes over the progression in the key of A.

Improvisation

- ☐ Focus on chord-tone soloing using the Patterns IV and II minor 7(♭5) arpeggios to outline chord tones in the progression provided.

UNIT 5

Learning Modules

> **Theory** - Harmonizing the natural minor scale with 7th chords

> **Fretboard Logic** - Patterns II, IV, and V major 7 arpeggios, Patterns II and IV minor 7 barre chords

> **Technique** - Diatonic 3rds sequence exercise

> **Rhythm Guitar** - Reggae rhythm guitar

> **Money Makers** - Pattern III money makers over a progression in A

> **Improvisation** - Soloing with chord tones in F

> **Practice** - Continue practice routine development

THEORY

You have learned to harmonize both the major and natural minor scales with triads as well the major scale with 7th chords. In this Unit you will harmonize the natural minor scale with 7th chords. This will help you understand how 7th chords function together within minor diatonic harmony.

Harmonizing the Natural Minor Scale with 7th Chords

To harmonize the seven-note natural minor scale with 7th chords, start on the 1st scale degree and find the diatonic notes from the scale a 3rd, a 5th, and a 7th higher. A 7th chord is formed with these four notes. Its quality is determined by the combination of qualities of the 3rd, 5th, and 7th.

Here is the C natural minor scale with the scale degrees numbered one through seven.

C Minor Scale

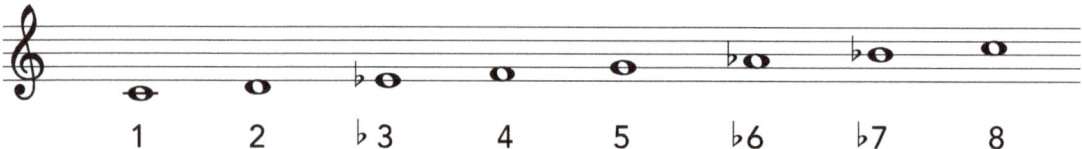

The I Chord

Start with the 1st scale degree, C.

The I Chord

Find the note a 3rd above the root, and it has to be from the key, which is C minor. That note is E♭. Next, find the note a 5th above C from the C minor scale, too. That note is G. Next, find the note a 7th above C, B♭.

The I Chord

Analyze the intervals and then compare them to the 7th chord interval formulas. E♭ is a minor 3rd above C, G is a perfect 5th above C, and B♭ is a minor 7th above C.

The 7th chord with a minor 3rd, a perfect 5th, and minor 7th is a minor 7 chord.

I Chord

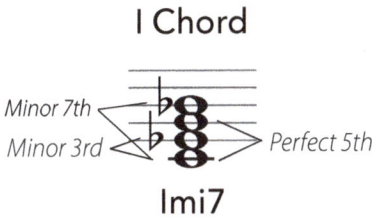

Imi7

Conclusion: The I chord is minor 7. Label it Imi7.

The II Chord

Next, build the II chord. Begin with the 2nd scale degree, D.

From the key of C minor, find the note a 3rd above D: F. Find the note a 5th above D: A♭. Find a note a 7th above D: C.

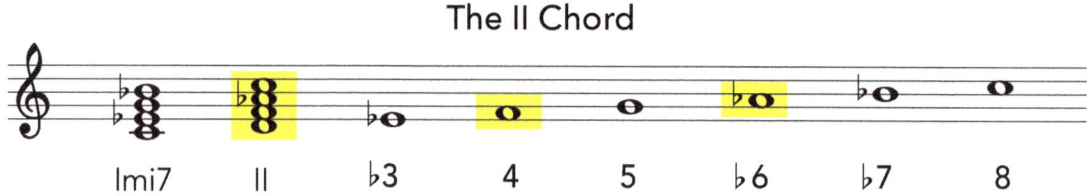

Analyze the intervals and then compare them to the 7th chord interval formulas. F is a minor 3rd above D, A♭ is a diminished 5th above D, and C is a minor 7th above D.

The 7th chord with a minor 3rd, diminished 5th, and a minor 7 is a minor 7(♭5) chord.

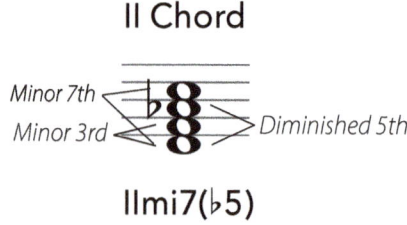

Conclusion: The II chord is minor 7(♭5). Label it IImi7(♭5), or half diminished.

The ♭III Chord

Let's build a chord on the minor 3rd scale degree. It is labeled ♭III because it is built on the minor 3rd, and it's common to say flatted or flat 3rd scale degree.

Start with the ♭3rd scale degree which is E♭. From the key of C minor, find the note a 3rd above E♭: G. Find the note a 5th above E♭: B♭. Find the note a 7th above E♭: D.

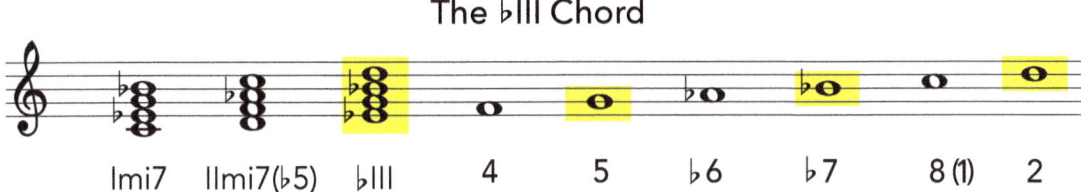

Analyze the intervals and then compare the them to the 7th chord interval formulas. G is a major 3rd above E♭, B♭ is a perfect 5th above E♭, and D is a major 7th above E♭.

The 7th chord with a major 3rd, perfect 5th, and major 7th is a major 7 chord.

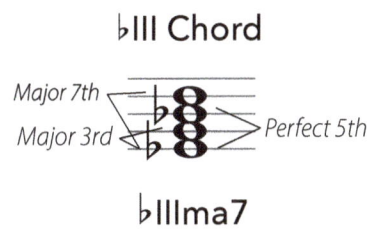

Conclusion: The ♭III chord is major 7. Label it ♭IIIma7.

The IV Chord

Build a chord on the 4th scale degree, F.

The IV Chord

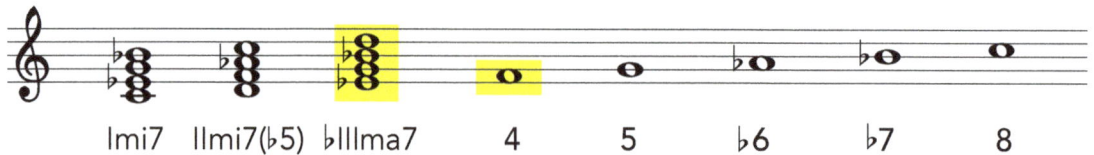

From the key of C minor, find the note a 3rd above F: A♭. Find the note a 5th above F: C. Find the note a 7th above F: E♭.

IV Chord

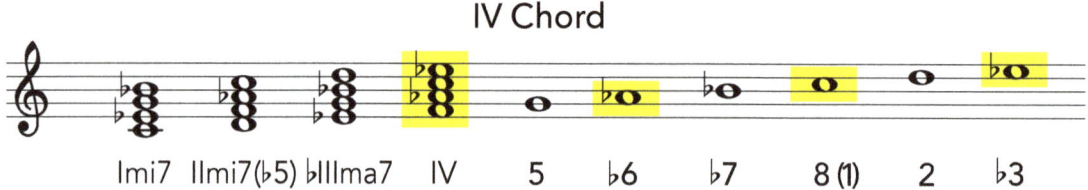

Analyze the intervals and then compare them to the 7th chord interval formulas. A♭ is a minor 3rd above F, C is a perfect 5th above F, and E♭ is a minor 7th above F.

The 7th chord with a minor 3rd, a perfect 5th, and minor 7th is a minor 7 chord.

IV Chord

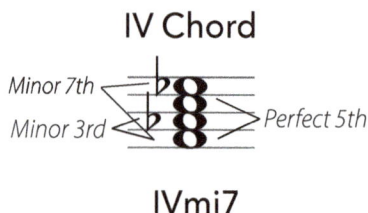

IVmi7

Conclusion: The IV chord is minor 7. Label it IVmi7

The V Chord

Build a chord on the 5th scale degree, G.

The V Chord

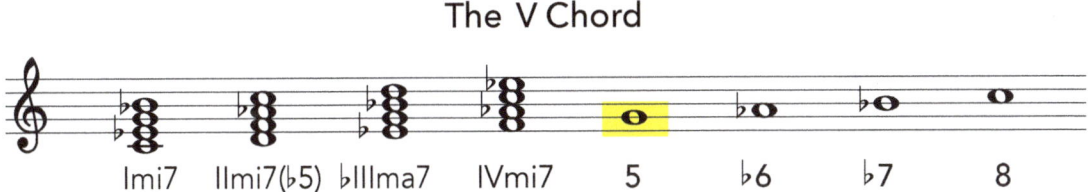

From the key of C minor, find the note a 3rd above G: B♭. Find the note a 5th above G: D. Find the note a 7th above G: F.

V Chord

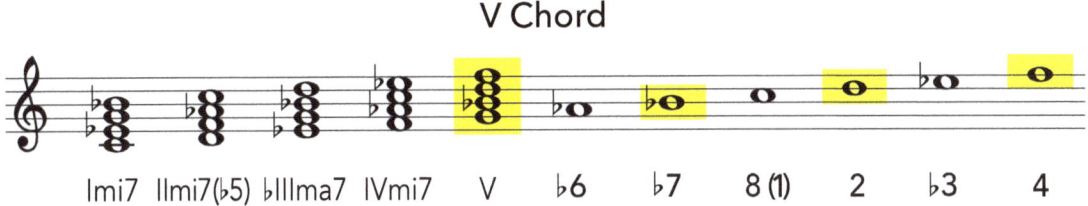

Analyze the intervals and then compare them to the 7th chord interval formulas. B♭ is a minor 3rd above G, D is a perfect 5th above G, and F is a minor 7th above G.

The 7th chord with a minor 3rd, a perfect 5th, and minor 7th is a minor 7 chord.

V Chord

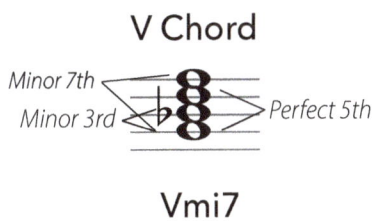

Vmi7

Conclusion: The V chord is minor 7. Label it Vmi7.

It is important to point out that the V chord in a minor key often appears as a dominant 7 chord.

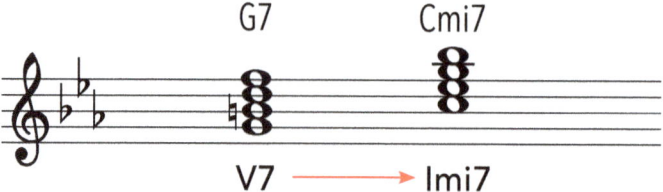

This is a result of a brief entrance into the harmonic minor scale for the duration of the V chord only. It introduces what is called the leading tone. A leading tone is the major 7th degree of a scale.

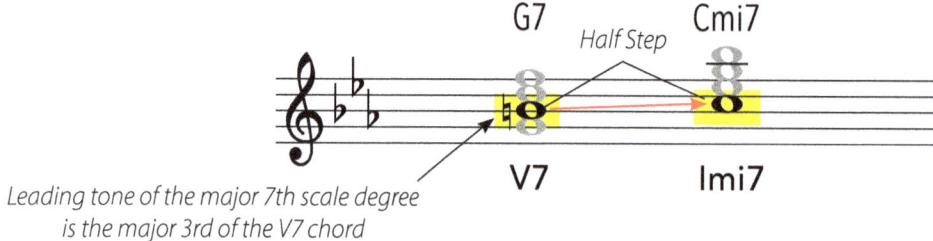

Leading tone of the major 7th scale degree is the major 3rd of the V7 chord

This major 7th scale degree has a powerful effect on the listener because it leads the ear up a half step to resolution on the tonic. Play it to hear the effect.

Because the natural minor scale formula calls for a minor 7, the leading tone effect is absent.

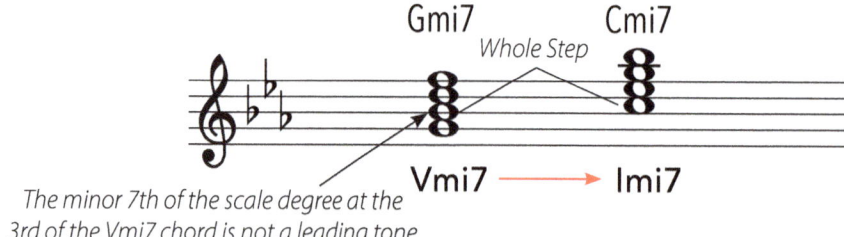

The minor 7th of the scale degree at the 3rd of the Vmi7 chord is not a leading tone

Composers and songwriters often use a V7 in place of a Vmi7 to achieve this leading tone effect. For example, in the key of C minor, that diatonic V chord is Gmi7, which is labeled Vmi7. It is quite common to replace it with a G7. This topic is discussed this topic in great detail in later level.

The ♭VI Chord

Build the ♭VI chord on the flatted 6th scale degree, A♭.

The ♭VI Chord

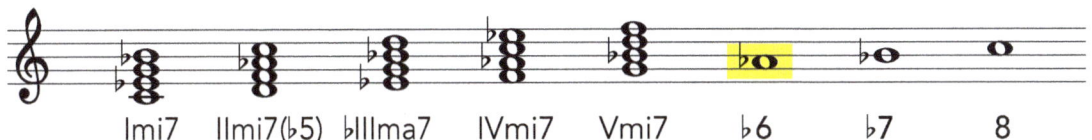

Find a note the 3rd above A♭: C. Find the note a 5th above A♭: E♭. Find the note a 7th above A♭: G.

The ♭VI Chord

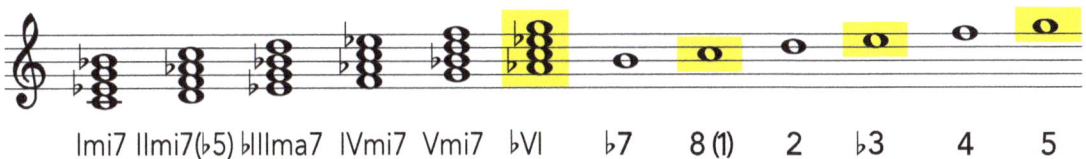

Analyze the intervals and then compare them to the 7th chord interval formulas. C is a major 3rd above A♭, E♭ is a perfect 5th above A♭, and G is a major 7th above A♭.

The 7th chord with a major 3rd, perfect 5th, and major 7th is a major 7 chord.

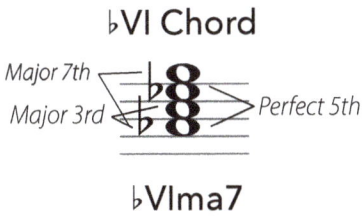

Conclusion: The ♭VI chord is major7 Label it ♭VIma7.

The ♭VII Chord

Build the ♭VII chord on the flatted 7th scale degree, B♭.

The ♭VII Chord

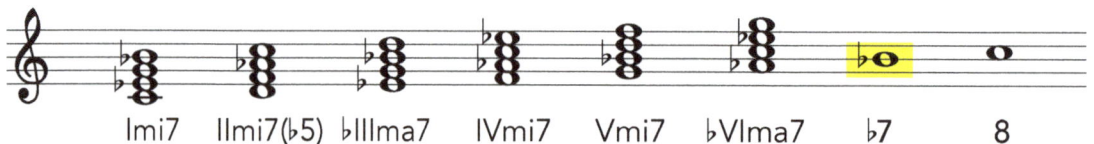

From the C minor scale, find the note a 3rd above B♭: D. Find the note a 5th above B♭: F. Find the note a 7th above B♭: A♭.

♭VII Chord

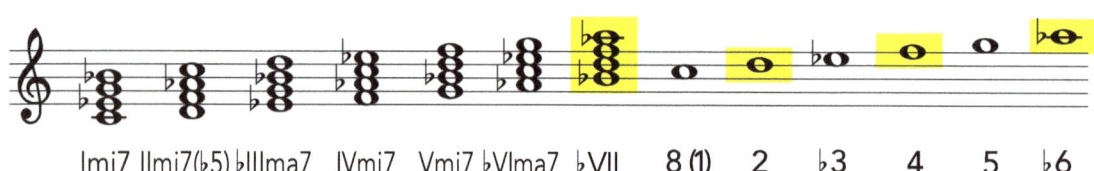

Analyze the intervals and then compare them to the 7th chord interval formulas. D is a major 3rd above B♭, F is a perfect 5th above B♭, and A♭ is a minor 7th above B♭.

The 7th chord with a major 3rd, perfect 5th, and minor 7th is a dominant 7 chord.

♭VII Chord

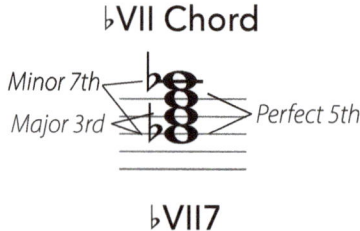

Conclusion: The ♭VII chord is dominant. Label it ♭VII7.

The Harmonized C Minor Scale with 7th Chords

The Harmonized C Minor Scale with 7th Chords

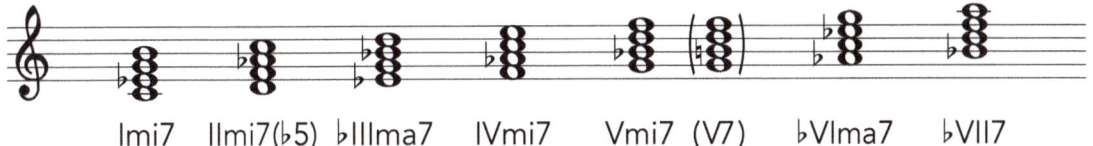

Imi7   IImi7(♭5)   ♭IIIma7   IVmi7   Vmi7 (V7)   ♭VIma7   ♭VII7

Here are the chords of the harmonized C minor scale:
- I chord is Cmi7
- II chord is Dmi7(♭5), sometimes called half diminished
- ♭III chord is E♭ma7
- IV chord is Fmi7
- V chord is Gmi7 or sometimes G7
- ♭VI chord is A♭ma7
- ♭VII chord is B♭7

These chords, other than V7, are diatonic to the key of C natural minor. This process can be repeated with the natural minor scale on any other tonic and the result will be the same: the I chord will always be minor 7, the II chord will always be minor 7(♭5), the ♭III chord will always be major 7, the IV chord will always be minor 7, the V chord can be minor 7 or dominant 7, the ♭VI chord will always be major 7, the ♭VII chord will always be dominant 7.

Memorize this. Here's a little trick that might help:
- In minor, the I, IV, and V chords are minor 7
- II is minor 7(♭5)
- ♭III and ♭VI are major 7
- ♭VII is dominant

In the next Units you will be learning about harmonic analysis for chord progressions using 7th chords in minor keys. This skill is important for understanding what to play when improvising, playing chords, or arranging in minor keys. You need to know what chords belong to all minor keys.

Because key signatures determine the notes of every key and because the qualities of the chords built on each scale degree is the same in all minor keys, any chord (I through ♭VII) in any minor key can be identified easily making it possible to understand the harmony of a song. To prepare for this, quiz yourself on the chords in every minor key.

If you know the quality of the chord built on each scale degree and know all the minor scales (through your understanding of key signatures), you can you know what chords belong to any and all minor keys.

Try a few.

- What is the II chord in G minor?
- What is the V chord in D minor
- What is the ♭VII chord in C# minor?
- What is IV chord in F minor?
- What is the ♭III chord in E♭ minor?
- What is the ♭VI chord in B♭ minor?

Now you know both the harmonized major and minor scales with triads and 7th chords. These are important milestones. If you are not understanding any part of this, go back and review the last few Units until you are comfortable. It is pointless to go on without a thorough understanding of all the important foundational material you have studied so far.

Here is some context about where all of this information takes you. Through your study of scale construction, key signatures, triad and 7th chord construction, and the harmonized major and minor scales, you have a working understanding of the major and minor diatonic systems.

After several more Units, the Theory Modules gradually move into the study of non-diatonic harmony. The term "non-diatonic harmony" sounds more complicated than it is. With a solid foundation in diatonic harmony, it is not hard to grasp. Most of the music you have heard in your life uses at least a few chords and notes from outside the diatonic systems. Non-diatonic notes and chords are part of what makes music interesting. Here is the point: Non-diatonic harmony can't really be studied until you have a grasp on diatonic harmony; that is, the major and minor diatonic systems.

This program moves through the material in a deliberate way so that when non-diatonic harmony is presented, you will have a strong foundation in diatonic harmony.

FRETBOARD LOGIC

Arpeggios

In this module you will learn the remaining three major 7 chord arpeggios: Patterns II, IV, and V.

Start with the Pattern II major triad arpeggio. Next, add a major 7th everywhere possible within the octave shape. The result is a Pattern II major 7 arpeggio. Practice this with alternate picking starting and ending on the root.

Pattern II Major Triad Arpeggio   Pattern II Major 7 Arpeggio

Here is a Pattern IV major triad arpeggio. Add a major 7th everywhere possible within the octave shape to build a Pattern IV major 7 arpeggio. Practice this with alternate picking starting and ending on the root.

Pattern IV Major Triad Arpeggio   Pattern IV Major 7 Arpeggio

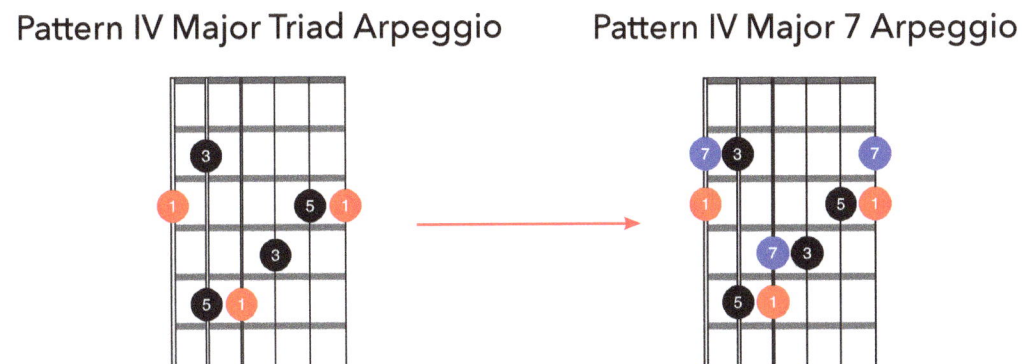

Here is the Pattern V major triad arpeggio. To the major triad, add a major 7th everywhere possible within the octave shape to build a Pattern V major 7 arpeggio.

Again, practice this with alternate picking starting and ending on the root.

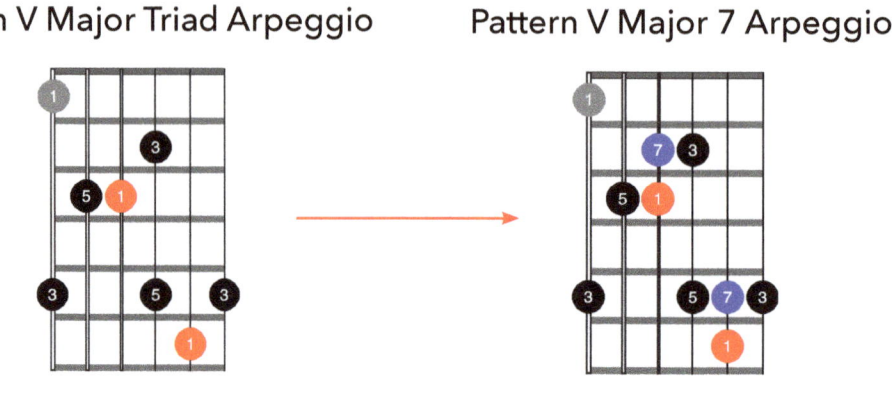

Pattern V Major Triad Arpeggio   Pattern V Major 7 Arpeggio

Chords

There are two minor 7 chords derived from the Patterns IV and II barre chords. Here is a Pattern IV minor barre chord with the chord tones labeled. To create a minor 7 chord within this shape. Replace the root on the 4th string with a minor 7th. The result is a Pattern IV minor 7 chord, and it is movable anywhere on the fretboard. You can add another minor 7th on the 2nd string as an option.

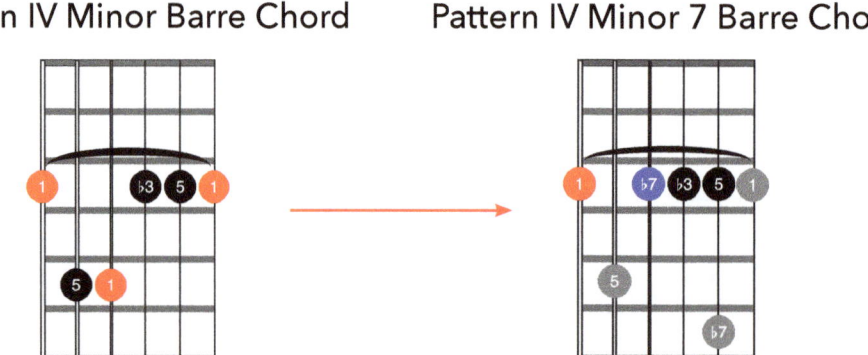

Pattern IV Minor Barre Chord   Pattern IV Minor 7 Barre Chord

Here is a Pattern II minor barre chord with the chord tones labeled. Create a minor 7 chord within this shape. Next, replace the root on the 3rd string with a minor 7th. The result is a Pattern II minor 7 chord, and it is movable anywhere on the fretboard. You can add another minor 7th on the 1st string as another option.

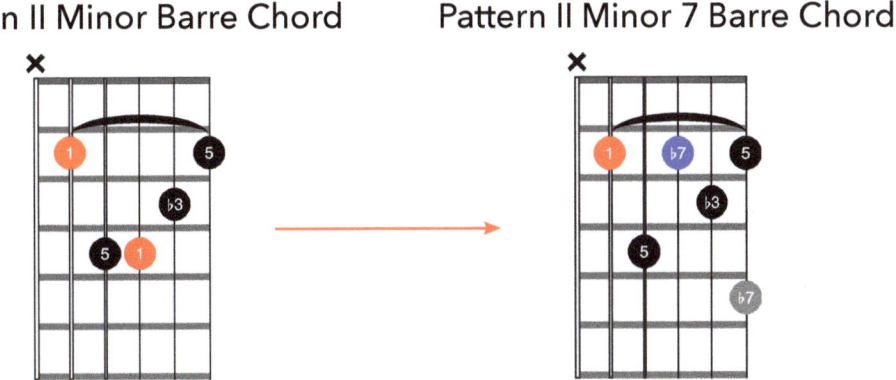

Be sure to check in on the Family Tree as you progress and see how the new information you learn fits in.

TECHNIQUE

This module introduces a new kind of sequence. Instead of moving step-wise, this sequence moves by interval. It is called the "diatonic 3rds sequence" because it moves though the scale in 3rds. Use the Pattern IV major scale in the key of A with 8th-notes.

Diatonic 3rds Sequence

It is best to see the notes of the scale in pairs that are a 3rd apart. Play the 1st scale degree and then a diatonic note a 3rd above it. Then play the 2nd scale degree and then a diatonic note a 3rd above it. Then play the 3rd scale degree and then a diatonic note a 3rd above it, and so on.

Ascending this sequence will look like this:

Diatonic 3rds Sequence Exercise - Ascending

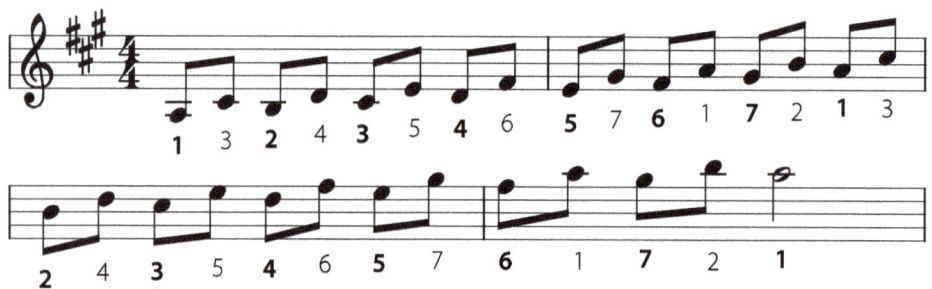

Continue ascending with this pattern until you reach the highest note available in the pattern. Then descend in reverse order like this:

Diatonic 3rds Sequence Exercise - Descending

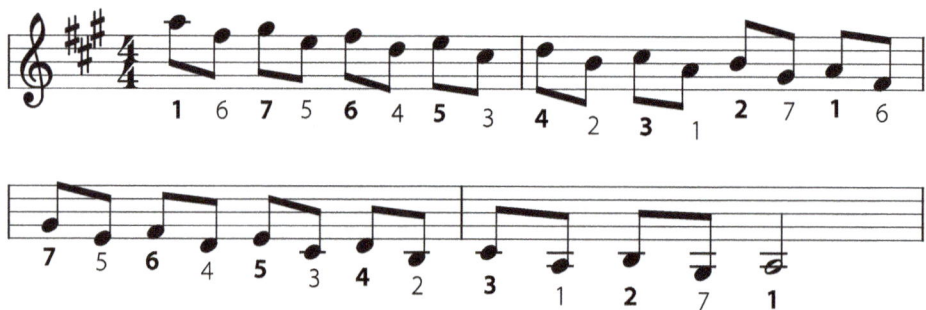

Continue descending with this pattern until you reach the lowest note available in the pattern. Be consistent with alternate picking. Interval sequences are excellent alternate-picking exercises. When you feel like you're ready, set your metronome at slow tempo – perhaps 50 to 60 bpm.

RHYTHM GUITAR

We conclude the series of Rhythm Guitar modules on Reggae with another example with two guitar parts. You will learn another kind of guitar part that can be played along with the chop.

In this example, the secondary guitar part functions more like a melodic percussion instrument. It is a repetitive and muted kind of part sometimes called "popcorn". This idea has been imported into Reggae from Funk and Pop music. It is common in Pop music that is Reggae-influenced.

Progression in C Minor

Here's a two-bar progression in C minor with a swung-16th groove.

C Minor Progression

Like in the first three examples, the chop part is essential.

Chop Part

The popcorn part is a short melodic line built inside the Pattern IV C minor pentatonic scale. The popcorn line functions as a percussive counterpoint melody under the main melody.

Popcorn Line

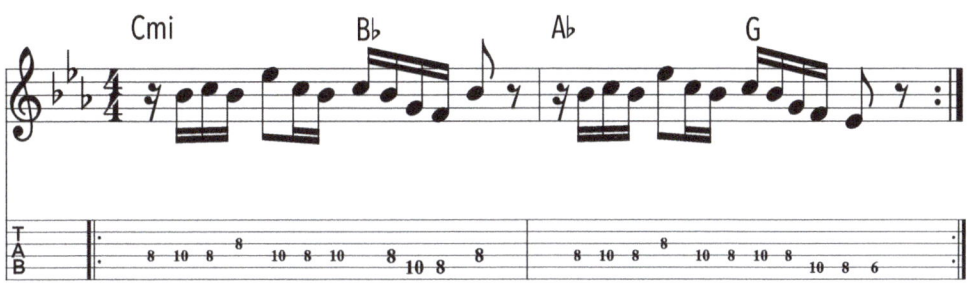

First, play the chop part. Next play the popcorn line, which should cut through the mix, so use a moderately bright tone and mute it through a combination of light fretting hand pressure and palm mute. Alternate picking is essential to keeping the time and groove.

This concludes our introduction to Reggae. As with all styles, I suggest you spend time listening and transcribing after you have the background you've learned here. Reggae rhythm guitar is about groove and feel and fitting in with the rest of the rhythm section.

MONEY MAKERS

Here are more 6th interval ideas to add to the Pattern III money makers. Keep working with the progression in the key of A that was used in the last Money Makers module. It has three chords, A, D, and E. Your goal, as in the last Money Makers module, is to play specific double-stop combinations over specific chords. Here is the progression and analysis.

A Major Progression

The ideas you learn in this Module can be referenced to Pattern III of the key but some of them venture outside of the pattern.

Shapes over the I major chord (A)

Over A, the I chord, start where you did in the last Money Makers module:

1. 2nd finger at the 6th fret of the 3rd string. That is the 3rd, C#. The 1st finger at the 5th fret of the 1st string. That is the root and tonic, A.

2. Without taking those fingers off the fretboard, place your 3rd finger at the 7th fret of the 3rd string (the 4th) and your 4th finger at the 7th fret of the 1st string (the 9th). Both your 3rd and 4th fingers are at the 7th fret.

3. Next, slide that shape to your destination: 3rd finger at the 9th fret of the 3rd string (the 5th) and 4th finger at the 9th fret of the 1st string (the 3rd).

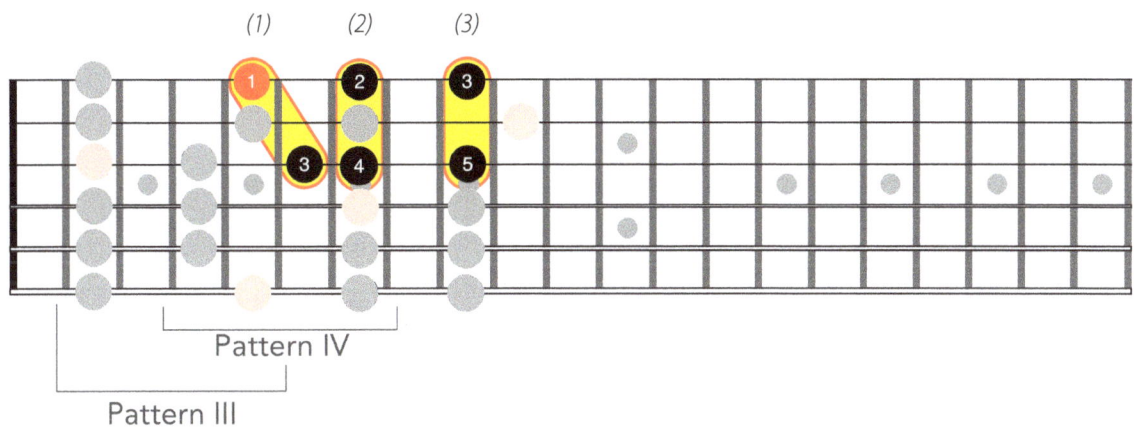

Shapes over the IV major chord (D)

Over the IV chord D, start here:

1. Place your 2nd finger at the 4th fret of the 4th string. That is the 3rd of the D chord, F#. Place your 1st finger at the 3rd fret of the 2nd string. That's the root of the D chord, D.

2. Without taking those fingers off the fretboard, put your 3rd finger at the 5th fret of the 4th string and your 4th finger at the 5th fret of the 2nd string. Both your 3rd and 4th fingers are at the 5th fret.

3. Next, slide that shape to your destination: 3rd finger at the 7th fret of the 4th string (the 5th) and 4th finger at the 7th fret of the 2nd string (the 3rd).

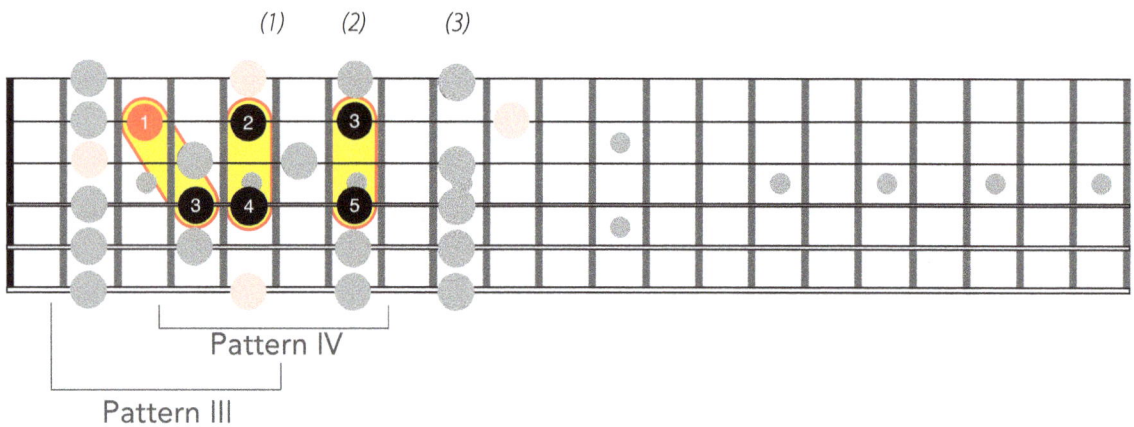

Shapes over the V major chord (E)

Over the V chord E, play the same move you did on D:

1. Place your 2nd finger at the 6th fret of the 4th string. That is the 3rd of the E chord, G#. Also place your 1st finger at the 5th fret of the 2nd string. That is the root of the E chord, E.

2. Without taking those fingers off the fretboard, place your 3rd finger at the 7th fret of the 4th string and 4th finger at the 7th fret of the 2nd string. Both your 3rd and 4th fingers are at the 7th fret.

3. Next, slide that shape to your destination: 3rd finger at the 9th fret of the 4th string (the 5th) and 4th finger at the 9th fret of the 2nd string (the 3rd).

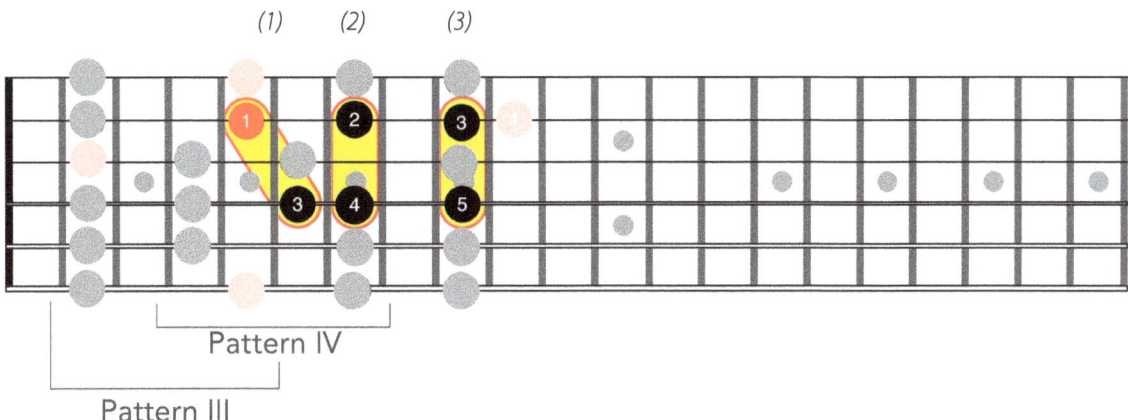

You now have many Money Maker options based in and around the Pattern III octave shape. Practice these licks with all the tracks used so far in the Money Maker modules and any other tracks that are in a major key. These ideas will stay with you for your entire career. And remember, these ideas are transposable to all major keys.

Level 3 Unit 5 • Money Maker Demo

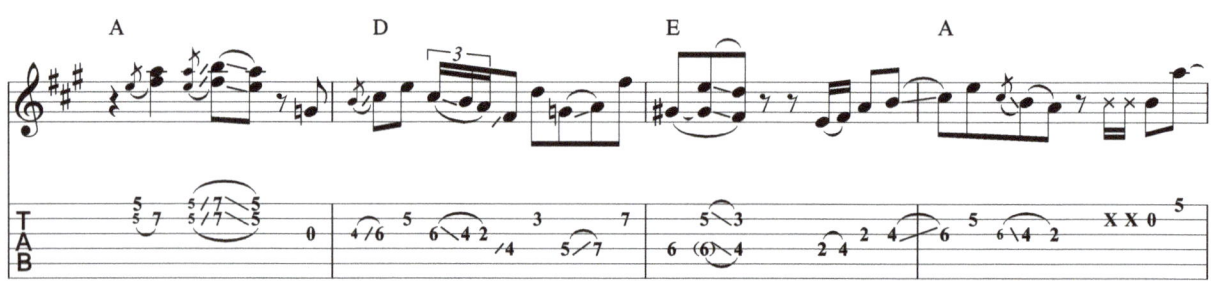
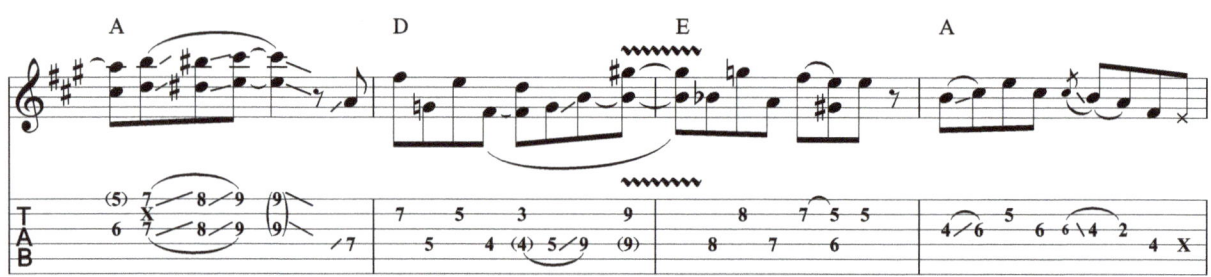

©2020 Fretboard Biology • fretboardbiology.com

Fretboard Biology — Level 3 • Unit 5: Money Makers

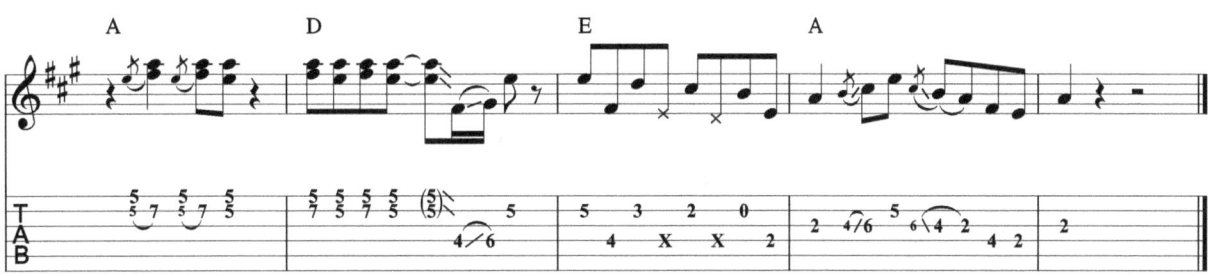

IMPROVISATION

In this and the next few Units you will solo with chord tones over progressions that have include different quality chords.

Here's a simple two-chord progression: Fma7 to Gmi7. It is in the key of F and if you play a key-center solo over this, your source of notes will be the F major or F major pentatonic scale. I suggest you first play a key-center solo over the track to get acquainted with the track and get a feel for the changes.

F Major Progression

Next use the chord-tone approach. Work in two different locations on the fretboard. First, over the Ma7, use the Pattern I Fma7 arpeggio, which places you in 5th position. Next, over the Gmi7, play the Pattern IV Gmi7 arpeggio, which places you in 3rd position. You will need to shift from 5th position to 3rd position. This is not ideal, but do it for now, since you are comfortable with these two arpeggio shapes.

As with the previous progressions it is a good idea to play just the arpeggios over the chords to start. This is the best way to locate and visualize the chord tones.

F Major Progression

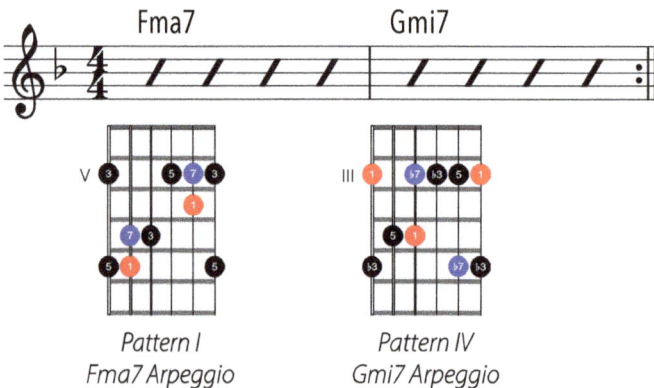

Pattern I
Fma7 Arpeggio

Pattern IV
Gmi7 Arpeggio

Take another segment of your practice and create short motifs that blend chord tones and scale tones.

Next, solo in a different location on the fretboard. Over the Ma7 play the Pattern III Fma7 arpeggio, which places you in 10th position. Next over the Gmi7, play the Pattern II Gmi7 arpeggio, which also places you in 10th position. You won't need to shift position to play these two shapes. This is the ultimate goal.

F Major Progression

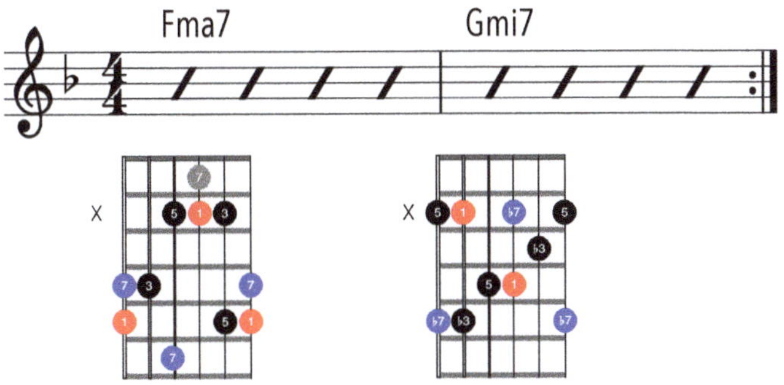

| Fma7 | Gmi7 |

Pattern III
Fma7 Arpeggio

Pattern II
Gmi7 Arpeggio

Later in Level 3 you will learn how to play any arpeggio in any position on the fretboard. This is a great help in trying to transition from one arpeggio to the next when using chord tones. Keep working on your chord tones!

Level 3 Unit 5 • Improv Demo 1

Level 3 Unit 5 • Improv Demo 2

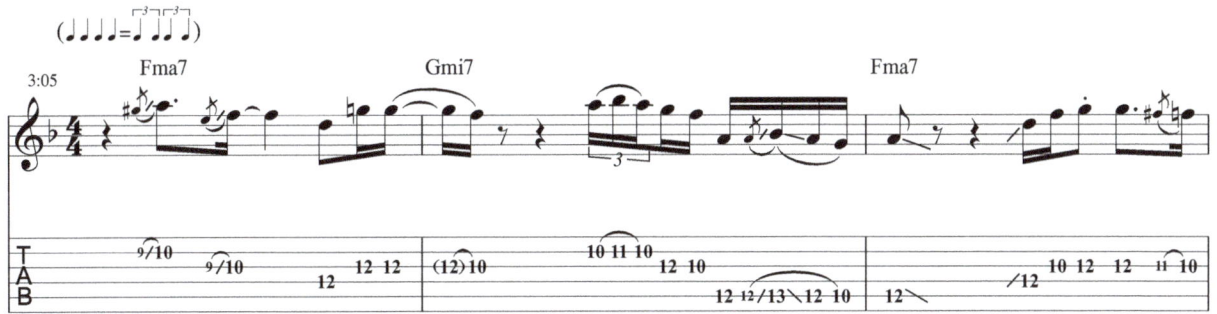

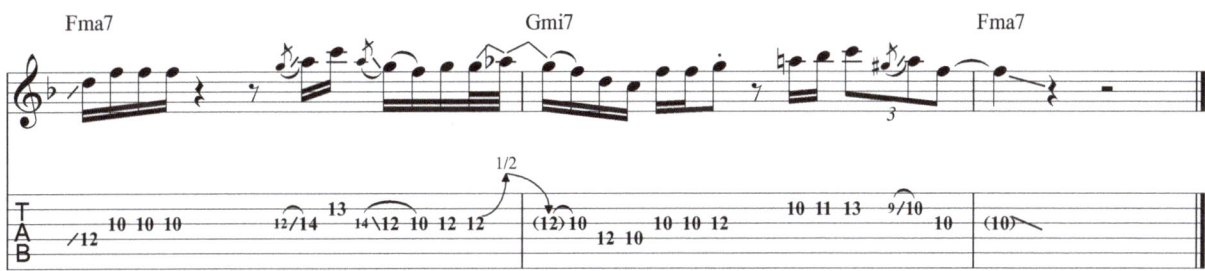

PRACTICE

Theory

- ❑ Go to the tabs below the Theory video on the website and complete the quiz.
- ❑ Learn how to harmonize the minor scale with 7th chords.

Fretboard Logic

- ❑ Learn the Patterns II, IV, and V major 7 arpeggios. Add these to your practice routine.
- ❑ Learn the Patterns II and IV minor 7 barre chords. Add these to your practice routine.

Technique

- ❑ Learn the diatonic 3rds sequence exercise and add it to your practice routine.

Rhythm Guitar

- ❑ Practice the chop and popcorn parts in Reggae rhythm guitar.

Money Makers

- ❑ Learn the Pattern III money maker shapes over the progression in the key of A.

Improvisation

- ❑ Focus on chord-tone soloing over the progression provided using Patterns I and III major 7 and Patterns II and IV minor 7 arpeggios.

UNIT 6

Learning Modules

> **Theory** - Harmonic analysis in minor key progressions with 7th chords, chord families with 7th chords in minor keys

> **Fretboard Logic** - Patterns II, IV, and V dominant 7 arpeggios, Patterns IV and II minor 7(♭5) barre chords

> **Technique** - Diatonic 4ths sequence exercise

> **Rhythm Guitar** - Introduction to Country rhythm guitar

> **Money Makers** - Licks in Pattern IV minor pentatonic

> **Improvisation** - Soloing with chord tones in G minor

> **Practice** - Continue practice routine development

THEORY

Chord Families

In this Unit you will learn about harmonic analysis when a progression in a minor key has 7th chords. You learned about chord families in minor keys when we harmonized the minor scale in triads. The next step is to add the 7th chords to chord family chart.

- The Tonic family in minor consists of Imi7 and ♭IIIma7
- The Subdominant family in minor consists of IImi7(♭5), IVmi7, and ♭VIma7
- The Dominant family in minor consists of Vmi7 (sometimes V7) and ♭VII7.

FAMILY	MEMBERS	EMOTIONAL EFFECT
Tonic	Imi7, ♭IIIma7	At home, resolved
Subdominant	IImi7(♭5), IVmi7, ♭VIma7	Moving away from tonic
Dominant	Vmi7, V7, ♭VII7	Moving toward tonic

Here is a progression in a minor key. To start, take the methodical approach to harmonic analysis. Determine all of the keys to which each chord could belong.

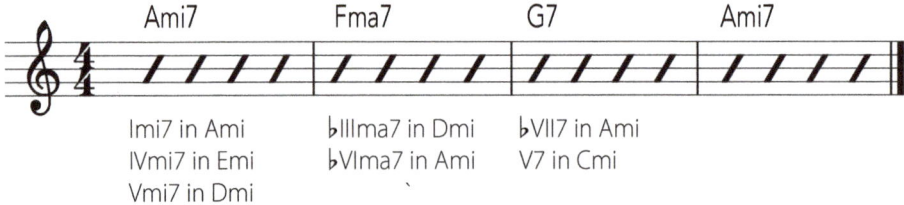

Ami7	Fma7	G7	Ami7
Imi7 in Ami	♭IIIma7 in Dmi	♭VII7 in Ami	
IVmi7 in Emi	♭VIma7 in Ami	V7 in Cmi	
Vmi7 in Dmi			

There is one key to which all chords belong: A minor

Here is another. Determine all of the keys to which each chord could belong.

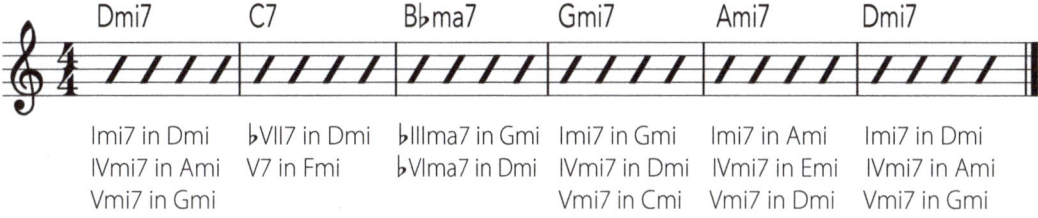

There is one key to which all chords belong: D minor.

Shortcuts to Finding the Key

There are other clues in both of these progressions:

The last chord offers a good clue, as it is often the tonic chord, but that indicator is not 100% reliable.

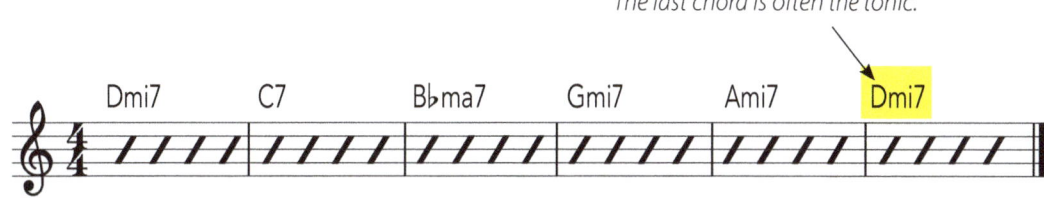

The roots of the Gmi7 and Ami7 in the last progression are a whole step apart. There is only one place in the harmonized minor scale where two minor 7 chords are positioned one whole step apart: IVmi7 and Vmi7.

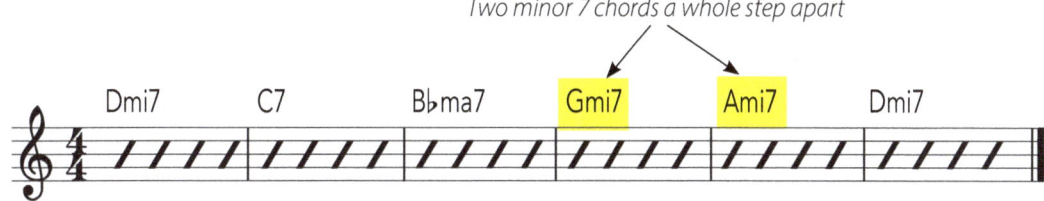

One of the best clues is the C7. There is only one dominant 7th chord in the harmonized minor scale: the ♭VII7 chord.

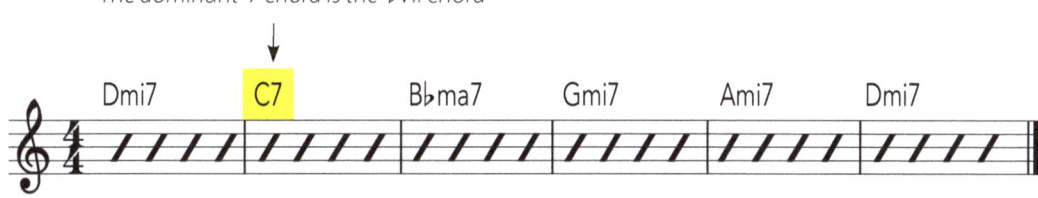

Here is what you have learned about harmonic analysis so far. You have learned a slow and reliable method for analyzing progressions made up of triads and 7th chords in both major and minor keys. With this method you determine the single key to which all chords in a progression could belong. The extra clues just discussed can speed up the process in minor keys as well; clues like locating a dominant 7 chord or locating two minor 7 chords a whole step apart.

Common Chord Groups

In minor keys, groups of chords tend to "hang out together", as they do in major keys Your recognition will improve over time because you will see them together so often. It's only logical that you see them together frequently because they part of the same key and are used in combination over and over, again and again, in song after song.

Harmonic analysis should be a habit. It should be automatic every time you learn a new song. The ability to quickly analyze chords provides important benefits:

- Understanding the function indicates the "family" each chord belongs to and therefore its emotional tendency.
- As with major keys, we can sometimes substitute chords within a family and this offers reharmonization options, which is a chord from the same family substituted for the chord originally written.
- Another benefit of this knowledge is to use the arpeggio of another chord within the family as a melodic device.

Harmonic Analysis Exercise

The next few pages contain an exercise to help you develop your skills in quickly analyzing progressions in minor keys. The example will show you how to fill out this worksheet. Your goal is to identify three things: 1) the key of the progression, 2) the number of each chord in the progression, and 3) the chord family to which each chord belongs.

Fretboard Biology · Level 3 • Unit 6: Theory · 153

Progression Analysis Exercise

Answer key located on Page 278

Step One: Make a tentative determination of the key.
Step Two: Based on this, determine the number (function) of each chord.
Step Three: Confirm and label the key and function of each chord.

EXAMPLE:

Key: F#mi

F#mi7	Ama7	Dma7	C#mi7	F#mi7
Imi7	bIIIma7	bVIma7	Vmi7	Imi7
☒ Tonic	☒ Tonic	☐ Tonic	☐ Tonic	☒ Tonic
☐ Subdominant	☐ Subdominant	☒ Subdominant	☐ Subdominant	☐ Subdominant
☐ Dominant	☐ Dominant	☐ Dominant	☒ Dominant	☐ Dominant

Key: _____

Ami7	Fma7	Emi7	Ami7
_____	_____	_____	_____
☐ Tonic	☐ Tonic	☐ Tonic	☐ Tonic
☐ Subdominant	☐ Subdominant	☐ Subdominant	☐ Subdominant
☐ Dominant	☐ Dominant	☐ Dominant	☐ Dominant

Key: _____

Emi7	D7	Cma7	Bmi7	Emi7
_____	_____	_____	_____	_____
☐ Tonic	☐ Tonic	☐ Tonic	☐ Tonic	☐ Tonic
☐ Subdominant	☐ Subdominant	☐ Subdominant	☐ Subdominant	☐ Subdominant
☐ Dominant	☐ Dominant	☐ Dominant	☐ Dominant	☐ Dominant

©2020 Joe Elliott • FretboardBiology.com

Progression Analysis Exercise

Key: _____

| Gmi7 | Ami7 | B♭ma7 | Ami7 | Dmi7 |

Number: _____ _____ _____ _____ _____

Family:
- ☐ Tonic
- ☐ Subdominant
- ☐ Dominant

- ☐ Tonic
- ☐ Subdominant
- ☐ Dominant

- ☐ Tonic
- ☐ Subdominant
- ☐ Dominant

- ☐ Tonic
- ☐ Subdominant
- ☐ Dominant

- ☐ Tonic
- ☐ Subdominant
- ☐ Dominant

Key: _____

| D♭ma7 | B♭mi7 | Cmi7 | Fmi7 |

Number: _____ _____ _____ _____

Family:
- ☐ Tonic
- ☐ Subdominant
- ☐ Dominant

- ☐ Tonic
- ☐ Subdominant
- ☐ Dominant

- ☐ Tonic
- ☐ Subdominant
- ☐ Dominant

- ☐ Tonic
- ☐ Subdominant
- ☐ Dominant

Key: _____

| Gmi7 | E♭ma7 | D7 | Gmi7 |

Number: _____ _____ _____ _____

Family:
- ☐ Tonic
- ☐ Subdominant
- ☐ Dominant

- ☐ Tonic
- ☐ Subdominant
- ☐ Dominant

- ☐ Tonic
- ☐ Subdominant
- ☐ Dominant

- ☐ Tonic
- ☐ Subdominant
- ☐ Dominant

Key: _____

| Ami7 | Cma7 | Fma7 | Emi7 | Ami7 |

Number: _____ _____ _____ _____ _____

Family:
- ☐ Tonic
- ☐ Subdominant
- ☐ Dominant

- ☐ Tonic
- ☐ Subdominant
- ☐ Dominant

- ☐ Tonic
- ☐ Subdominant
- ☐ Dominant

- ☐ Tonic
- ☐ Subdominant
- ☐ Dominant

- ☐ Tonic
- ☐ Subdominant
- ☐ Dominant

©2020 Joe Elliott • FretboardBiology.com

Progression Analysis Exercise

Key: _____

| Dmi7 | B♭ma7 | Gmi7 | Ami7 | Dmi7 |

Number: _____ _____ _____ _____ _____

Family:
- ☐ Tonic / ☐ Subdominant / ☐ Dominant
- ☐ Tonic / ☐ Subdominant / ☐ Dominant
- ☐ Tonic / ☐ Subdominant / ☐ Dominant
- ☐ Tonic / ☐ Subdominant / ☐ Dominant
- ☐ Tonic / ☐ Subdominant / ☐ Dominant

Key: _____

| Emi7 | Cma7 | F♯mi7(♭5) | B7 | Emi7 |

Number: _____ _____ _____ _____ _____

Family:
- ☐ Tonic / ☐ Subdominant / ☐ Dominant
- ☐ Tonic / ☐ Subdominant / ☐ Dominant
- ☐ Tonic / ☐ Subdominant / ☐ Dominant
- ☐ Tonic / ☐ Subdominant / ☐ Dominant
- ☐ Tonic / ☐ Subdominant / ☐ Dominant

Key: _____

| B♭ma7 | D7 | Gmi7 | Cmi7 | F7 | Gmi7 |

Number: _____ _____ _____ _____ _____ _____

Family:
- ☐ Tonic / ☐ Subdominant / ☐ Dominant
- ☐ Tonic / ☐ Subdominant / ☐ Dominant
- ☐ Tonic / ☐ Subdominant / ☐ Dominant
- ☐ Tonic / ☐ Subdominant / ☐ Dominant
- ☐ Tonic / ☐ Subdominant / ☐ Dominant
- ☐ Tonic / ☐ Subdominant / ☐ Dominant

Key: _____

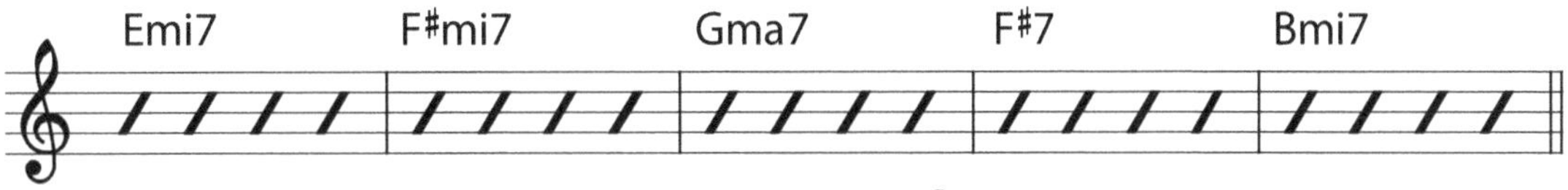

| Emi7 | F♯mi7 | Gma7 | F♯7 | Bmi7 |

Number: _____ _____ _____ _____ _____

Family:
- ☐ Tonic / ☐ Subdominant / ☐ Dominant
- ☐ Tonic / ☐ Subdominant / ☐ Dominant
- ☐ Tonic / ☐ Subdominant / ☐ Dominant
- ☐ Tonic / ☐ Subdominant / ☐ Dominant
- ☐ Tonic / ☐ Subdominant / ☐ Dominant

FRETBOARD LOGIC

Arpeggios

In this module you will learn the remaining three dominant 7 chord arpeggios – Patterns II, IV, and V.

Here is a Pattern II major triad arpeggio. Add a minor 7th everywhere possible within the octave shape to build a Pattern II dominant 7 arpeggio.

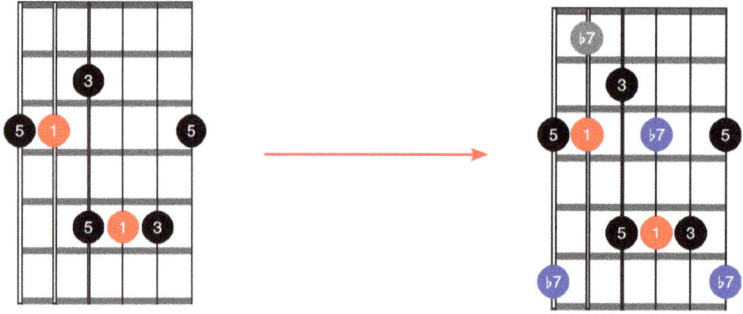

Practice this with alternate picking starting and ending on the root.

Here is a Pattern IV major triad arpeggio. Add a minor 7th everywhere possible within the octave shape to build a dominant 7 arpeggio.

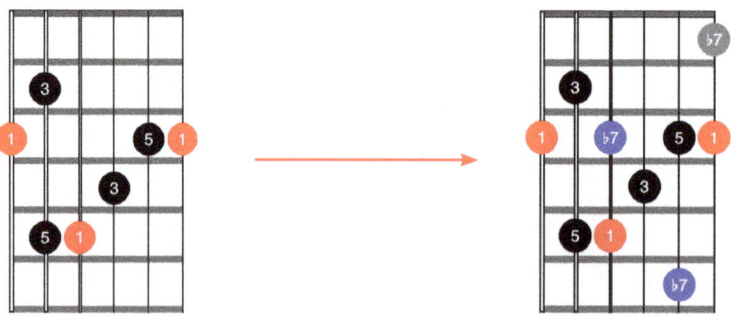

Practice this with alternate picking starting and ending on the root.

Fretboard Biology — Level 3 • Unit 6: Fretboard Logic

Here is a Pattern V major triad arpeggio. Add a minor 7th everywhere possible within the octave shape to build a dominant 7 arpeggio.

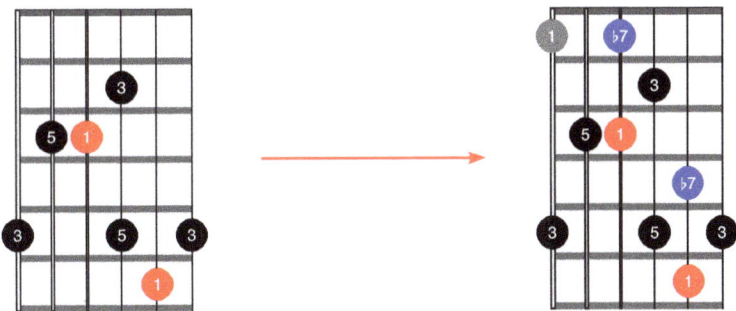

Practice this with alternate picking starting and ending on the root.

Chords

Minor 7(♭5) chords can derived from the Patterns IV and II barre chords. Here is a Pattern IV minor barre chord with the chord tones labeled. Creating a minor 7(♭5) chord within this shape will require a couple adjustments to the barre chord. Replace the root on the 4th string with a minor 7th. Replace the 5th on the 2nd string with a flatted 5th. Omit the 5th on the 5th string and also omit the root on the 1st string. The result is a Pattern IV minor 7(♭5) chord, and it's movable anywhere on the neck.

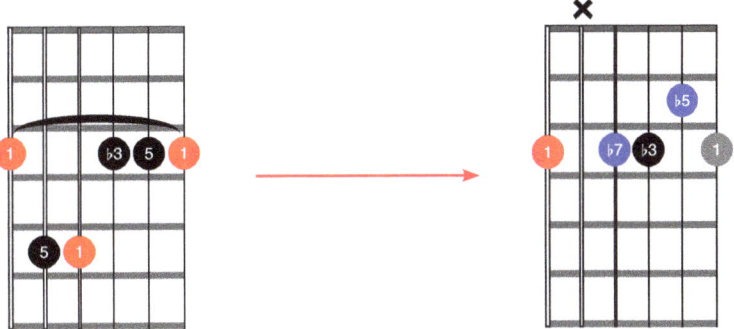

Here is a Pattern II minor barre chord with the chord tones labeled. Creating a minor 7(♭5) chord within this shape requires a couple of adjustments to the barre chord. Replace the root on the 3rd string with a minor 7th. Replace the 5th on the 4th string with a flatted 5th. Omit the 5th on the 1st string. The result is a Pattern II minor 7(♭5) chord, and it's movable anywhere on the neck.

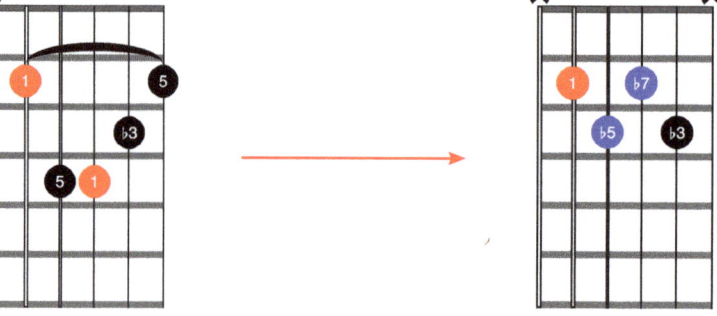

Pattern II Minor Barre Chord → Pattern II Minor 7(♭5) Barre Chord

TECHNIQUE

In this module you will learn another interval sequence. This one is called the "diatonic 4ths sequence" because it is based in moving though the scale in 4ths. Use the Pattern IV major scale in the key of A with 8th-notes.

Diatonic 4ths Sequence

Work your way up the scale playing notes in pairs. Play the 1st scale degree and then a diatonic note a 4th above it. Then play the 2nd scale degree and then a diatonic note a 4th above it. Then play the 3rd scale degree and then a diatonic note a 4th above it, and so on through the scale.

Ascending this sequence will look like this:

Diatonic 4ths Sequence Exercise - Ascending

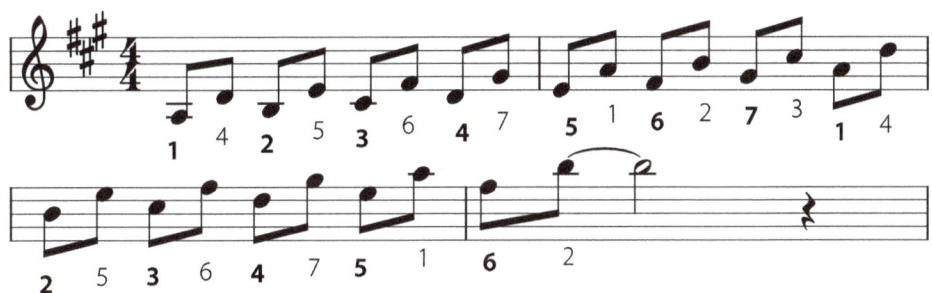

Continue ascending with this pattern until you reach the highest note available in the pattern. Then descend in reverse order like this:

Diatonic 4ths Sequence Exercise - Descending

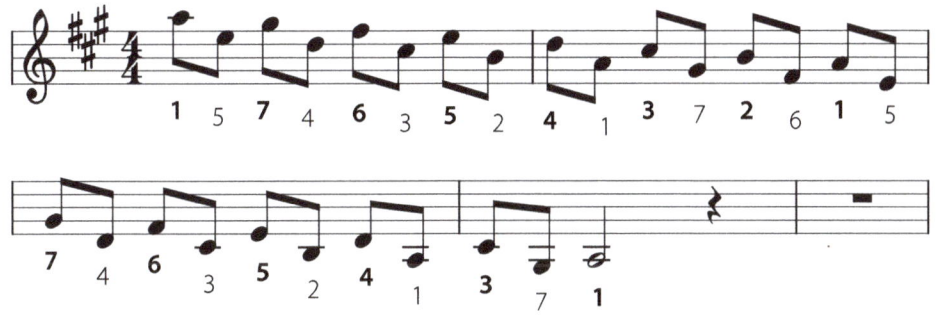

Continue descending with this pattern until you reach the lowest note available in the pattern. Focus on alternate picking. When you feel like you're ready, set your metronome at a slow tempo and work through these patterns again.

RHYTHM GUITAR

Country

In the next few units you will learn the basics of traditional Country rhythm guitar. You will notice a few similarities with the Folk Rhythm Guitar modules from an earlier Level. All the strumming and fingerpicking you learned in Folk is also applicable in Country. The difference here is that more examples will be played with a flat pick.

All Rhythm Guitar modules are intended to introduce you to the basics of a particular genre; in this case, Country. This curriculum does not begin with the complicated stuff. There are a lot of flashy rhythm guitar parts you will want to learn over time. They will be easier once you have a solid understanding of fundamental rhythm guitar.

Boom-Chick Pattern

Start with a basic boom-chick pattern. It can be used with all open string voicings and barre chords. In 4/4 time play the lowest root in the chord voicing on beat one, strum the chord on beat 2, then on beat three play the root again or the 5th if you choose, and then on beat four strum the chord again.

When you strum the chord on beats two and four, avoid the 5th string because the note found there is in a low register and can muddy the sound of the chord. The challenge is to find and play the roots and 5ths cleanly with your flat pick.

I suggest you work through each chord individually before putting them together in progressions. You will recall from your work with fingerpicking that the roots and 5ths are on different strings for different chords. That makes the movement of your flat pick challenging.

Work through the open chords in alphabetical order just with triads:

Open A Chord

The root is on the open 5th string and the 5th is on the open 6th string.

One-Bar Pattern

There is another option. You can play a two-bar pattern.

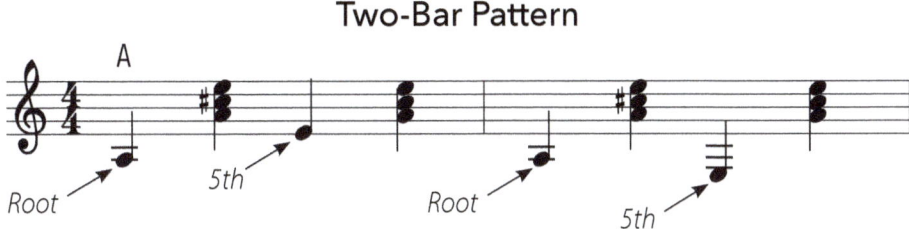

In measure one of this pattern:
- On beat one, play the root on open 5th string
- On beat two, strum the chord
- On beat three, play the 5th on the 4th string at the 2nd fret
- On beat four, strum the chord

In measure two:
- On beat one, play the root on open 5th string
- On beat two, strum the chord
- On beat three, play the 5th on the open 6th string
- On beat four, strum the chord

Open A Minor Chord

For A minor, play the same way as you did for A.

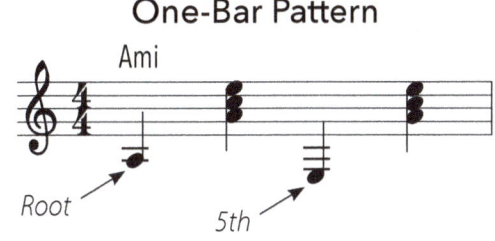

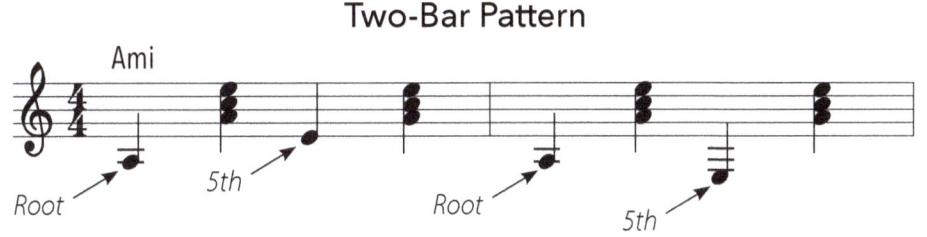

Open C Chord

The root is at the 3rd fret of the 5th string played with your 3rd finger. The 5th is played on the 6th string at the 3rd fret and you will need to move your 3rd finger to play it.

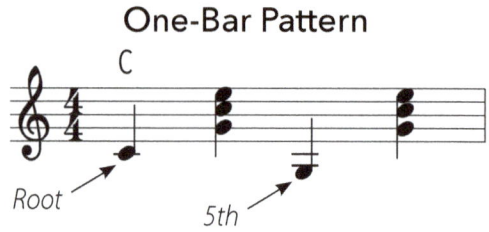

Open D Chord

The root is on the open 4th string and the 5th is on the open 5th string.

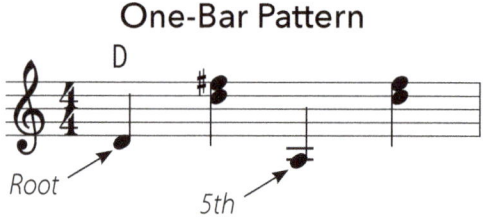

There is another option here, too: You can play a two-bar pattern.

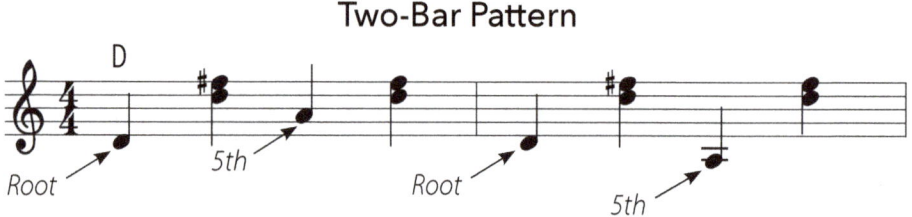

In measure one of this pattern:
- On beat one, play the root on open 4th string
- On beat two, strum the chord
- On beat three, play the 5th on the 3rd string at the 2nd fret
- On beat four, strum the chord

In measure two:
- On beat one: play the root on open 4th string
- On beat two: strum the chord
- On beat three: play the 5th on the open 5th string
- On beat four: strum the chord

Open D Minor Chord

These patterns are the same for D minor.

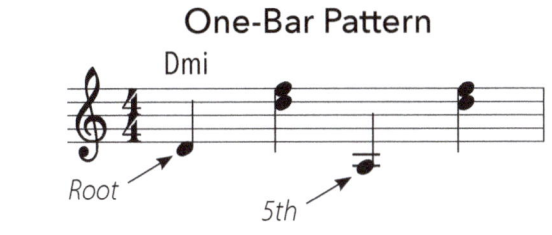

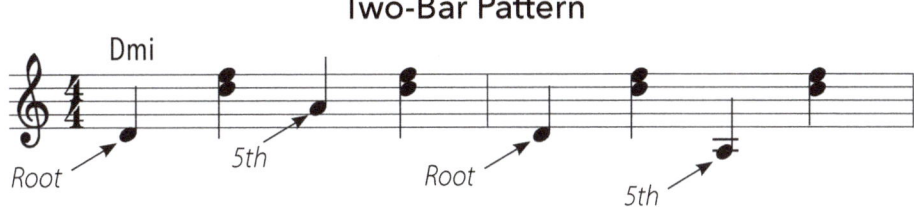

Open E Chord

The root is on the open 6th string and the 5th is played with the 2nd finger at the 2nd fret of the 5th string.

Again, there is another option: You can play a two bar phrase.

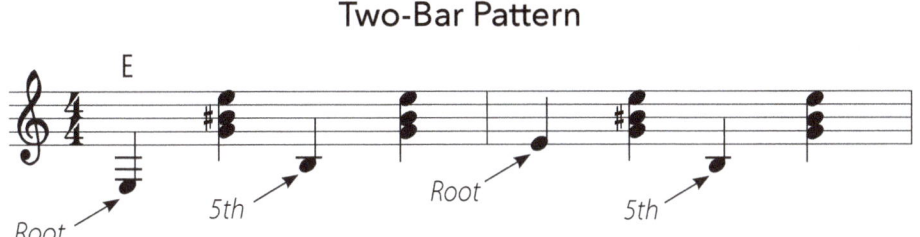

In measure one of this pattern:
- On beat one, play the root on open 6th string
- On beat two, strum the chord
- On beat three, play the 5th on the 5th string at the 2nd fret
- On beat four, strum the chord

In measure two:
- On beat one, play the root on the 4th string at the 2nd fret
- On beat two, strum the chord
- On beat three: play the 5th on the 5th string at the 2nd fret
- On beat four: strum the chord

Open E Minor Chord

These patterns are the same for E minor.

One-Bar Pattern

Two-Bar Pattern

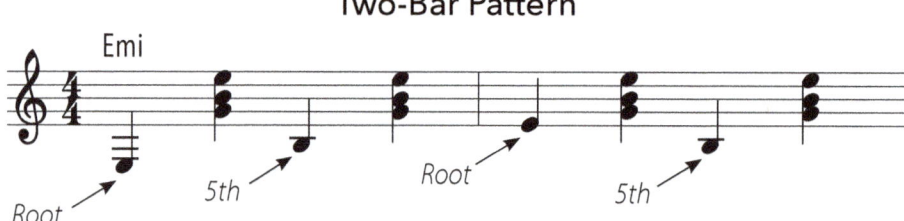

Open G Chord

The root is on the 3rd fret of the 6th string and the 5th is played on the open 4th string.

One-Bar Pattern

Boom-Chick Pattern with Barre Chords

When playing boom-chick with at Pattern IV barre chord, your picking hand should make the same motion as it does on an open E or Emi: The root is on the 6th string and the 5th is on the 5th string.

When playing boom-chick with a Pattern II barre chord your picking hand should make the same motion as it does on an open A or Ami: The root is on the 5th string and the 5th is on the 6th string.

With both open and barre chords, experiment with the duration of both the bass notes and chords. You can do this by using a palm mute (where you rest the palm of your picking hand on the strings near the bridge), or by releasing pressure in your fretting hand, or a combination of both.

Boom-Chick Pattern with 8th Notes

You can also add to the chord rhythm by playing two 8th notes on beats two and four instead of just the quarter note.

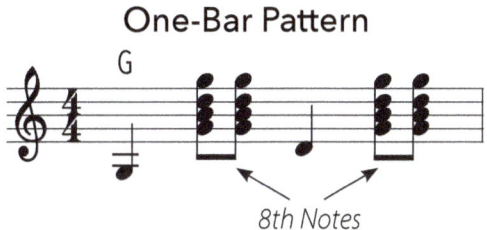

One-Bar Pattern

8th Notes

I suggest working on each of these chords individually so you get comfortable with each one before doing any multi-chord progressions.

Grooves in Country

The time feel in Country is usually straight-8th note or shuffled-8th note, and the time signature is either 4/4 or 3/4.

Drums

In 4/4 time in Country, as with most Pop styles, the bass drum pattern includes beats one and three. There may be other attacks that precede or follow. Often the bass drum plays four quarter notes or "four on the floor" in music written for dancing. The snare drum plays on beats two and four and that is called the back beat. An alternative to a full snare attack is the cross stick, which is a lighter attack.

The hi-hat usually plays an 8th-note pattern. Sometimes in place of the hi-hat, the ride cymbal plays an 8th-note pattern to contrast between sections. For example, the hi-hat is usually played on verses and the ride cymbal on choruses and solos.

Bass

The bass player primarily plays the root and 5th of the chord. The root is played on beats one and three and the 5th on beats two and four. While this is not complicated, there are many nuances that are overlooked by musicians who don't listen to or play a lot of Country. Duration of the notes is an important. Where the bass player cuts off the note makes a difference. Cutting a note off in order to leave a space for another sound to be featured like the back beat is important. If the bass note played on beat one cuts off at the start of beat two, the space on beat two is cleared for the snare or cross stick to stand out.

Keyboards

The keyboard player, whether it's an organ or piano, usually plays the chords.

Guitar

The rhythm guitar parts you learn in these Modules are really the glue that holds together the harmony of the song meaning keyboard parts are normally secondary to the guitar parts. Always be aware of what is happening around you. Listen to all parts when learning a song.

Example Progressions

Here are a few examples using the boom-chick guitar part. All of the chords you just worked through are used in at least one of these progressions so you can practice using each of them. Some of these grooves are straight-8th note and some are shuffle-8th note. Your goal is to be comfortable with both.

A Major Progression

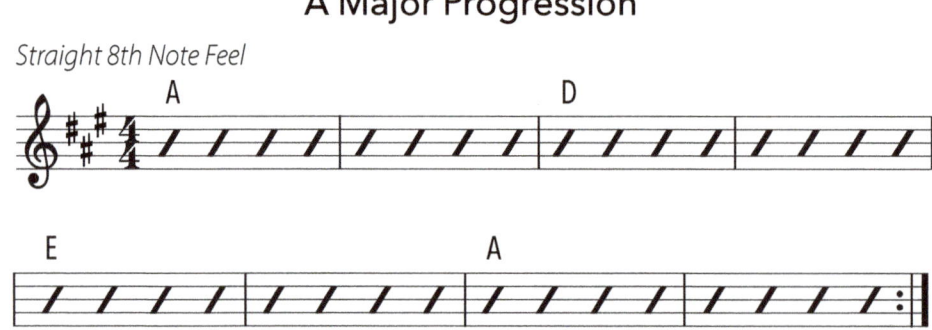

C# Minor Progression

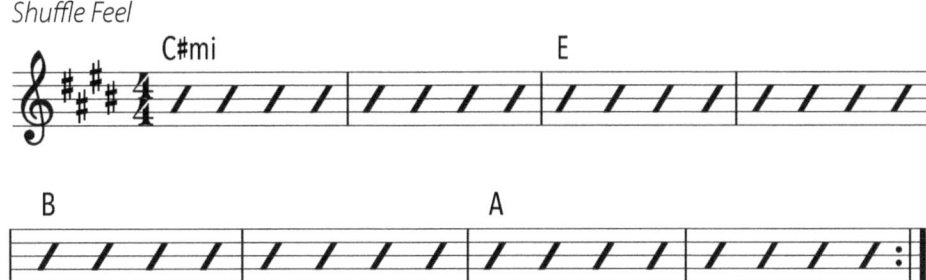

G Major Progression

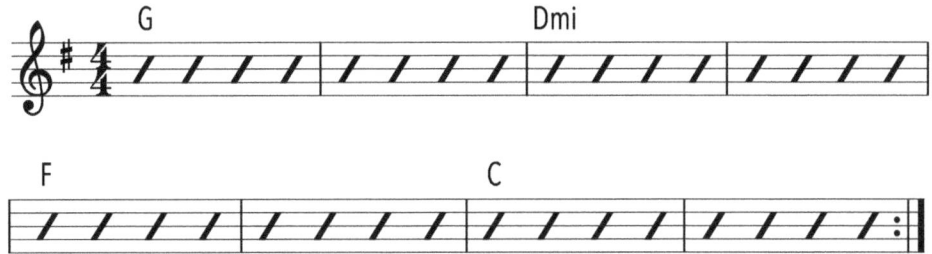

C Major Progression

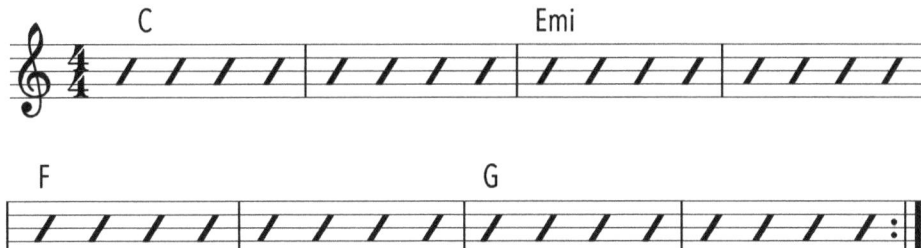

The boom-chick pattern can also be played with thumb and fingers instead of the flat pick. This is another valuable technique that gives you a lot picking hand control of dynamics and the duration of the chords.

The picking-hand thumb is assigned to the root and 5th pattern. Put your 1st, 2nd, and 3rd fingers together in sort of a claw shape. They will work together as a unit to play one of two string sets. You can assign them to string set 1, 2, and 3 or string set 2, 3, and 4. Practice the thumb-and-claw idea over all the progressions, too.

MONEY MAKERS

The Money Makers in Units 1 through 5 are in major keys. Now we will turn our attention to ideas that work in minor keys. We will go through each of the five minor pentatonic shells over the next five modules. The goal is to learn the cliché melodic gems that live inside each of these shapes. This will not be comprehensive – that's not the point. The idea is to point out some of the convenient Bluesy-sounding licks in each shape. From these ideas you can come up with all kinds of licks, either written, worked out, or on the fly.

One of the challenges of learning a lick from a recording is figuring out where to play it on the fretboard. There are so many places on the guitar to play the exact same notes. But some licks physically lay nicely in one shape and are nearly impossible to play in others. That's just the way the fretboard is so it is important to learn some classic licks that are unique to each minor pentatonic shape. That's the goal over the next five Money Maker Modules.

Licks in Pattern IV Minor Pentatonic

This Module's examples are in the Pattern IV minor pentatonic shell. This is the shape where most guitarists first learn to solo. Not only is this the first place many guitarists learn to solo, but it stays the go-to pattern throughout entire careers, and there's nothing wrong with that.

Pattern IV Minor Pentatonic Scale

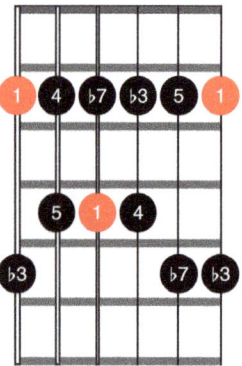

Let's start by learning a few licks over a 12-bar Blues progression.

Fretboard Biology — Level 3 • Unit 6: Money Makers

A 12-Bar Blues Progression

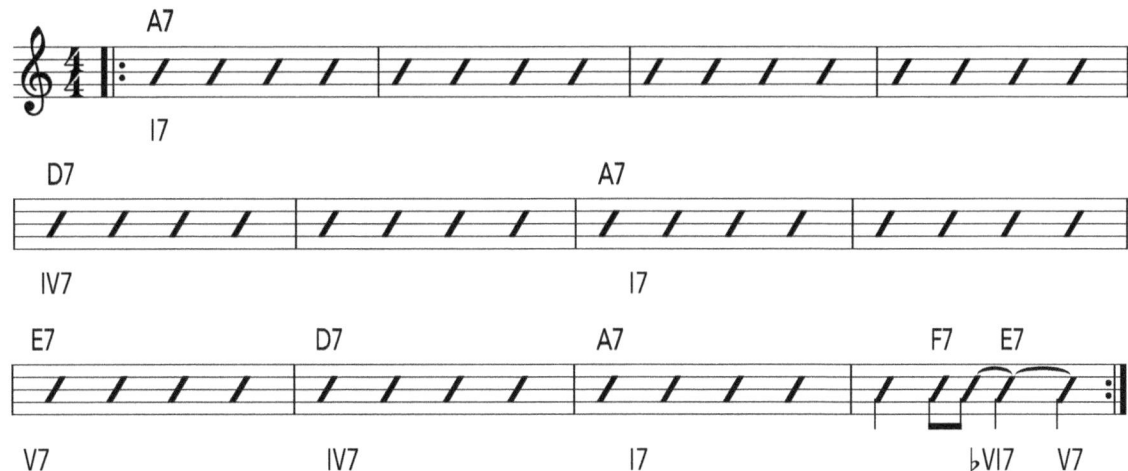

Pattern IV Blues Lick 1

Pattern IV Blues Lick 2

Pattern IV Blues Lick 3

Pattern IV Blues Lick 4

Work on getting the licks in this module under your fingers. On the next page, you will see a demo solo that uses these licks so you can see how they work in the context of a solo.

One more thing before we go deeper: At this point we are not concerning ourselves too much with chord tones. Although that would be nice, it's too much to try and do all at once. The licks you will use will work over any of the three chords in Blues in a crude kind of way. Work hard on these.

Level 3 Unit 6 • Money Maker Demo

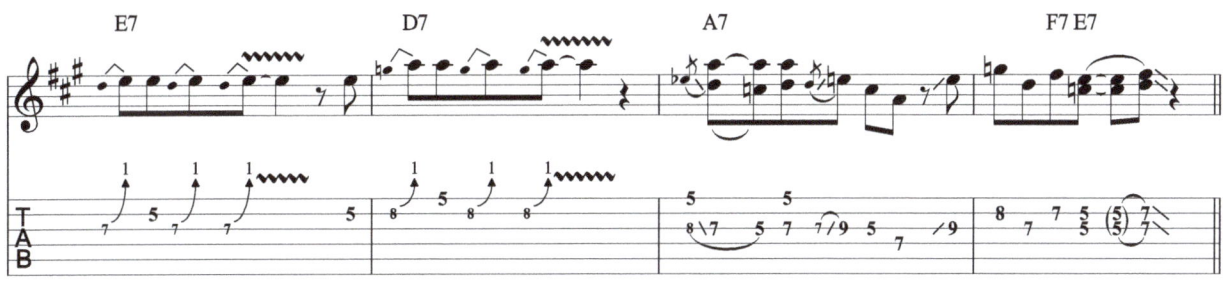

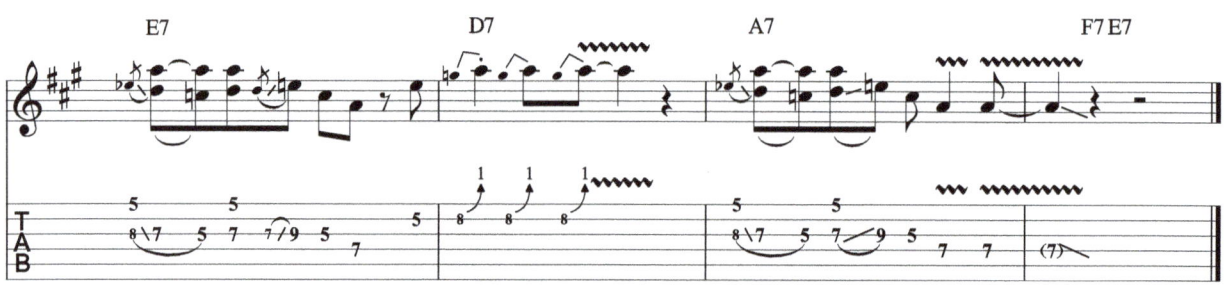

IMPROVISATION

This module continues to use chord tones in solos over progressions that have different quality chords. Examine this two-chord progression: Gmi7 to D7. It is in the key of G minor and if you play a key-center solo over this, your source of notes can be the G minor pentatonic scale. It won't fit perfectly over the D7 because of the F# in the D7. It is not in the G minor pentatonic scale, but you can make it work. First play a key-center solo over the track to get acquainted with the groove and to get a feel for the changes.

Next use the chord-tone approach and work in two different locations on the fretboard. To start, over the minor 7 chord use the Pattern IV Gmi7 arpeggio, which places you in 3rd position. Next, over the D7 chord, play the Pattern I D7 arpeggio, which places you in 2nd position. You won't have to move your hand very far between these two shapes.

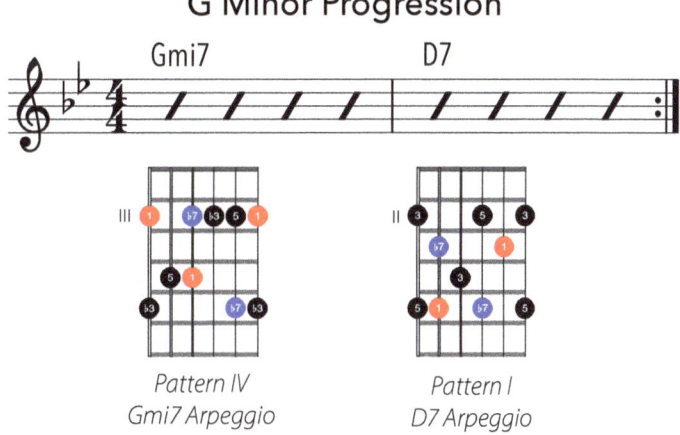

As with the previous progressions it is a good idea to play just arpeggios over the chords as an exercise to get familiar with the location of the arpeggios. Then take another segment of your practice and create short motifs that blend chord tones and scale tones.

Next, play this in a different location on the fretboard. Over the Gmi7 chord use the Pattern II Gmi7 arpeggio, which places you in 10th position. Next, over the D7 chord, play the Pattern III D7 arpeggio, which places you in 7th position so you will need to shift from 10th to 7th position.

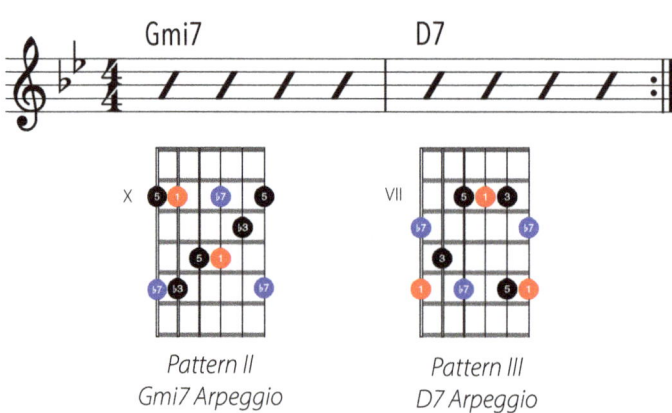

Pattern II Gmi7 Arpeggio

Pattern III D7 Arpeggio

This position shift is not ideal, but later in Level 3 you will learn how to organize arpeggios in such a way to give access to any quality arpeggio in every position on the fretboard. This is an enormous help in trying to transition from one arpeggio to the next when using chord tones. Keep working on your chord tones!

Level 3 Unit 6 • Improv Demo 1

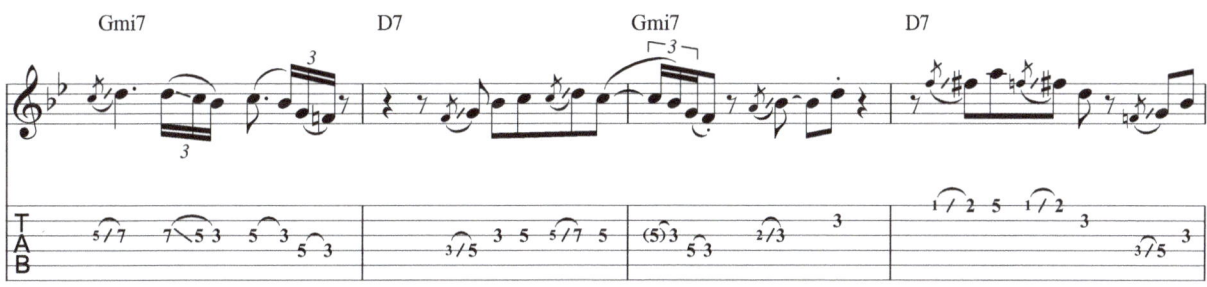

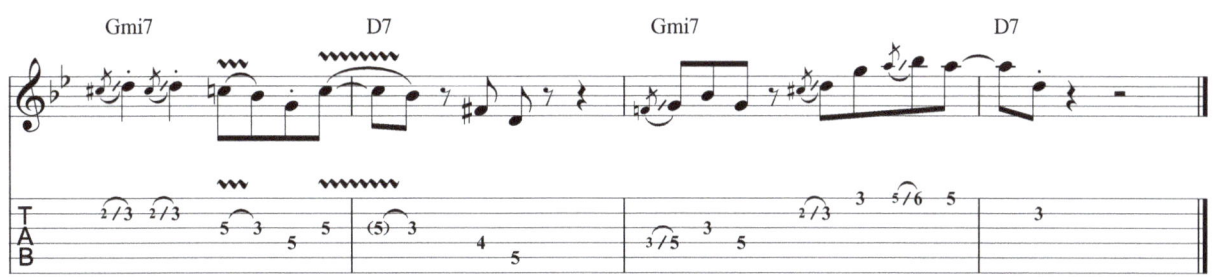

Level 3 Unit 6 • Improv Demo 2

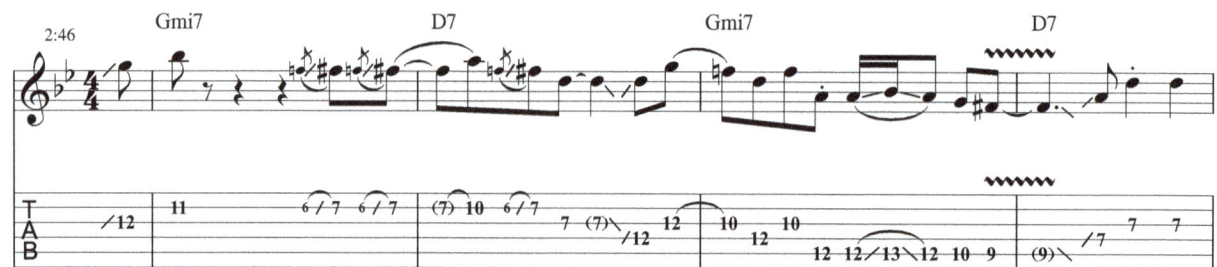
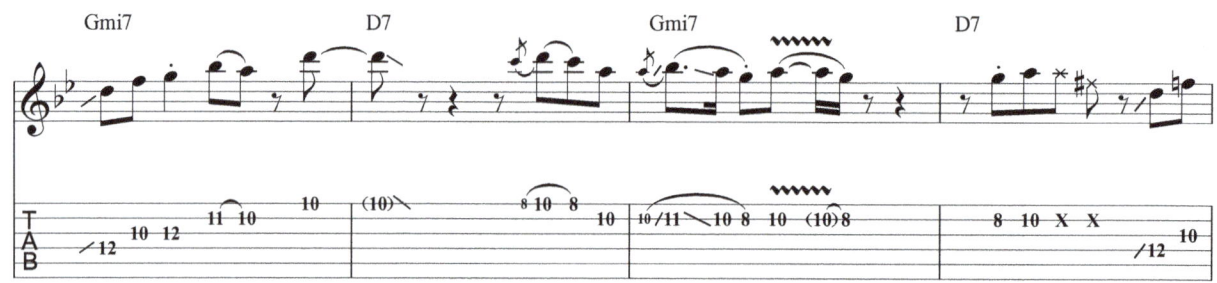
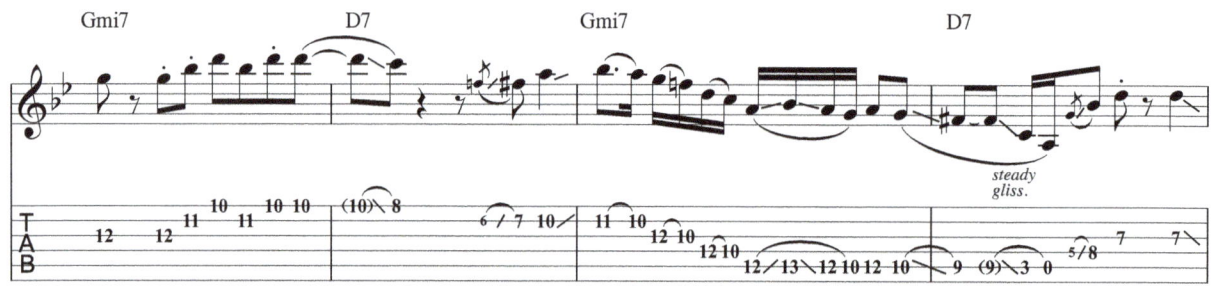
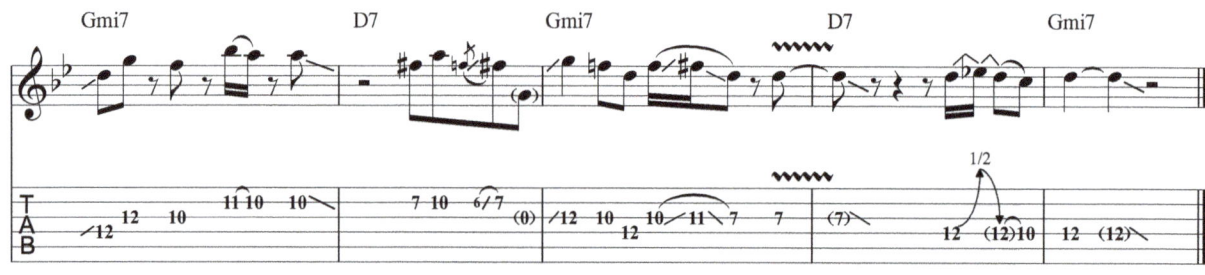

PRACTICE

Theory

- ☐ Go to the tabs below the Theory video on the website and complete the quiz.
- ☐ Memorize the 7th chord families in minor keys.
- ☐ Work through the Progression Analysis Exercise and check your work with the answer key in the Appendix.

Fretboard Logic

- ☐ Learn the Pattern II, IV, and V dominant 7 arpeggios. Add these to your practice routine.
- ☐ Learn the Patterns IV and II minor 7(♭5) chords. Add these to your practice routine.

Technique

- ☐ Learn the diatonic 4ths sequence and add it to your practice routine.

Rhythm Guitar

- ☐ Learn the different strumming patterns in Country rhythm guitar.

Money Makers

- ☐ Learn the Pattern IV minor pentatonic licks and practice playing them.

Improvisation

- ☐ Focus on chord-tone soloing over the progression provided using Patterns II and IV minor 7 arpeggios and I and III dominant 7 arpeggios.

UNIT 7

Learning Modules

> **Theory** - Analyzing minor chord progressions with 7th chords

> **Fretboard Logic** - Patterns I, III, and V minor 7 arpeggios, Patterns II and IV 7th chord shapes, using movable 7th chords in progressions

> **Technique** - Diatonic 5ths sequence exercise

> **Rhythm Guitar** - 3/4 time in Country rhythm guitar

> **Money Makers** - Pattern V minor pentatonic licks

> **Improvisation** - Chord tone soloing in D major

> **Practice** - Continue practice routine development

THEORY

In the last Theory module you learned about harmonic analysis of chord progressions in minor keys that have 7th chords. This module provides more progressions for demonstration and practice. In addition to identifying the number of each chord, determine the chord family to which each of these chords belong.

Progression 1

Here is the first progression:

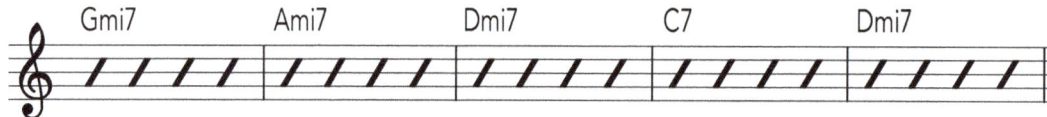

One common indication of the key of a progression is the final chord, which is often the I chord. Consider this the first clue. Dmi7 is the final chord. That implies D as the tonic.

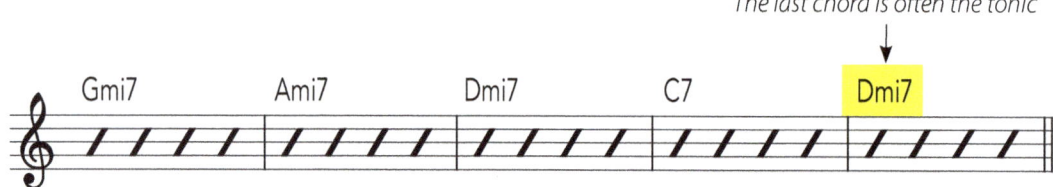

Another very common clue is a dominant 7th chord. In major diatonic harmony there is only one dominant 7th chord, the ♭VII7. This progression has C7. There is only one key in which C7 can be ♭VII7 and that is D minor.

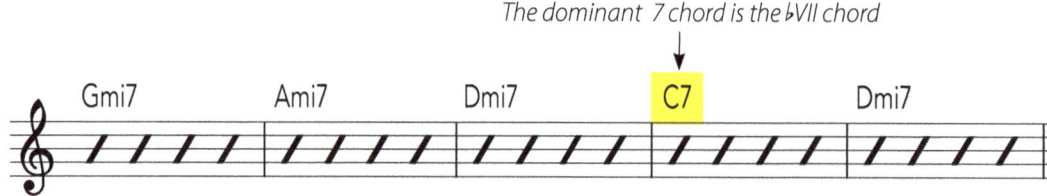

Another very common clue is where two minor 7 chords are a whole step apart. In major diatonic harmony there is only one place this occurs: between II minor 7 and III minor 7. Dmi7 and Emi7 are two minor 7 chords a whole step apart in the key of D minor.

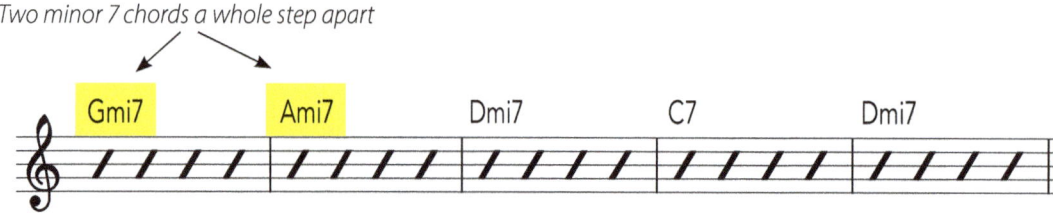

Because of these clues, start with the assumption that this progression is in the key of D minor. Here is the analysis:

- Gmi7 is the 4th scale degree in D minor, and the IV chord in a minor key is minor 7. Therefore, Gmi7 is IVmi7.
- Ami7 is the 5th scale degree in D minor, and the V chord in a minor key is minor 7. Therefore, Ami7 is Vmi7.
- Dmi7 is the 1st scale degree in D minor, and the I chord in a minor key is minor 7. Therefore, Dmi7 is Imi7.
- You determined that C7 is ♭VII7 in the key of D minor.
- The last chord, Dmi7, again is Imi7.

Key: D Minor

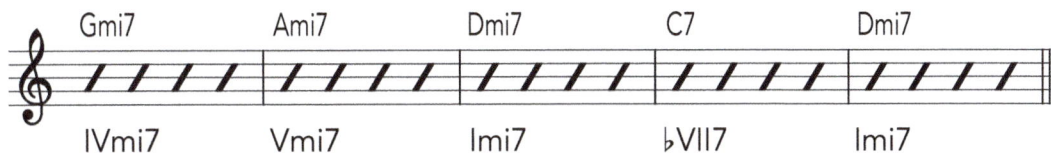

Progression 2

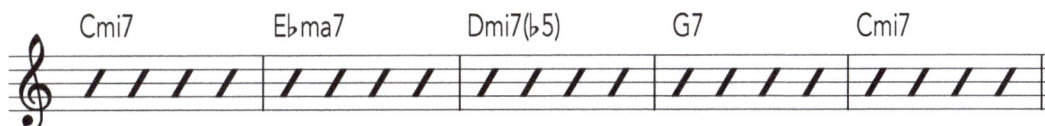

Look at the last chord, as it is often the I chord in the key. The last chord in this progression is Cmi7. Start with the assumption that Cmi7 is the I chord and C is the tonic.

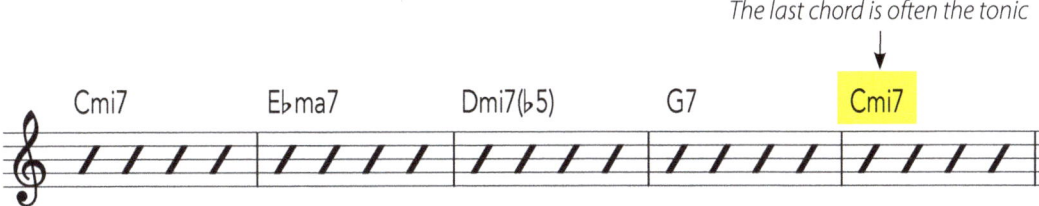

Another clue is a dominant 7th chord which can either be the ♭VII7 or the V7 in a minor key. This progression has G7. Since there is no Ami7 in the progression, we have to assume that the G7 is V7 and that the key is C minor.

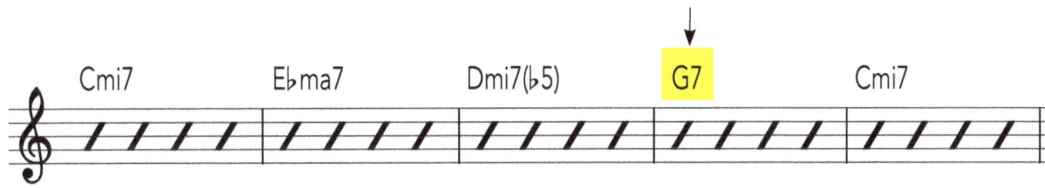

Because of these two clues, start with the assumption that this progression is in the key of C minor. Here is the analysis:

- Cmi7 is the 1st scale degree in C minor, and the I chord in a minor key is minor 7. Therefore, Cmi7 is Imi7.
- E♭ma7 is the 3rd scale degree in C minor and the ♭III chord in a minor key is a major 7. Therefore, E♭ma7 is the ♭IIIma7.
- Dmi7(♭5) is next and fits as the IImi7(♭5) in D.
- You determined that G7 is V7 and the final chord, Cmi7, is Imi7.

Progression 3

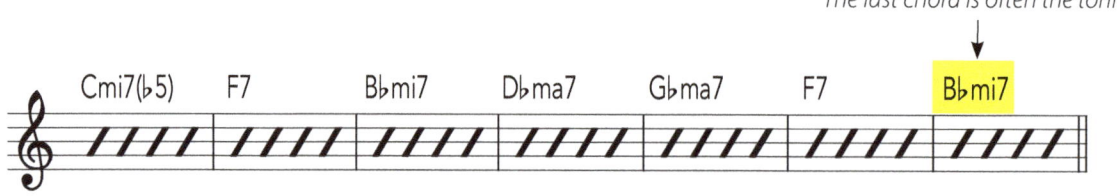

Because the last chord is B♭mi7, start with tentative the assumption that it is the I chord and the tonic is B♭.

The last chord is often the tonic

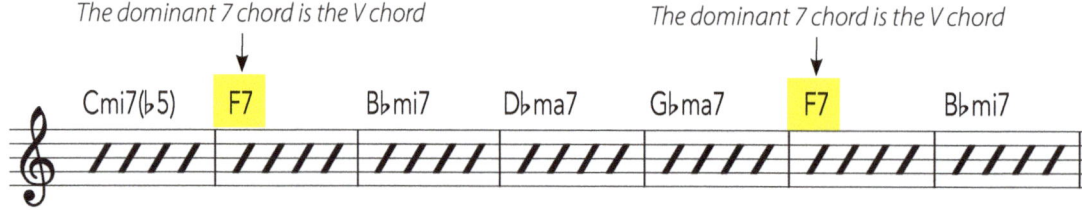

Another clue is the dominant 7th chord which is usually the ♭VII7 or V7 in a minor key. This progression has an F7. There are only two places where the a dominant 7 chord can occur in diatonic harmony: the ♭VII7 or V7. In this case, the F7 is the V7 in B♭ minor.

There is also a mi7(♭5) chord, which in a minor key is the II chord. Here the Cmi7(♭5) is the II chord in B♭ minor.

Fretboard Biology — Level 3 • Unit 7: Theory

The minor 7(♭5) chord is the II chord

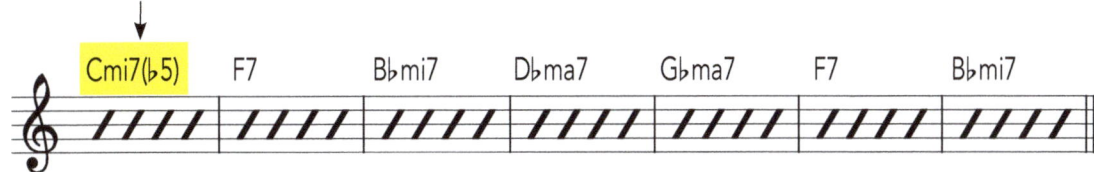

Because of these clues, start with the assumption that this progression is in the key of B♭ minor. Here is the analysis:

- C is the 2nd scale degree in B♭ minor, and the II chord in a minor key is minor 7(♭5). Therefore, Cmi7(♭5) is IImi7.
- You determined that F7 is V7 in B♭ minor.
- B is the tonic in B♭ minor, and the I chord in a minor key is minor 7. Therefore, B♭mi7 is Imi7.
- D♭ is the 3rd scale degree in B♭ minor, and the ♭III chord in a minor key is major 7. Therefore, D♭ma7 is ♭IIIma7.
- G♭ is the 6th scale degree in B♭ minor, and the ♭VI chord in a minor key is major 7. Therefore, G♭ma7 is ♭VIma7.
- You determined that F7 is V7, and the final chord, B♭mi7, is Ima7.

Key: B♭ Minor

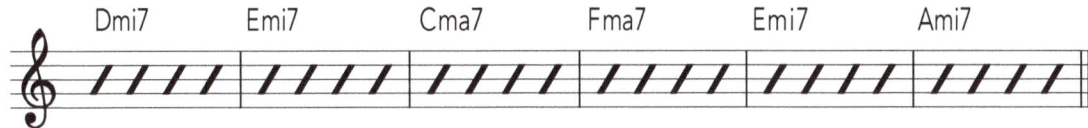

Progression 4

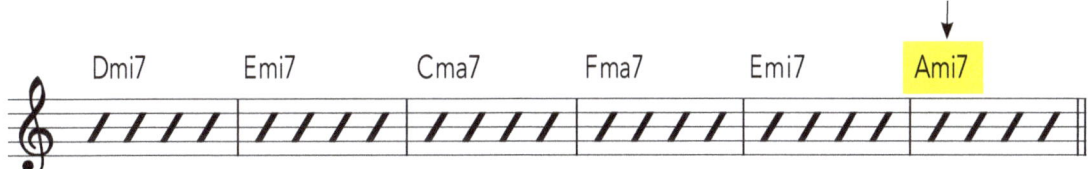

Because the last chord is Ami7, think of it as Imi7 in the key of A minor to start.

The last chord is often the tonic

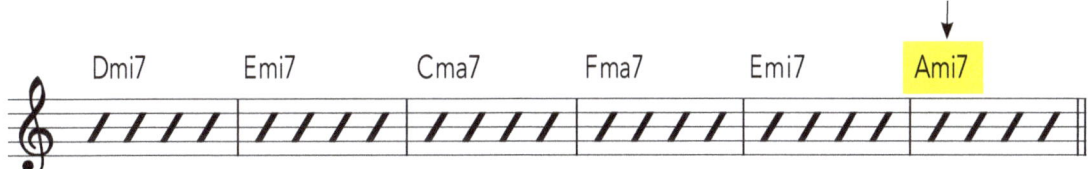

This progression has two minor 7 chords a whole step apart, which only happens between the IV and V chords in a minor key. So, Dmi7 and Emi7 are the IVmi7 and Vmi7 chords in A minor.

Two minor 7 chords a whole step apart

| Dmi7 | Emi7 | Cma7 | Fma7 | Emi7 | Ami7 |

Because of these clues, start with the assumption that this progression is in the key of A minor. Here is the analysis:

- Dmi7 is built on D, the 4th scale degree in A minor, and the IV chord is minor 7.
- Emi7 is built on E, the 5th scale degree in A minor, and the V chord is minor 7.
- Cma7 is built on C, the 3rd scale degree in A minor, and the ♭III chord is major 7.
- Fma7 is built on F, the 6th scale degree in A minor, and the ♭VI chord is major 7.
- You determined that Emi7 is Vmi7.
- Ami7 is built on the tonic and is the Imi7 chord.

Key: A Major

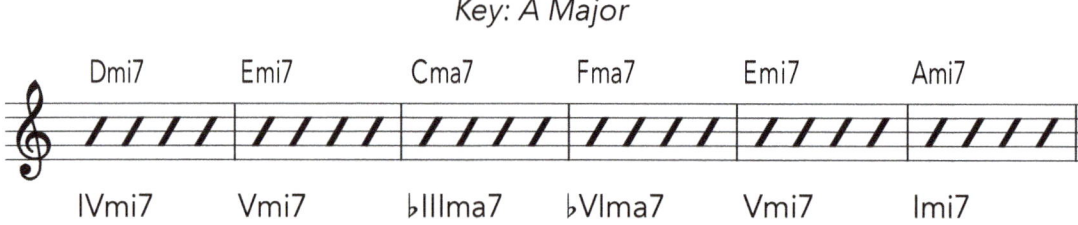

Get in the habit of analyzing every chord progression you see. In the short term there will progressions that you don't fully understand because you have only worked with progressions that use all diatonic chords. As you progress through the Fretboard Biology Theory Modules, you will learn about the non-diatonic chords that are commonly used. This is a gradual process that relies on your understanding of diatonic harmony. Make sure you're solid with it.

Progression Analysis Exercise

The next few pages contain an exercise to help you develop your skills in quickly analyzing progressions. The example will show you how to fill out this worksheet. Your goal is to identify two things: 1) the key of the progression and 2) the number of each chord in the progression. Once you complete the exercise, you can check the answer key in the Appendix of this book. If you struggle with this exercise, keep working at it until it becomes second-nature.

Fretboard Biology — Level 3 • Unit 7: Theory — 185

Progression Analysis Exercise

Answer key located on Page 281

Step One: Make a tentative determination of the key.
Step Two: Based on this, determine the number (function) of each chord.
Step Three: Confirm and label the key and function of each chord.

EXAMPLE:

Key: A minor

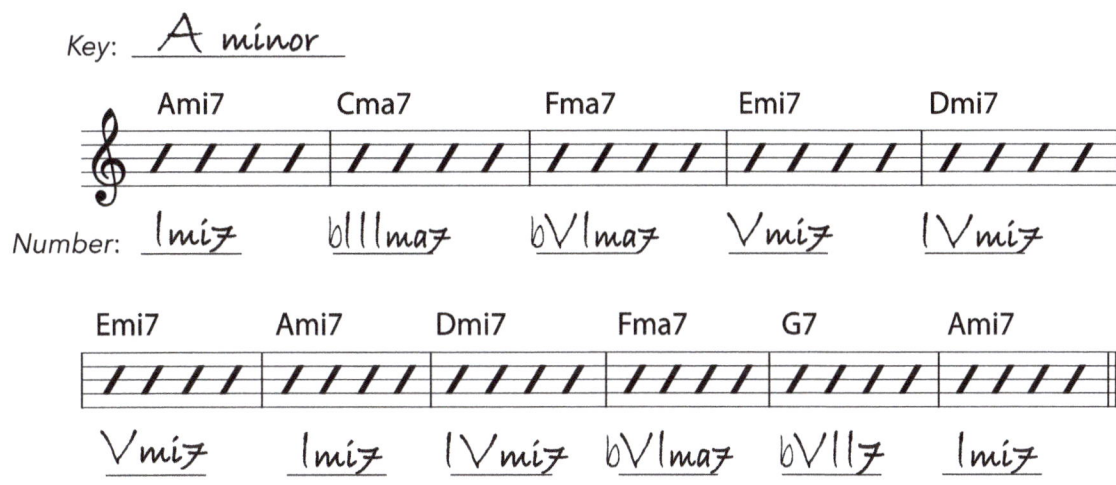

Key: _____

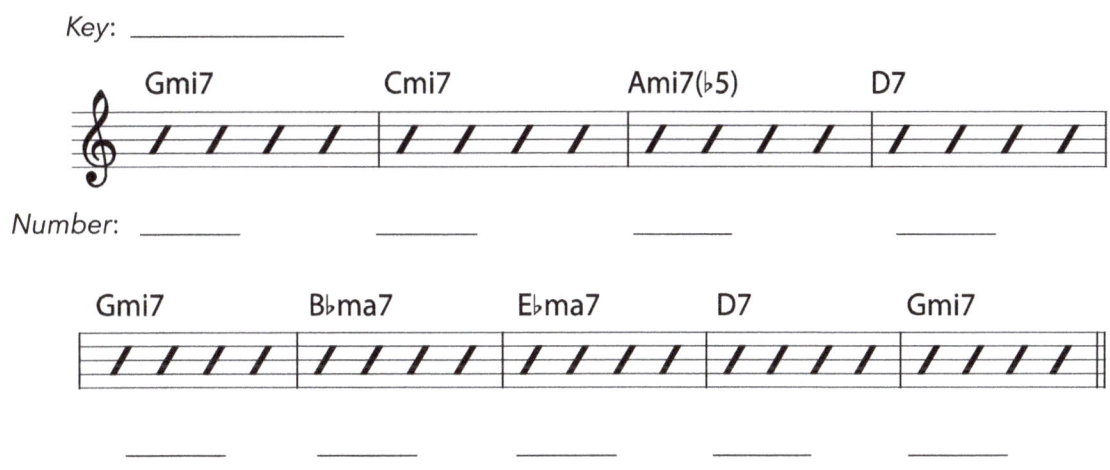

©2020 Joe Elliott • FretboardBiology.com

Progression Analysis Exercise

Key: _____

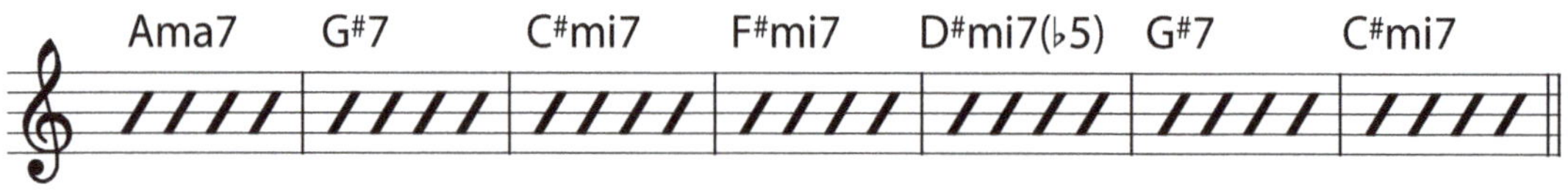

| Ama7 | G#7 | C#mi7 | F#mi7 | D#mi7(♭5) | G#7 | C#mi7 |

Number: _____ _____ _____ _____ _____ _____ _____

Key: _____

| Dmi7 | C7 | B♭ma7 | Ami7 |

Number: _____ _____ _____ _____

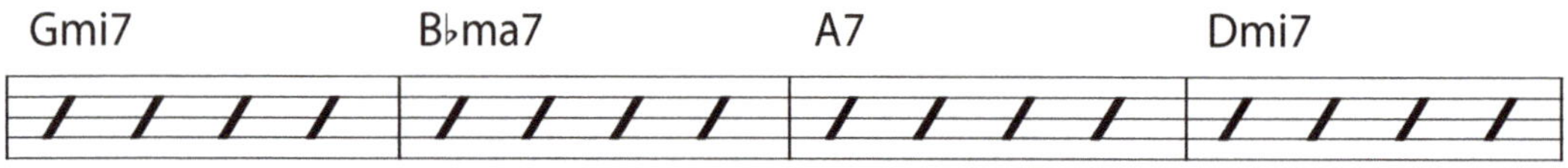

| Gmi7 | B♭ma7 | A7 | Dmi7 |

_____ _____ _____ _____

Key: _____

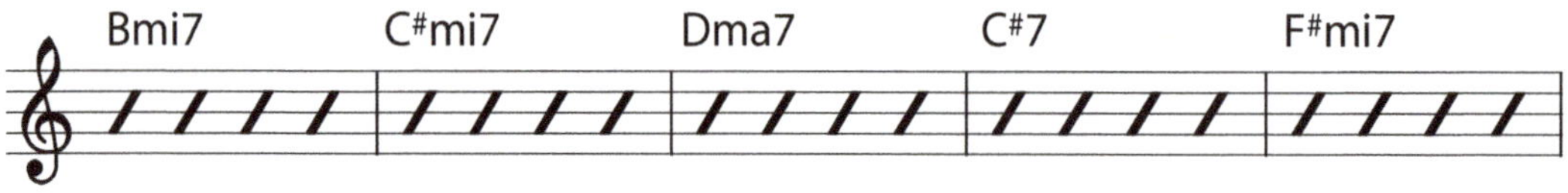

| Bmi7 | C#mi7 | Dma7 | C#7 | F#mi7 |

Number: _____ _____ _____ _____ _____

| Dma7 | Ama7 | Bmi7 | G#mi7(♭5) | C#7 | F#mi7 |

_____ _____ _____ _____ _____ _____

Fretboard Biology
Level 3 • Unit 7: Theory
187

Progression Analysis Exercise

Key: _____

| Dmi7(♭5) | G7 | Cmi7 | Fmi7 |

Number: _____ _____ _____ _____

| A♭ma7 | Gmi7 | Fmi7 | G7 |

_____ _____ _____ _____

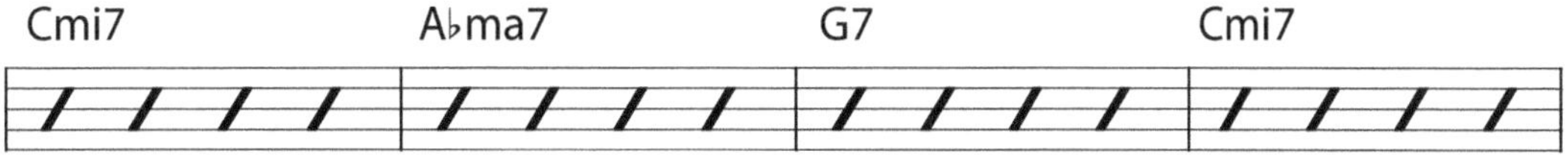

| Cmi7 | A♭ma7 | G7 | Cmi7 |

_____ _____ _____ _____

Key: _____

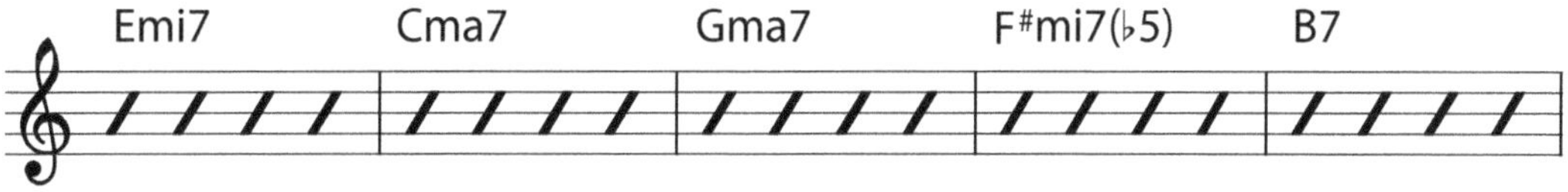

| Emi7 | Cma7 | Gma7 | F#mi7(♭5) | B7 |

Number: _____ _____ _____ _____ _____

| Emi7 | Ami7 | Bmi7 | Cma7 | D7 | Emi7 |

_____ _____ _____ _____ _____ _____

FRETBOARD LOGIC

Arpeggios

In this module you will learn the remaining three minor 7 chord arpeggios: Patterns I, III, and V. Here is a Pattern I minor triad arpeggio. Now, add a minor 7th everywhere possible within the octave shape to build Pattern I minor 7 arpeggio.

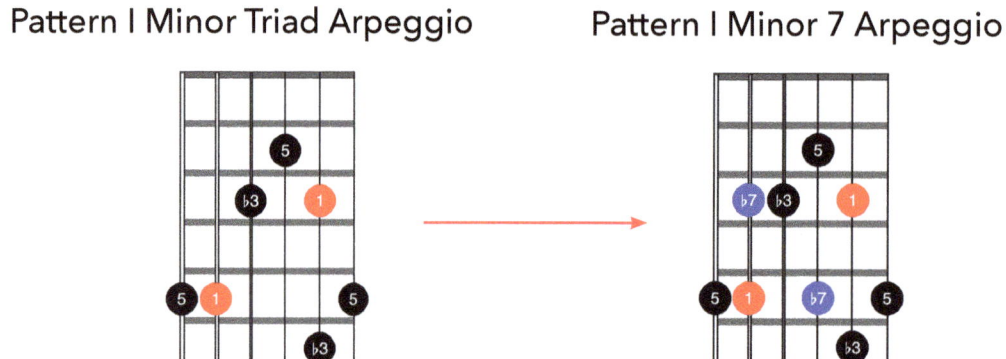

Practice this with alternate picking starting and ending on the root.

Next, let's look at a Pattern III minor triad arpeggio. Add a minor 7th everywhere possible within the octave shape to build a Pattern III minor 7 arpeggio.

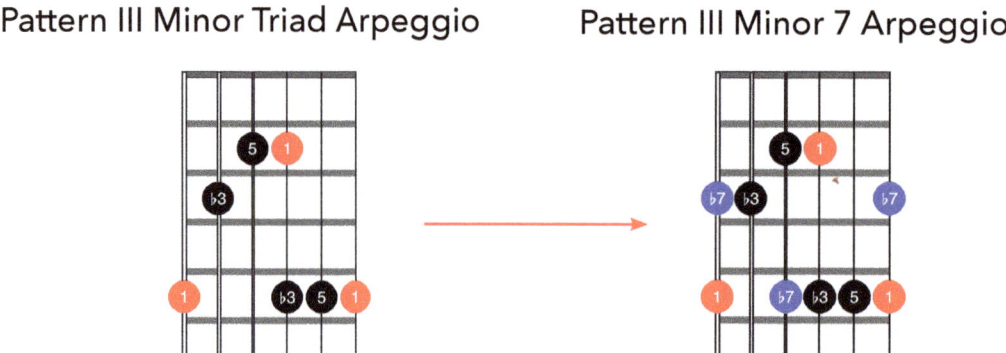

Practice this with alternate picking starting and ending on the root.

Here's a pattern V minor triad arpeggio. Now, add a minor 7th everywhere possible within the octave shape to build a Pattern V minor 7 arpeggio.

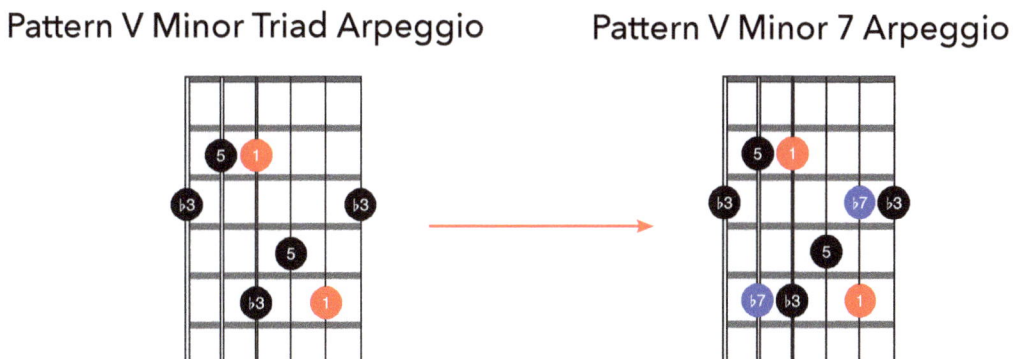

Practice this with alternate picking starting and ending on the root.

Chords

You have learned the most common movable major 7, dominant 7, minor 7, and minor 7(♭5) chords derived from the Patterns IV and II barre chord. This demonstrates that if you have command of the simple structures like triads or pentatonic shells, you can expand them to make more complex structures.

Pattern II 7th Chord Shapes

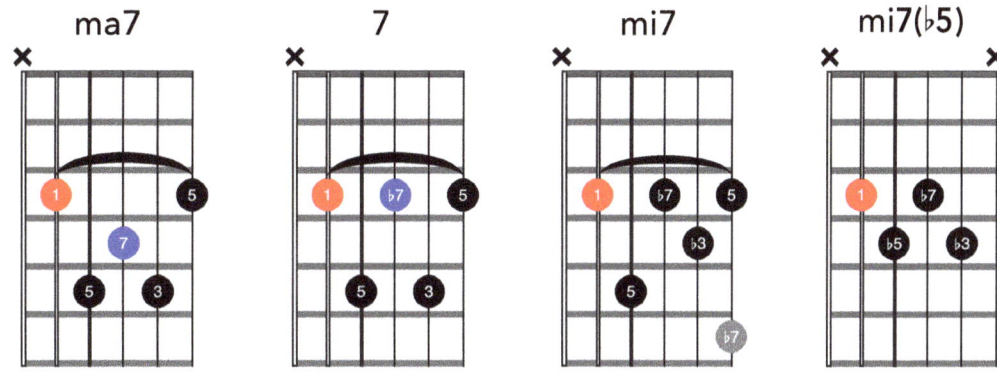

Pattern IV 7th Chord Shapes

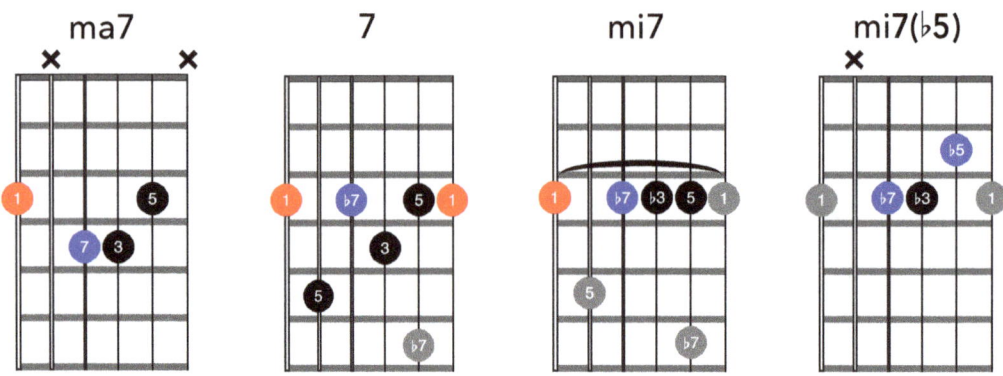

The Patterns II and IV movable 7th chord shapes were introduced first because you know the barre chords they are derived from so well and therefore this is an easy transition from triad to 7th chord. Practice them in progressions as you did when you learned the basic barre chords. The goal in following progressions is to move between chords with as little movement and effort as possible using both patterns II and IV chord shapes.

Look at the exercise tabs below and practice these examples moving as efficiently as possible from chord to chord.

Movable 7th Chord Shape Practice Progressions

Progression 1

Progression 2

Progression 3

Progression 4

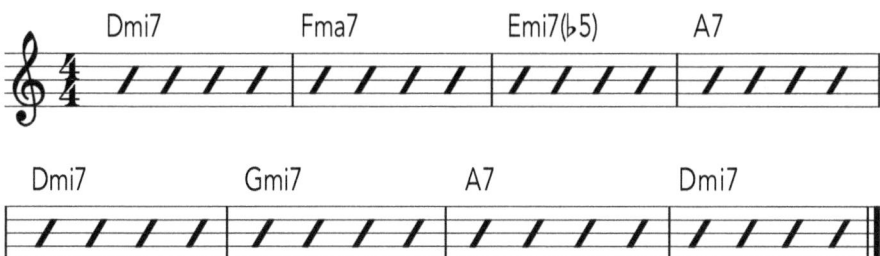

Progression 5

Progression 6

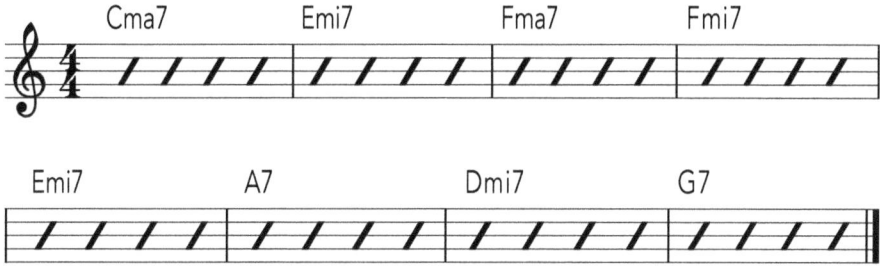

TECHNIQUE

In this module you will learn the "diatonic 5ths" interval sequence. This sequence moves though the scale in 5ths. Use the Pattern IV major scale in the key of A using 8th notes. Work your way up the scale playing notes in pairs.

Diatonic 5ths Sequence

Play the 1st scale degree and then a diatonic note a 5th above it. Then play the 2nd scale degree and then a diatonic note a 5th above it. Then play the 3rd scale degree and then a diatonic note a 5th above it, and so on through the scale.

Ascending this sequence looks like this:

Diatonic 5ths Sequence Exercise - Ascending

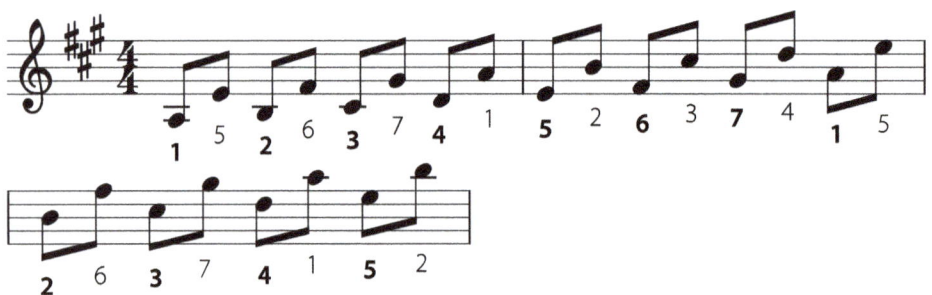

Continue ascending with this pattern until you reach the highest note available in the pattern. Then descend in reverse order like this:

Diatonic 5ths Sequence Exercise - Descending

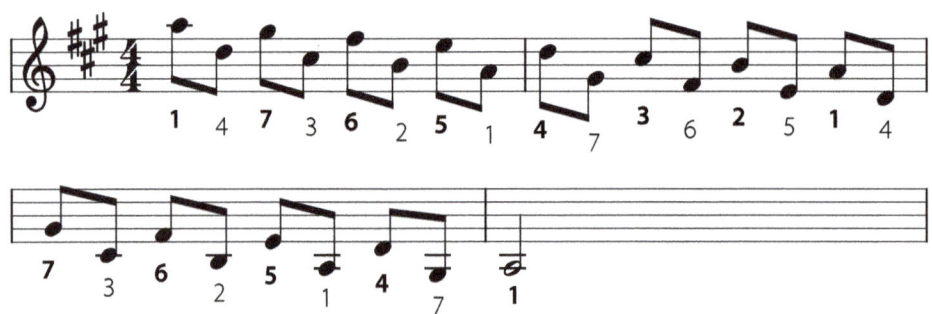

Continue descending with this pattern until you reach the lowest note available in the pattern. Focus on your alternate picking. When you feel like you're ready, set your metronome at slow tempo and go through the patterns again.

RHYTHM GUITAR

3/4 Time in Country

This module continues with basic traditional Country rhythm guitar but focuses on the 3/4 time signature. 3/4 time is pretty common in traditional Country music and it usually swings. It is essentially a waltz.

Drums

The bass drum plays on beat one. The snare or cross stick plays on beat three and the high hat or ride cymbal plays quarter notes and sometimes the 8th note that precedes beat one, which is the swung "and" of beat three.

Bass

The bass player plays the root and the 5th as in 4/4 time but in 3/4, it is played as a two-bar phrase. The root is played on beat one of the first measure and the 5th is played on beat one of the second measure.

Keyboards

The keyboard player, whether it is an organ or piano, normally plays the chords.

Guitar

The basic rhythm guitar part in 3/4 is simple. With flat pick, just strum three quarter notes or insert some 8th notes on the "ands". If you want the boom-chick sound, think of it as more of boom-chick-chick boom-chick-chick. In this case, think about a two-bar phrase as with the bass part described above. In the first measure play the root on beat one and strum the chord on beats two and three. In the second measure play the 5th on beat one and strum the chord on beats two and three again.

3/4 Boom-Chick Pattern 1

Boom Chick Chick   Boom Chick Chick

This example uses an open A chord to demonstrate. You can insert 8th notes on the "ands" in a couple of places, too, as in the examples below.

The boom-chick-chick pattern can be played with thumb and fingers. The picking-hand thumb is assigned to the root and 5th and your fingers work together in sort of a claw shape.

MONEY MAKERS

We are working through each of the five minor pentatonic shells with the goal of understanding the cliché melodic gems that live in side each of these shapes. This is not meant to be comprehensive, but only to point out some of the convenient Bluesy-sounding licks in each shape. From these short licks you can come up with all kinds of other licks, either planned in advance or on the fly.

Licks in Pattern V Minor Pentatonic

This module will focus on the Pattern V minor pentatonic shell. This shape is adjacent to Pattern IV minor pentatonic, the pattern where most guitarists first learn to solo, so it's a natural place to turn next.

Pattern V Minor Pentatonic Scale

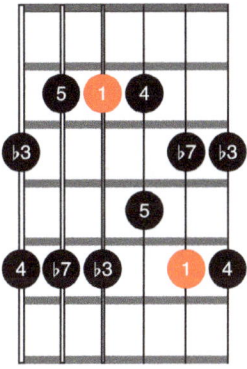

Here are the licks that we will learn in this unit.

Pattern V Blues Lick 1

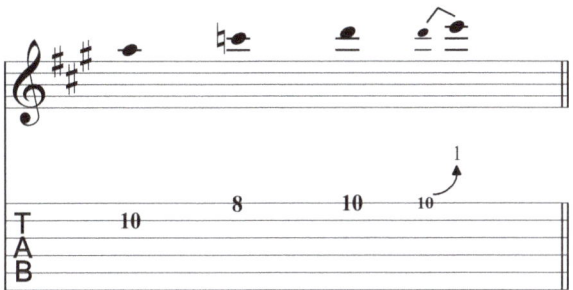

Pattern V Blues Lick 2

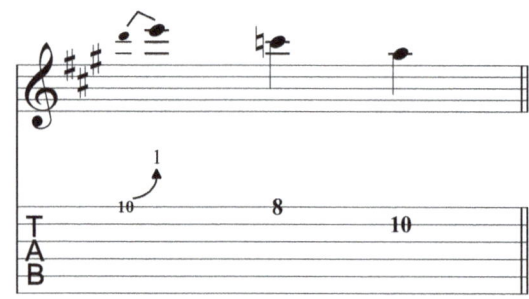

Pattern V Blues Lick 3

Pattern V Blues Lick 4

Work on getting these short mini-licks under your fingers. Practice building your own solo with the new vocabulary as well as the pattern IV vocabulary. On the next page, you will see a demo solo that uses these licks so you can see how they work in the context of a solo.

Fretboard Biology — Level 3 • Unit 7: Money Makers

Level 3 Unit 7 • Money Maker Demo

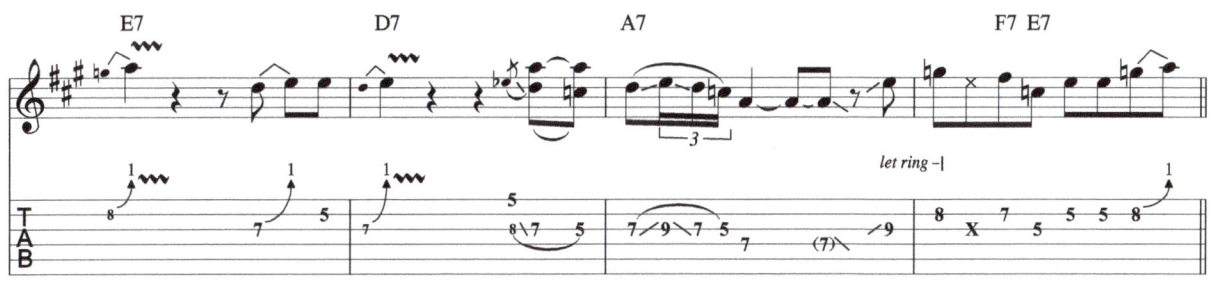

*Played as straight eighth notes.

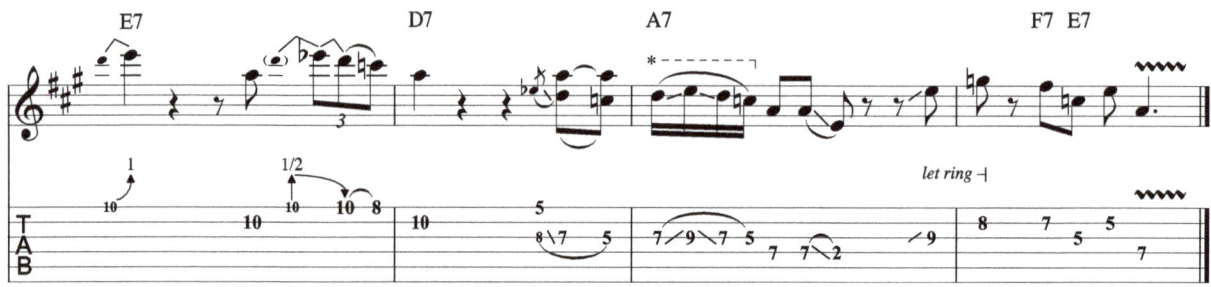

*Played as straight eighth notes.

IMPROVISATION

In this unit and the next we'll continue working on using chord tones in solos over progressions that have several different quality chords.

Here's another simple two-chord progression: Dma7 to A7. For a key center solo, just pick notes from the D major pentatonic scale. As always, I suggest you first play a key-center solo over the track to get acquainted with the track and feel for the changes.

D Major Progression

Next try the chord-tone approach in two different locations on the fretboard. To start, over the Dma7, use the Pattern I Dma7 arpeggio, which places you in 2nd position. Next, over the A7, play the Pattern III A7 arpeggio, which is also in 2nd position. There is no need for movement between these two chords as the arpeggios are in the same position.

D Major Progression

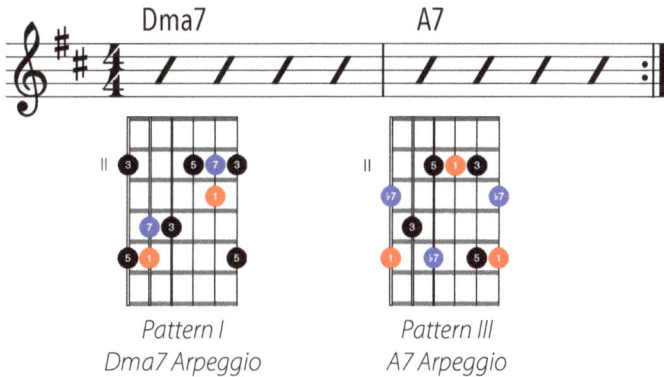

Pattern I Dma7 Arpeggio   *Pattern III A7 Arpeggio*

Play just the arpeggios over the chords as an exercise to start. Then take another segment of your practice and create short motifs that blend chord tones and scale tones.

Try this in a different location on the fretboard. Over the Dma7, use the Pattern III major 7 arpeggio, which is in 7th position. Next over the A7, play the Pattern I A7 arpeggio, which places you in 9th position so you will move two frets.

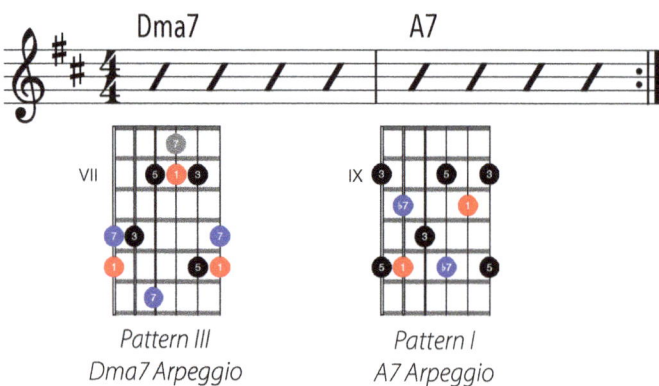

Later in Level 3 you will learn to organize arpeggios by position. This is an important concept for reducing movement between arpeggios when using chord tones.

As always, keep working on your chord tones.

Level 3 Unit 7 • Improv Demo

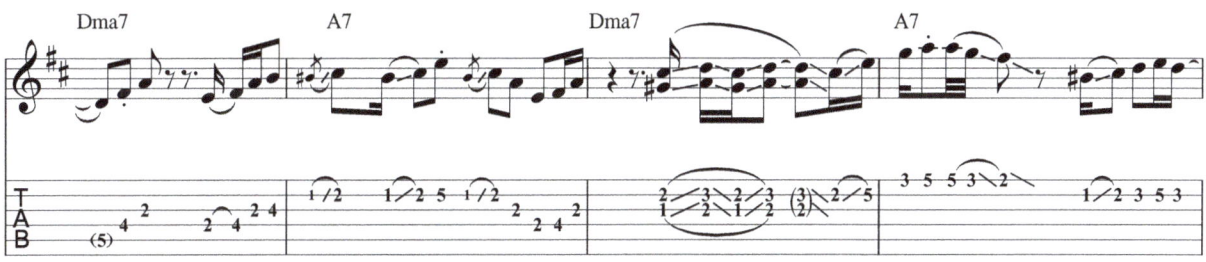

PRACTICE

Theory

- ❑ Go to the tabs below the Theory video on the website and complete the quiz.
- ❑ Practice analyzing minor chord progressions with 7th chords.

Fretboard Logic

- ❑ Learn the Patterns I, III, and V minor 7 arpeggios.
- ❑ Learn the Patterns II and IV movable 7th chord shapes.
- ❑ Practice playing the movable 7th chord shapes in the practice progressions.

Technique

- ❑ Learn and practice the diatonic 5ths sequence exercise.

Rhythm Guitar

- ❑ Learn how to play Country grooves in 3/4 time.

Money Makers

- ❑ Learn common Pattern V minor pentatonic licks.

Improvisation

- ❑ Focus on chord-tone soloing using Patterns I and III major 7 arpeggios and Patterns I and III dominant 7 arpeggios.

UNIT 8

Learning Modules

> **Theory** - Introduction to Blues harmony

> **Fretboard Logic** - Patterns I, III, and V minor 7(♭5) arpeggios, progressions using movable 7th chord shapes

> **Technique** - Diatonic 6ths sequence exercise

> **Rhythm Guitar** - Basic embellishments

> **Money Makers** - Pattern I minor pentatonic licks

> **Improvisation** - Chord tone soloing in D minor

> **Practice** - Continue practice routine development

THEORY

The process of identifying key centers and analyzing diatonic chord progressions is not difficult once you learn the major and minor diatonic systems. In most cases you find the dominant 7th chord and it points you to the tonic. Exceptions to strictly diatonic harmony are common. It makes sense to learn the diatonic systems first and then gradually start exploring situations that use non-diatonic chords and melody notes.

Blues Harmony

Not all music uses strictly diatonic chords and melody notes. Blues is full of exceptions to diatonic harmony. The Rhythm Guitar Modules in Level 1 were about comping in the Blues. Now that you have studied diatonic harmony, you can see that the chords in typical Blues don't fit the diatonic systems. Blues harmony blends European diatonic and African non-diatonic musical traditions.

Just as in diatonic major and minor harmony, the three primary chords in Blues harmony are I, IV, and V, but, the chord qualities are different. In major keys, the I and IV chords are major 7 and V is dominant 7. In minor keys, the I, IV, and V chords are all minor 7. In Blues, however, the I, IV, and V chords are all dominant 7. The result is that Blues harmony is both tonal (because you feel the strong attachment to a tonic) and permanently unresolved because of the dominant 7 chords, preparing your ear for motion even when it would seem to be at rest.

Look at the comparison of major and minor harmony with Blues harmony.

Major, Minor, and Blues Harmony

	I Chord	IV Chord	V Chord
Major Keys	Ima7	IVma7	V7
Minor Keys	Imi7	IVmi7	Vmi7
Blues	I7	IV7	V7

The three dominant 7 chords built on I, IV, and V in Blues create some interesting melodic opportunities and challenges. There are conflicts between chord tones and common melodic choices that are accepted as normal because we have grown up hearing them. Blues has made it acceptable to have both I and IV dominant 7th chords.

In the next Module, we'll look at melody note choices in the Blues.

FRETBOARD LOGIC

Arpeggios

In this module you will learn the remaining three minor 7(♭5) arpeggios: Patterns I, III, and V.

Here is a Pattern I minor triad arpeggio. First, add a minor 7th everywhere possible within the octave shape. Next, lower all the 5ths a half step so they are ♭5s. The result is a Pattern I minor 7(♭5) arpeggio.

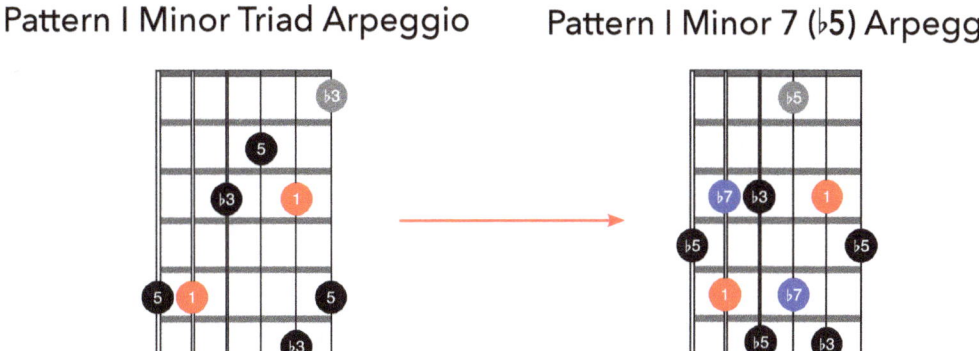

Practice this with alternate picking starting and ending on the root.

Here's a Pattern III minor triad arpeggio. First, add a minor 7th everywhere possible within the octave shape. Next, lower all the 5ths a half step so they are ♭5s. The result is a Pattern III minor 7(♭5) arpeggio.

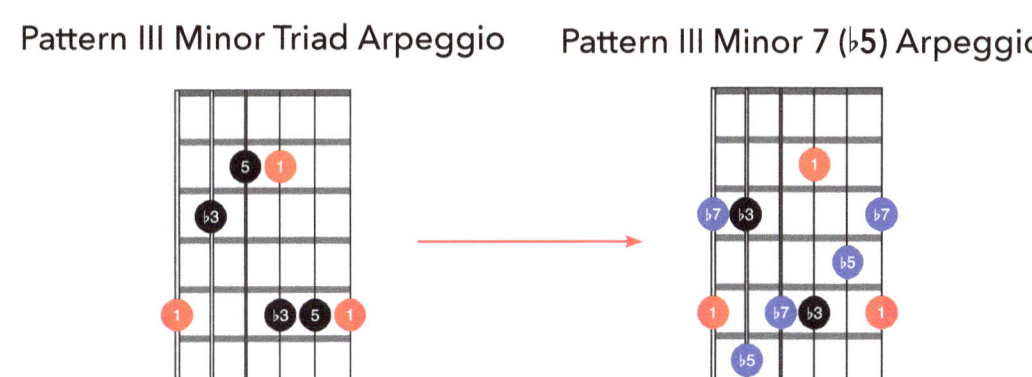

Practice this with alternate picking starting and ending on the root.

Here's a Pattern V minor triad arpeggio. First, add a minor 7th everywhere possible within the octave shape. Next, lower all the 5ths a half step so they are ♭5s. The result is a Pattern V minor 7(♭5) arpeggio.

Pattern V Minor Triad Arpeggio   **Pattern V Minor 7 (♭5) Arpeggio**

Practice this with alternate picking starting and ending on the root.

Chords

This module provides more practice opportunities using the movable 7th chords in progressions. Again, your goal in playing the following progressions is to move as little as possible from chord to chord using both Pattern II and IV chords.

Movable 7th Chord Shape Practice Progressions

Progression 1

Progression 2

Progression 3

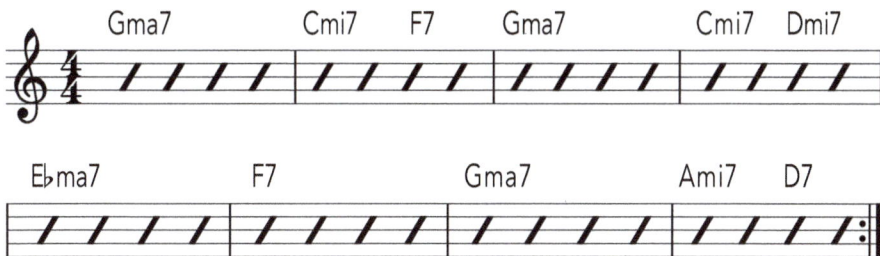

Progression 4

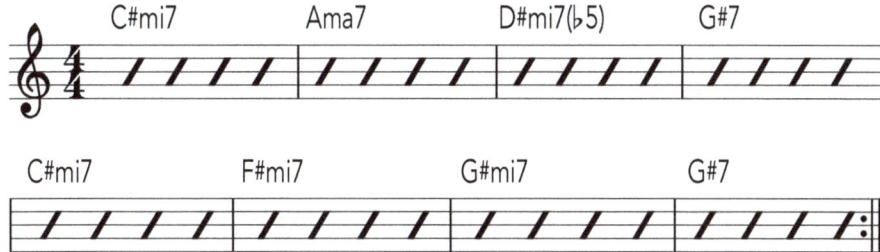

Progression 5

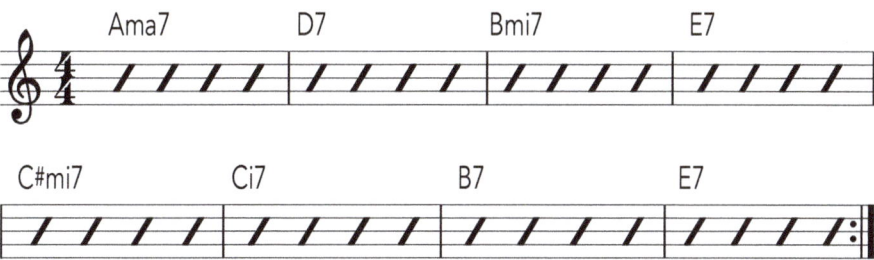

In the next module you will learn the critical concept of organizing arpeggios "in position". You will also learn all of the remaining practical 7th chord voicings within the octave shapes: Patterns I, III, and V. This will mark another milestone in advancing the chord sections of the Family Trees. The next module is a big one and very important.

TECHNIQUE

In this module you will learn the "diatonic 6th" interval sequence. Use the Pattern IV major scale in the key of A with 8th-notes. Work your way up the scale playing notes in pairs.

Diatonic 6ths Sequence

To start, play the 1st scale degree and then a diatonic note a 6th above it. Then play the 2nd scale degree and then a diatonic note a 6th above it. Then play the 3rd scale degree and then a diatonic note a 6th above it, and so on through the scale.

Ascending this sequence will look like this:

Diatonic 6ths Sequence Exercise - Ascending

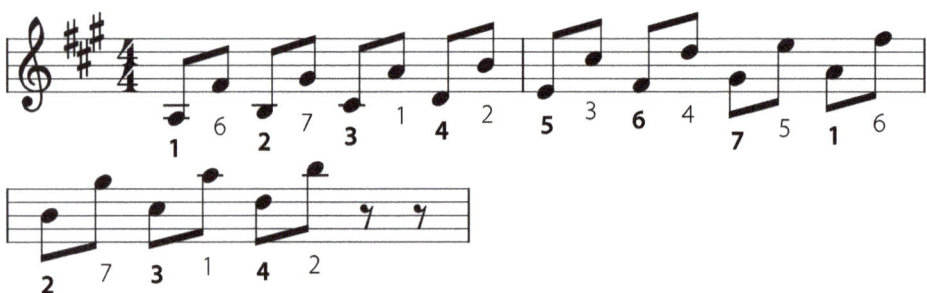

As before, continue ascending with this pattern until you reach the highest note available in the pattern. Then descend in reverse order like this:

Diatonic 6ths Sequence Exercise - Descending

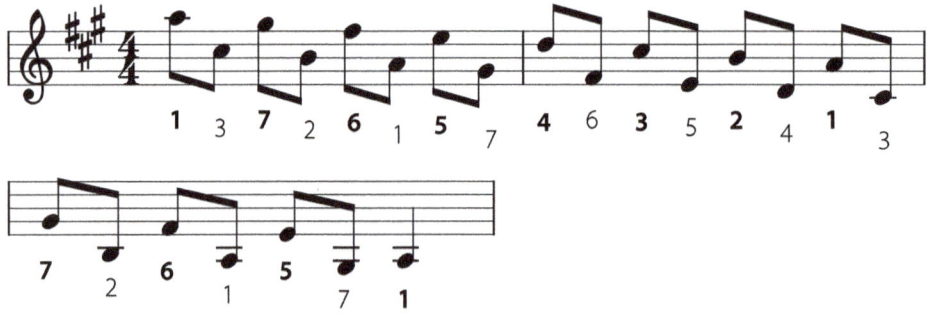

Continue descending with this pattern until you reach the lowest note available in the pattern. Focus on alternate picking. When you feel like you are ready, set your metronome at slow tempo and play through the sequences again.

RHYTHM GUITAR

Basic Embellishments

There are some useful embellishments you can integrate into your vocabulary quickly. You may have noticed that depending on how big your fingers are, and how wide your string spacing is near the nut, open voicings can be challenging to play cleanly. For example, the tighter the string spacing, the harder it is to play them cleanly, and if you have big fingers, too, it is even harder. You might try learning the ideas and example in this module on a nylon string guitar where the spacing is wider.

Here are some embellishments. It is best to practice them one chord at a time:

Open A Chord

First, look at an open A chord.

- On beat one, play the root on the open 5th string.
- On beat two, strum the chord.
- On beat three, hammer-on the 5th, E, with your first finger at the 2nd fret on the 4th string.
- On beat four, strum the chord.

One-Bar Pattern: Hammer-On Embellishment

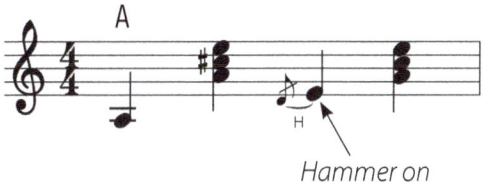

Hammer on

You can make it a two-bar pattern by doing this:

- One beat one, play the root on the open 5th string.
- On beat two, strum the chord.
- On beat three, hammer-on the 5th, E, with your first finger at the 2nd fret on the 4th string.
- On beat four, strum the chord.

In the second measure:

- On beat one, play the root on the open 5th string.
- On beat two, strum the chord.

- On beat three, play the 5th, E, on the open 6th string.
- On beat four, strum the chord.

Two-Bar Pattern: Hammer-On Embellishment

Open A Minor Chord

The same thing works for Ami, too.

One-Bar Pattern: Hammer-On Embellishment

Two-Bar Pattern: Hammer-On Embellishment

Open C Chord

Next learn this two-bar pattern for a C chord:
- On beat one, play the root on the 5th string and the 3rd fret.
- On beat two, strum the chord.
- On beat three, hammer-on the 3rd, E, with your second finger at the 2nd fret on the 4th string.
- On beat four, strum the chord.

In the second measure:

- On beat one, hammer-on the 6th, an A, with your third finger on the 3rd string at the second fret string.
- On beat two, strum the chord.

- On beat three, play the 5th, G, on the open 3rd string.
- On beat four, strum the chord – actually just the first and second strings.

Two-Bar Pattern: Hammer-On Embellishment

Hammer on

Hammer on

Open D Chord

Next look at an open D chord. Here, we can do two different embellishments. Let's start with a one-bar pattern:
- On beat one, play the root on the open 4th string.
- On beat two strum the chord.
- On beat three hammer-on the 5th, A, with your first finger at the 2nd fret on the 3rd string.
- On beat four strum the chord.

One-Bar Pattern: Hammer-On Embellishment

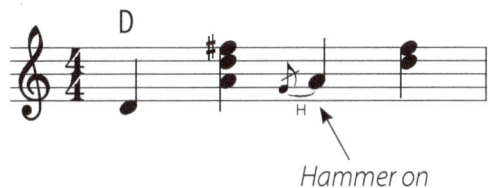

Hammer on

Next, let's do a two-bar embellishment by doing this:
- On beat one, play the root on the open 4th string
- On beat two, strum the chord.
- On beat three, hammer-on the 5th, A, with your first finger at the 2nd fret on the 3rd string.
- On beat four, strum the chord.

In the second measure:
- On beat one, play the root on the open 4th string again.
- On beat two strum the chord.
- On beat three play the 5th, A, on the open 5th string.
- On beat four strum the chord.

Two-Bar Pattern: Hammer-On Embellishment

Hammer on

Open D Minor Chord

The same patters work for D minor, too.

One-Bar Pattern: Hammer-On Embellishment

Two-Bar Pattern: Hammer-On Embellishment

Open E Chord

Let's look at an open E chord. We can do two different embellishments here as well. Let's start with a one-bar pattern:

- On beat one, play the root on the open 6th string.
- On beat two strum the chord.
- On beat three hammer-on the 5th, B, with your second finger at the 2nd fret on the 5th string.
- On beat four strum the chord.

One-Bar Pattern: Hammer-On Embellishment

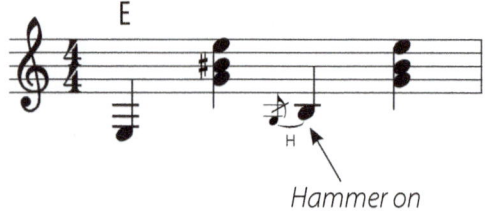

Hammer on

You can make it a two-bar pattern by doing this:
- On beat one, play the root on the open 6th string.
- On beat two, strum the chord.
- On beat three, hammer-on the 5th, B, with your second finger at the 2nd fret on the 5th string.
- On beat four, strum the chord.

In the second measure:
- On beat one, hammer-on the root on the 4th string at the second fret.
- On beat two, strum the chord.
- On beat three, hammer-on the 5th, B, on the 5th string at the second fret.
- On beat four, strum the chord.

Two-Bar Pattern: Hammer-On Embellishment

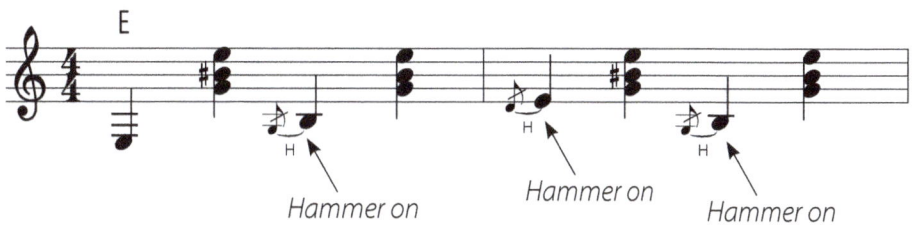

Open E Minor Chord

The same patterns works for E minor:

One-Bar Pattern: Hammer-On Embellishment

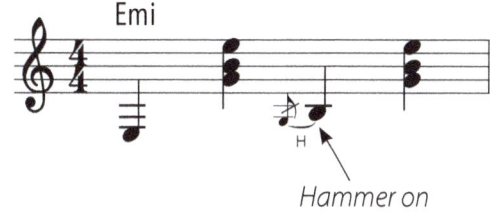

Two-Bar Pattern: Hammer-On Embellishment

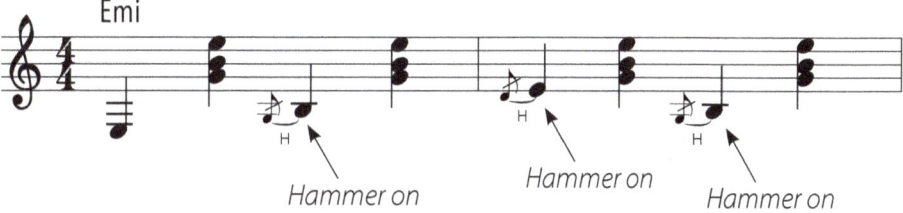

Open G Chord

Look at a G chord. This is the two-bar pattern:

- On beat one, play the root on the 6th string and the 3rd fret.
- On beat two, strum the chord.
- On beat three, hammer-on the 3rd, B, with your second finger at the 2nd fret on the 5th string.
- On beat four, strum the chord.

In the second measure:

- On beat one, hammer-on the 6th, E, with your 3rd finger on the 4th string at the second fret string.
- On beat two, strum the chord.
- On beat three, play the 5th, a D, on the open 4th string.
- On beat four, strum the chord – actually just the first and second strings.

Two-Bar Pattern: Hammer-On Embellishment

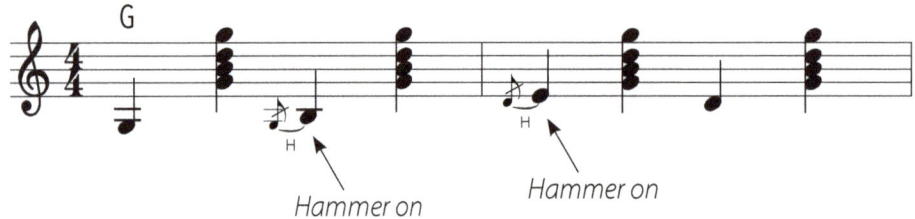

Practice these individually on isolated chords before trying them with some of the backing tracks. The tracks will be familiar – they are the ones used in the past two Modules.

MONEY MAKERS

Let's continue working through each of the five minor pentatonic shells finding the cliché melodic gems that live in side each of them.

Licks in Pattern I Minor Pentatonic

In this Module you will work in the Pattern I minor pentatonic shell. This shape has a lot of really great stuff packed into a really small area. The way the notes lay in the pattern makes for some really great possibilities. We'll work in this pattern the same way we did the Patterns IV and V.

Pattern I Minor Pentatonic Scale

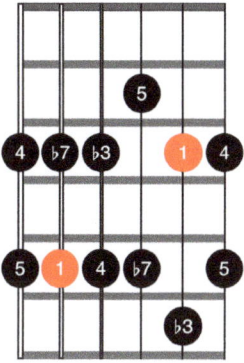

First let's learn some of these mini-licks now.

Pattern I Blues Lick 1

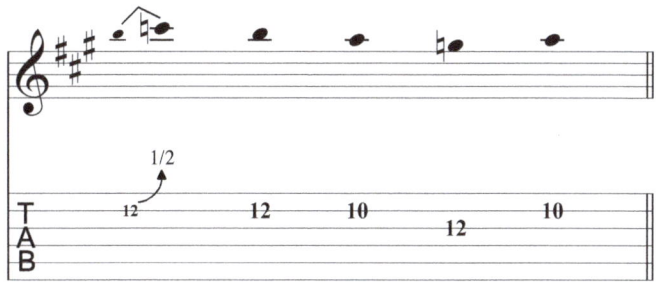

Pattern I Blues Lick 2

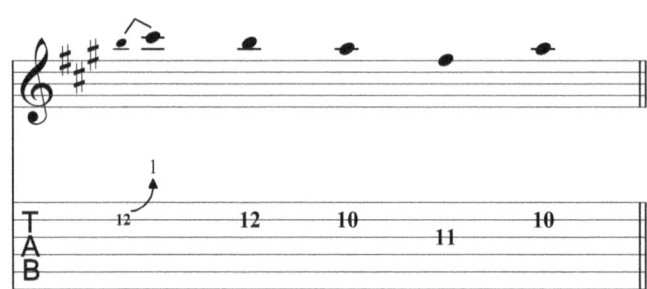

Pattern I Blues Lick 3

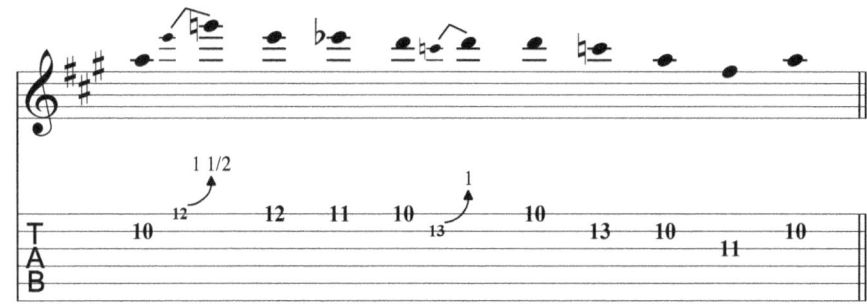

Pattern I Blues Lick 4

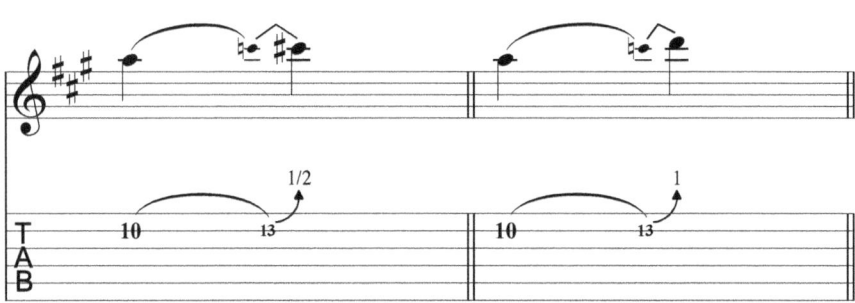

Pattern I Blues Lick 5

On the next page, you will see a demo solo that uses these licks so you can see how they work in the context of a solo.

Level 3 Unit 8 • Money Maker Demo

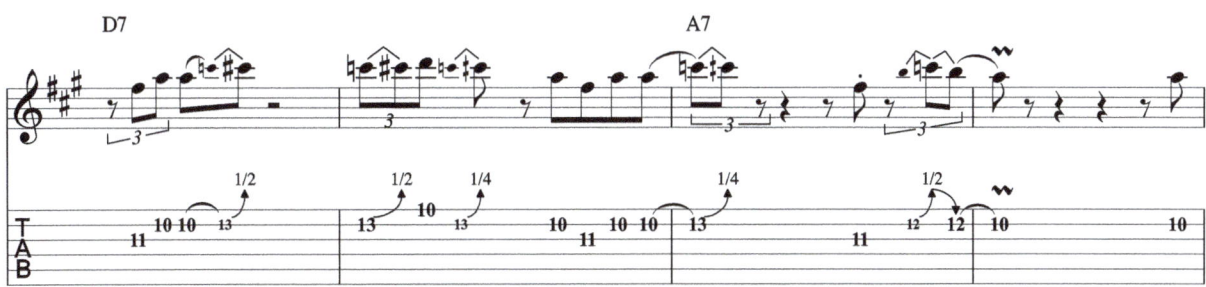
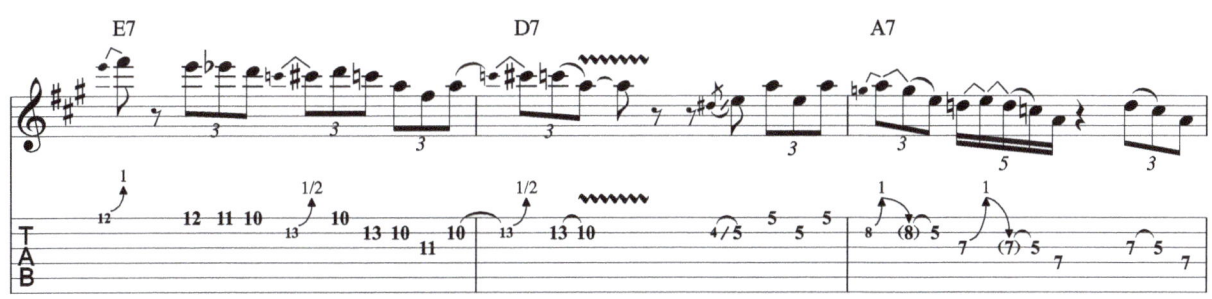

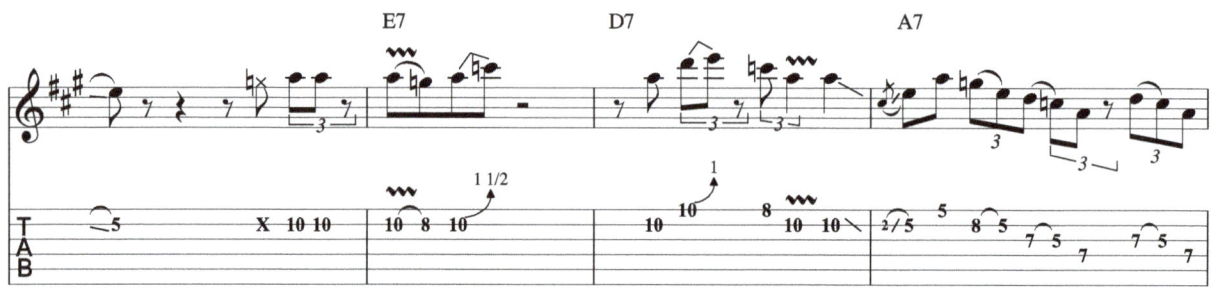

IMPROVISATION

In this module you will use chord tones in a progression with three chords. This progression is in D minor: Emi7(♭5), A7, and Dmi7. The source of notes for a key-center solo can be the D minor pentatonic scale. It's not perfect because the C# in the A7 conflicts, but you can make it work. I suggest you first play a key-center solo over the track in Pattern II D minor pentatonic to get acquainted with the track and to get a feel for the changes.

D Minor Progression

Next use the chord-tone approach and practice in two different locations on the fretboard. First, over the Em7(♭5) use the Pattern II minor 7(♭5) arpeggio, which places you in 7th position. Next, over the A7, play the Pattern III dominant 7 arpeggio, which places you in 2nd position. It is quite a distance between these two arpeggios and not ideal. Next, over the Dmi7, play the Pattern II minor 7 arpeggio, which places you in 5th position. You will have to move your hand from 2nd position for the A7 to 5th position for the Dmi7.

D Minor Progression

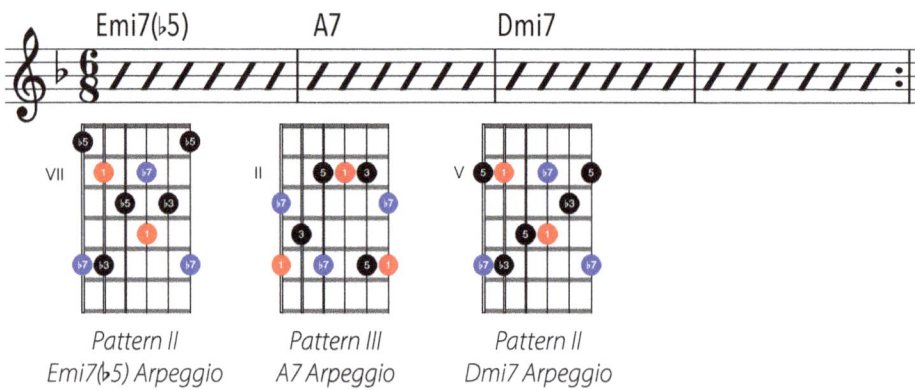

Practice using only arpeggios to start. Take another segment of your practice and create short motifs that blend chord tones and scale tones.

Next practice this in a different location on the fretboard. Over the Em7(♭5), use the Pattern IV minor 7(♭5) arpeggio, which places you in 12th position. Next, over the A7, play the Pattern I dominant 7 arpeggio, which places you in 9th position. It's a short move between Emi7(♭5) and A7. Next, over the Dmi7, play the Pattern IV minor 7 arpeggio, which places you in 10th position. It's a short move from the A7 in 9th position to 10th position for the Dmi7.

D Minor Progression

| Emi7(♭5) | A7 | Dmi7 |

Pattern IV
Emi7(♭5) Arpeggio

Pattern I
A7 Arpeggio

Pattern IV
Dmi7 Arpeggio

Compare the amount of movement from arpeggio to arpeggio in both of the locations where you just played this example. Moving a shorter distance is has advantages. Keep working on your chord tones!

Level 3 Unit 8 • Improv Demo 1

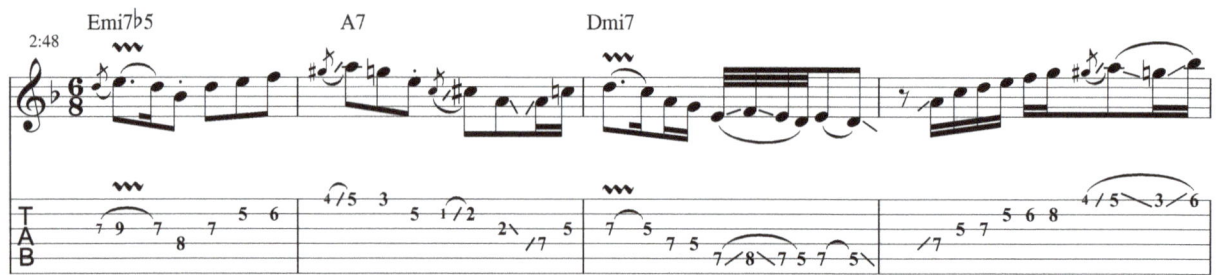

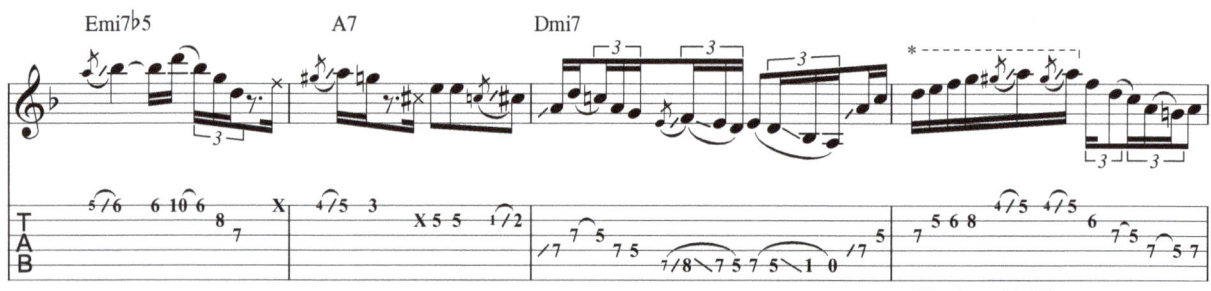

*Played as straight 16th notes.

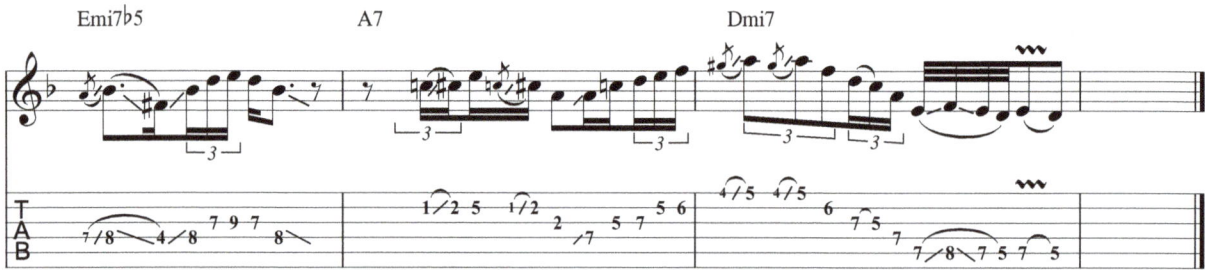

Level 3 Unit 8 • Improv Demo 2

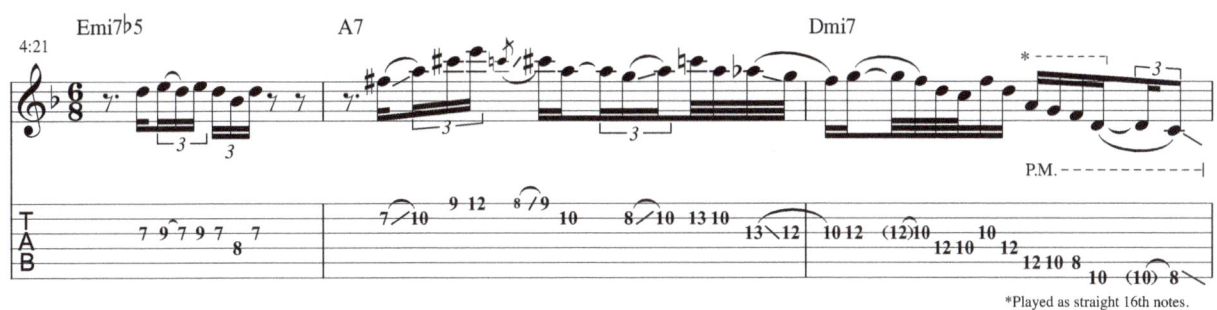

PRACTICE

Theory

- ❑ Learn how Blues harmony differs from major and minor harmony.
- ❑ Go to the tabs below the Theory video on the website and complete the quiz.

Fretboard Logic

- ❑ Learn the Patterns I, III, and V minor 7(♭5) arpeggios.
- ❑ Practice playing the movable 7th chord shapes in the practice progressions.

Technique

- ❑ Learn and practice the diatonic 6ths sequence exercise.

Rhythm Guitar

- ❑ Practice the basic embellishments shown in the Module.

Money Makers

- ❑ Learn common Pattern I minor pentatonic licks.

Improvisation

- ❑ Focus on chord-tone soloing using Patterns II and IV minor 7(♭5) arpeggios, Patterns I and III dominant 7 arpeggios, and Patterns II and IV minor 7 arpeggios.

UNIT 9

Learning Modules

> **Theory** - Constructing the Blues scale

> **Fretboard Logic** - Pattern I major in-position arpeggios, Patterns I, III, and V dominant 7th chords

> **Technique** - Diatonic 7th sequence exercise

> **Rhythm Guitar** - Imitating steel guitar

> **Money Makers** - Pattern II minor pentatonic licks

> **Improvisation** - Using Pattern I in-position arpeggios in F major

> **Practice** - Continue practice routine development

THEORY

Melodies that are diatonic use notes of the key. But as you learned in the last module, in popular music, including the Blues, exceptions to diatonic systems are the norm with respect to both harmony and melody. We focus on Blues melody in this module.

One of the striking aspects of Blues is found in the melody. Blues melodies contain unique inflections called Blue notes that fall between the written scale steps. The Blues scale is the minor pentatonic scale plus an extra note, the ♭5 (technically, this is a diminished 5th or augmented 4th). The ♭5 is wedged between the perfect 4th and perfect 5th in the scale.

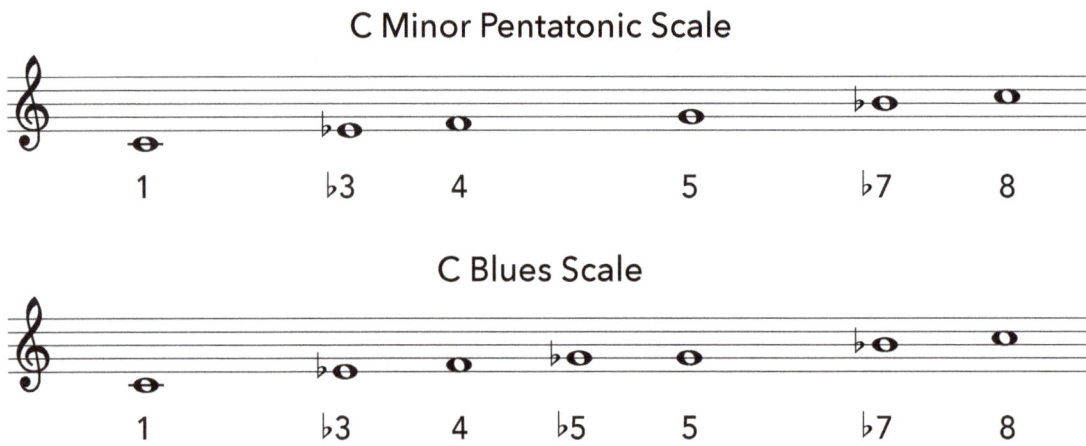

The Blues scale is only a starting point for creating Blues melodies. It is a simplified representation of Blues melody. One unique aspect of the Blues scale's sound lies in the interpretation of the Blue notes. The Blue notes are the minor 3rd, ♭5, and minor 7th. In Blues phrasing, Blue notes can be sung or bent slightly sharp to create notes that are in between diatonic scale steps.

These inflections create a dissonance not found in diatonic melodies, a feeling of tension that has become known simply as "Bluesy". Even with instruments that can't alter and stretch the Blue notes, as on a piano, the dissonance between the minor 3rd and ♭5 in the melody and the major third and perfect 5th in the dominant chord accompaniment create a similar tension.

Look closely at how the Blues scale aligns with the three chords in standard 12-bar Blues. Use the key of C and the C Blues scale.

- The I chord is C7 spelled C – E – G – B♭
- The IV chord is F7 spelled F – A – C – E♭
- The V chord is G7 spelled G – B – D – F

Next, let's compare the notes of each chord with the Blues scale.

I Chord

First, the I7 chord, C7: The C is in the Blues scale but the major 3rd, E, is not. In fact, the Blues scale has an E♭. The 5th, of the C7, G, is in the Blues scale as is the 7th, B♭.

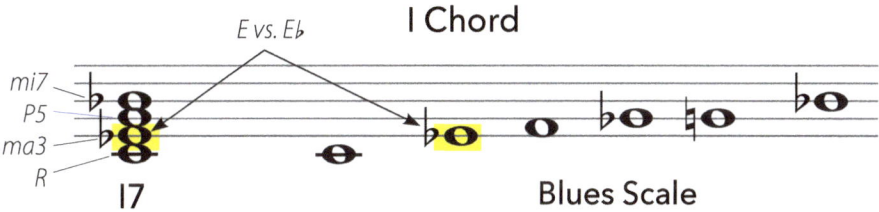

IV Chord

Next, the IV7 chord, F7: The F is in the Blues scale but the major 3rd, A, is not. The 5th of the F7, C, is in the Blues scale as is the ♭7th, E♭.

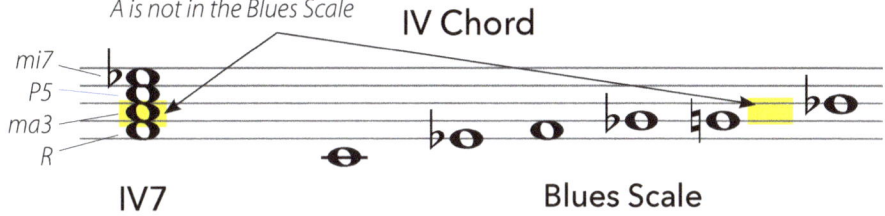

V Chord

Next, the V7 chord, G7: The B♭ is in the Blues scale but the major 3rd, B, is not. The D of the G7 is also not in the Blues scale. The ♭7th of the G7, F, is in the C Blues scale.

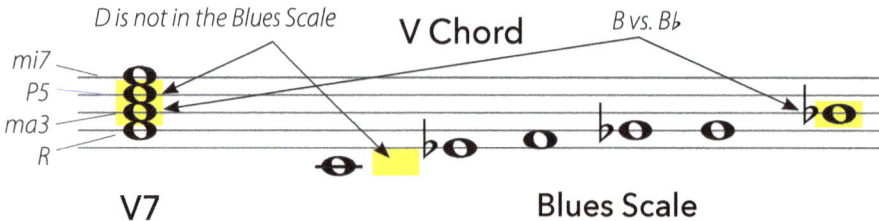

What should be noted is that none of the major 3rds of any of the three chords (I7, IV7, V7) is in the Blues scale. The dissonance created by the major 3rds of the chords conflicting the Blues scale is normal and accepted, and important to the sound of the Blues. It's completely acceptable to use the Blues scale over all three chords in the Blues – even with the discrepancies and contradictions. But it is rare for the Blues scale to be the only source of notes for Blues melodies and solos.

Often the Blues scale is stretched and expanded to accommodate the chord tones of each of the three dominant 7 chords: I, IV, and V.

In other words, when soloing in C Blues:

- For the I chord, C7, the Blues scale can be stretched to include E natural instead of E♭, or perhaps a note somewhere in between E♭ and E. That would be called a Blue note.
- For the IV chord, F7, the Blues scale can be expanded to include A, the major third of the F7.
- For the V chord, G7, the Blues scale can be stretched to include B instead of the B♭ that is in the scale, or perhaps a note somewhere in between B♭ and B. That would be called a Blue note. And the Blues scale can be expanded to include D, the 5th of the G7.

With this foundational information, the best way to approach Blues melody is to listen, transcribe, and use what you have learned here to understand the notes you hear.

FRETBOARD LOGIC

Arpeggios

This module teaches the most important information about how to uses arpeggios. You have learned five arpeggio shapes – major 7, dominant 7, minor 7, and minor 7(♭5) – and as of now you know them as individual entities assigned to the Family Tree structure.

In the Level 3 Improvisation modules you've learned about chord-tone soloing and how arpeggios are used to play chord tones. Certainly you recognize how much more brain power it requires to use chord tones rather than just wandering around the scale as in key-center soloing. The challenge with using chord tones is the result of having to play a specific arpeggio for each chord. The task is made even more challenging if you try to connect the arpeggios to one another smoothly.

If you know arpeggios only as individual entities sprinkled around the fretboard, it is difficult to use them for chord tones because they aren't organized in a logical way. It would be advantageous to have access to all the arpeggios of a key in one place on the fretboard. That can be done through a logical system of organization. The solution is remarkably simple. You simply need to organize the arpeggios by thinking of the harmonized scale within single octave shape.

In this Module, we will examine this idea within the pattern I octave shape. First look at the major scale and review the numbers of the scale degrees: 1, 2, 3, 4, 5, 6, 7, and the octave.

C Major Scale

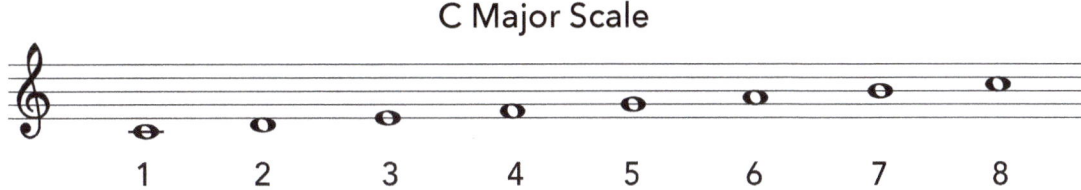

Next, review the quality of the chord built on each scale degree.

The Harmonized C Major Scale with 7th Chords

The goal is to be able to find and play all of the arpeggios of the harmonized major scale within the pattern I octave shape. And of course, this octave shape is movable to any key.

Pattern I Major Scale

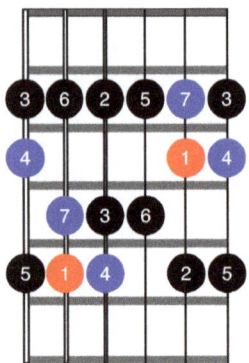

Before organizing arpeggios, review one more important fact which makes the system work: When you harmonize a major scale, the source of notes for each of these chords or arpeggios built on each scale degree is the scale itself.

- I – major 7
- II – minor 7
- III – minor 7
- IV – major 7
- V – dominant 7
- VI – minor 7
- VII – minor 7(♭5)

Consider this: If you can play all the notes of a scale within one octave shape, you should be able to play all of the seven arpeggios of the harmonized scale within the octave shape. Here is how it works.

Ima7 Arpeggio (In-Position)

In Pattern I of the major scale the tonic is played on the 5th string with the 4th finger. The quality of the chord built on the 1st scale degree is major 7. The major 7 arpeggio played with your 4th finger on the 5th string is a pattern I shape.

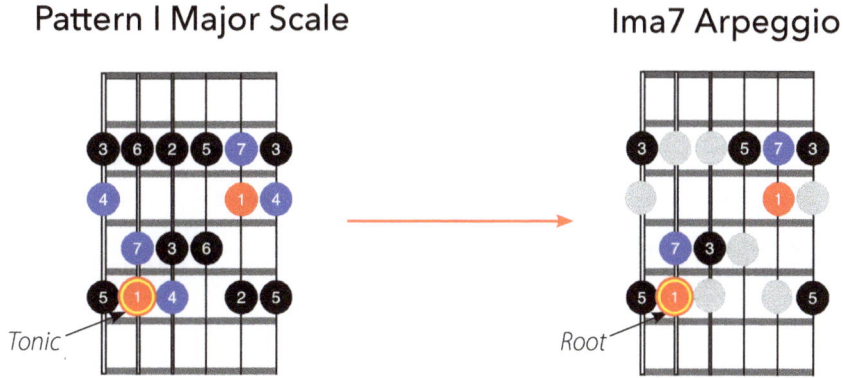

IImi7 Arpeggio (In-Position)

In Pattern I of the major scale the 2nd scale degree is played on the 4th string with the 1st finger. The quality of the chord built on the 2nd scale degree is minor 7. The minor 7 arpeggio played with your 1st finger on the 4th string is a Pattern V shape, but that's not what is important. What is important is that it lays right in the Pattern I major scale.

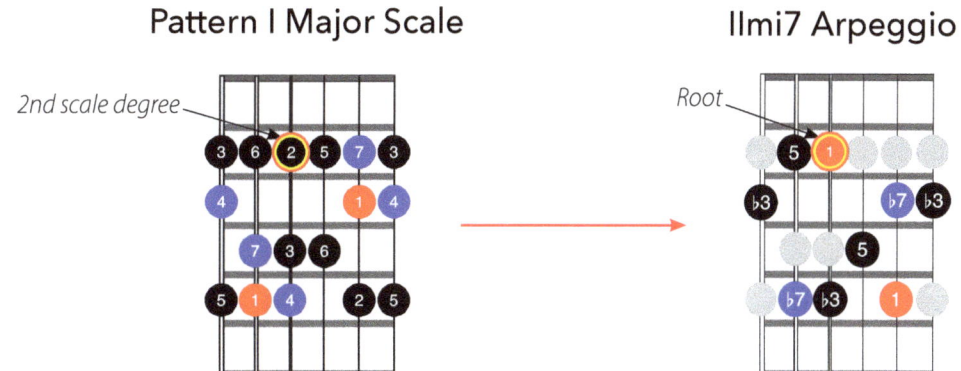

IIImi7 Arpeggio (In-Position)

In Pattern I of the major scale the 3rd scale degree is played on the 4th string with the 3rd finger but it can be played an octave lower on the 6th string within the pattern and with your 1st finger. The quality of the chord built on the third scale degree is minor 7. The minor 7 arpeggio played with your 1st finger on the 6th string is a Pattern IV shape, but the pattern is not what is important. What is important is that it lays right in the Pattern I major scale.

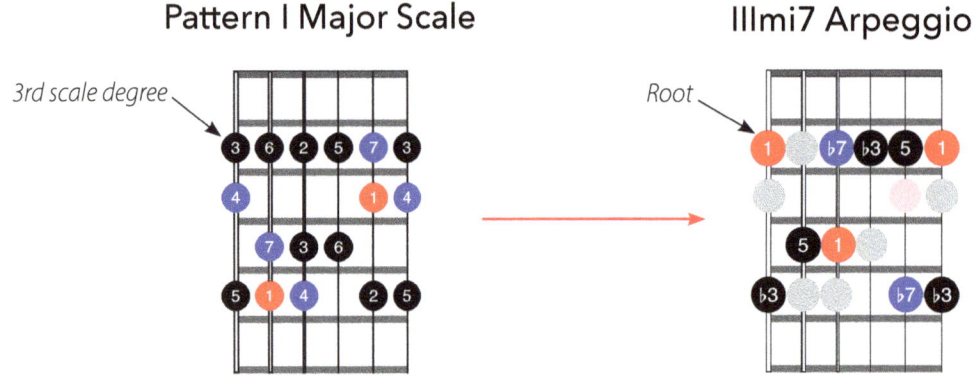

IVma7 Arpeggio (In-Position)

Find the 4th scale degree. It is played the 6th string with the 2nd finger. The quality of the chord built on the 4th scale degree is major 7. The major 7 arpeggio played with your 2nd finger on the 6th string is a Pattern IV shape, but again, that is not what is important. What is important is that it lays right in the Pattern I major scale.

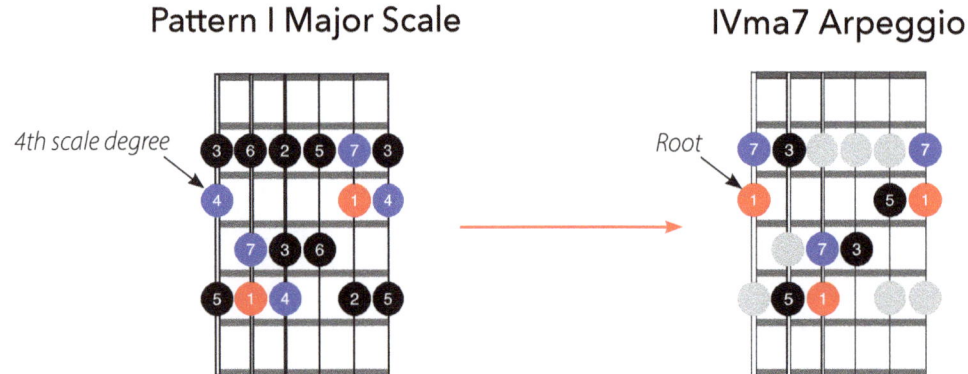

V7 Arpeggio (In-Position)

Find the 5th scale degree. It is played the 6th string with the 4th finger. The quality of the chord built on the 5th scale degree is dominant 7. The dominant 7 arpeggio played with your 4th finger on the 6th string is a Pattern III dominant 7 arpeggio and it fits in the Pattern I major scale.

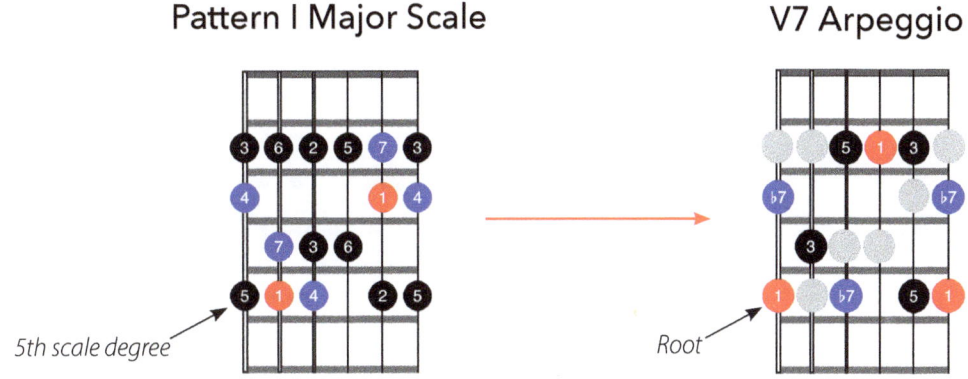

VImi7 Arpeggio (In-Position)

Find the 6th scale degree. It is played on the 5th string with the 1st finger. The quality of the chord built on the 6th scale degree is minor 7. The minor 7 arpeggio played with your 1st finger on the 5th string is Pattern II shape and it fits in the Pattern I major scale.

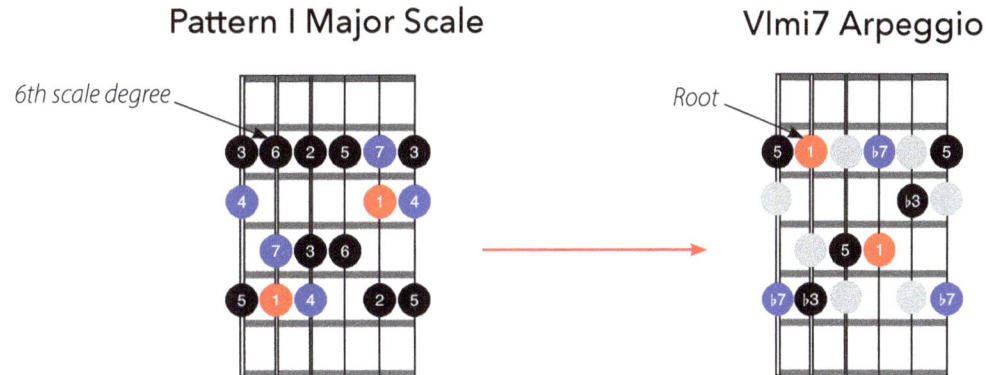

VIImi7(♭5) Arpeggio (In-Position)

And, finally, find the 7th scale degree. It is played the 5th string with the 3rd finger. The quality of a chord built on the 7th scale degree is minor 7(♭5). The minor 7(♭5) arpeggio played with your 3rd finger on the 5th string is a pattern I shape and it fits in the pattern I major scale.

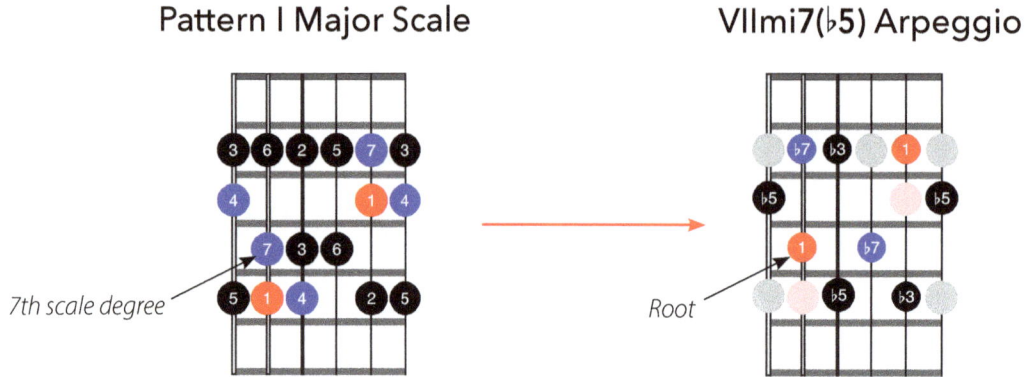

Examine how all 7 arpeggios of the harmonized scale fit nicely inside the major scale. This is because the source of notes for harmonizing the major scale is the major scale itself.

Pattern I In-Position Arpeggios

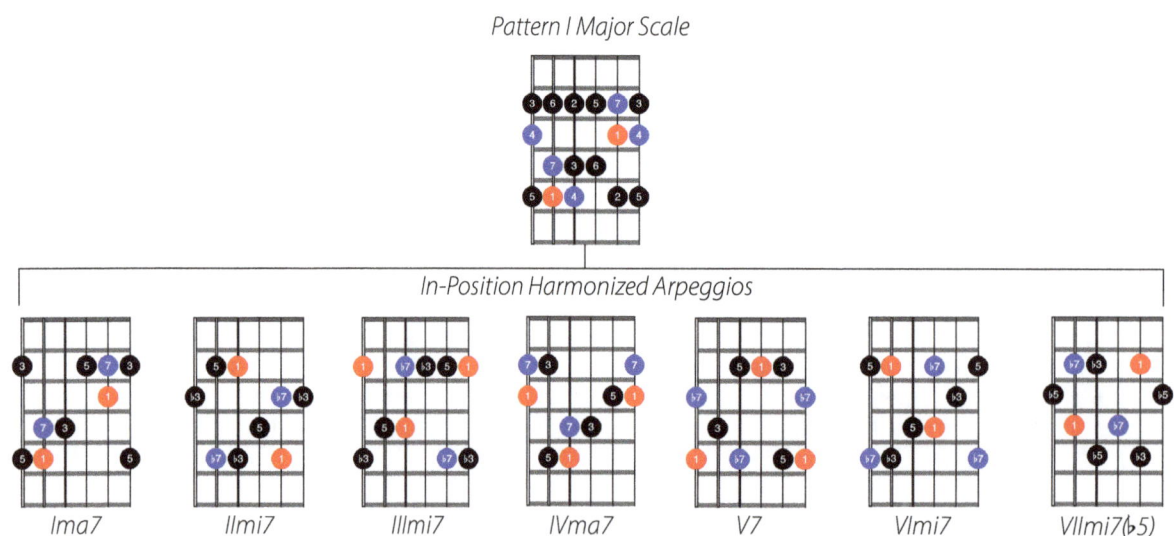

Fretboard Biology   Level 3 • Unit 9: Fretboard Logic   235

This new organization system shows the harmonized scale with "in position arpeggios". Your goal is to know all of the arpeggios of the harmonized major scale within the Pattern I octave shape. This saves you from the physical challenge of jumping around the fretboard. This process can be replicated in Patterns II through V as well. In the Improvisation Module for this Unit you will put this organization system to work.

My suggestion is from now on to practice your arpeggios "in position" rather than as independent shapes, because that is how you will use them. Think about it this way: If you have learned the five arpeggios presented in this Level (major 7, dominant 7, minor 7, and minor 7(♭5)), you will use all 20 of those by practicing the harmonized scale in each octave shape "in position". All in-position arpeggios for each octave shape can be found in the Appendix.

Chords

You have now learned the most common movable 7th chords. They are derived from the Patterns II and IV barre chords. Now complete your knowledge of 7th chord voicings and learn the other practical 7th chord shapes for the other patterns: Patterns I, III and V.

Here are the Pattern I major 7 and dominant 7 chords. Place these in the Pattern I Family Tree under the major triad chord.

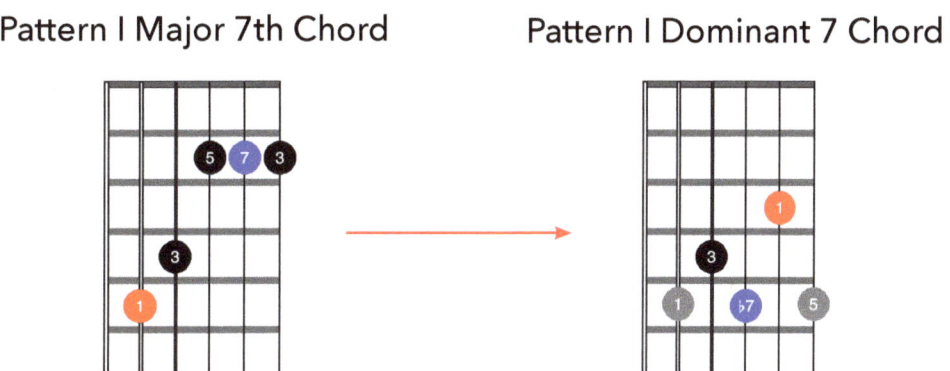

Here is the Pattern III major 7 for Pattern III and dominant 7 chords. Place these in the Pattern III Family Tree under the major triad chord.

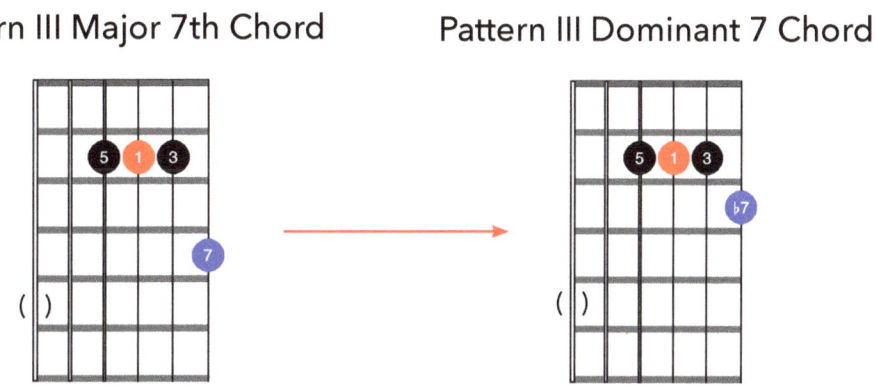

Next, let's have a look at major 7 and dominant 7 for Pattern V. Place these in the Pattern V Family Tree under the major triad chord.

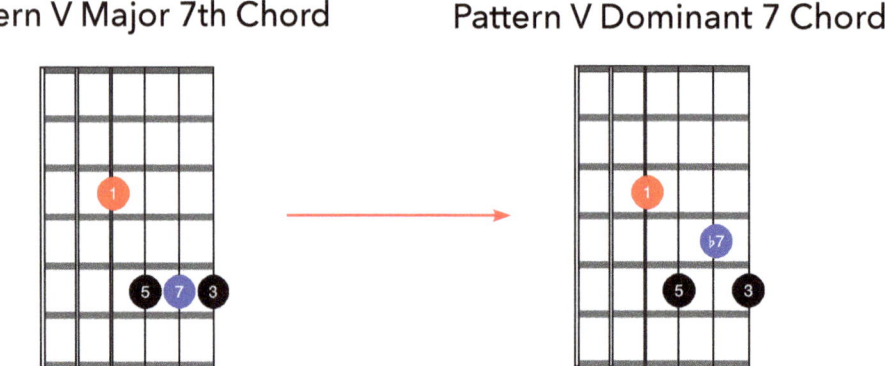

The next module is a really important milestone, too. You will learn the "in position" arpeggio system for minor chords and for the Blues as well.

TECHNIQUE

In this module you will learn the "diatonic 7ths" interval sequence. Again, use the Pattern IV major scale in the key of A and 8th-notes.

Diatonic 7ths Sequence

Work your way up the scale playing notes in pairs. Play the 1st scale degree and then a diatonic note a 7th above it. Then play the 2nd scale degree and then a diatonic note a 7th above it. Then play the 3rd scale degree and then a diatonic note a 7th above it, and so on through the scale.

Ascending this sequence will look like this:

Diatonic 7ths Sequence Exercise - Ascending

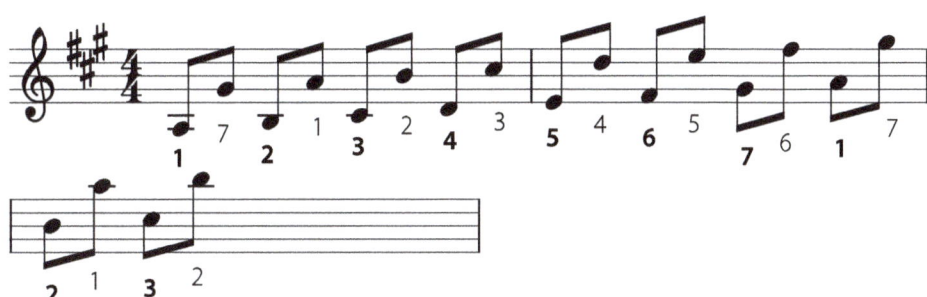

Continue ascending with this pattern until you reach the highest note available in the pattern. Then descend in reverse order like this:

Diatonic 7ths Sequence Exercise - Descending

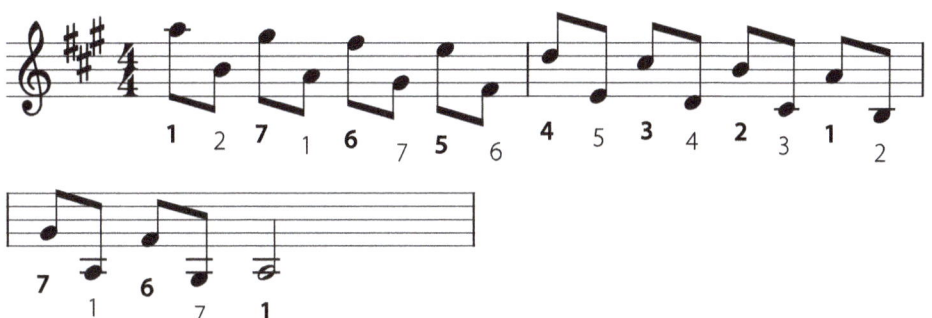

Continue descending with this pattern until you reach the lowest note available in the pattern. Focus on your alternate picking. When you feel like you're ready, set your metronome at slow tempo and play through it again. We'll see you in the next module.

RHYTHM GUITAR

Imitating Steel Guitar

In this module you will learn a few ways to imitate a pedal steel guitar without using a slide. The pedal steel guitar's role in a Country band ranges from playing solos, to playing fills and counterpoint lines around the lead vocal, to providing a broad harmonic pad under the arrangement.

Pad

A pad is a sustained chordal sound that fills out the harmony of the song behind the other instruments and lead vocal or lead instruments.

Pedal steel is a defining sound and texture in Country music. One way to imitate this sound with a six-string electric guitar is to combine the use of a volume pedal with bends and release bends, hammer-ons, and pull-offs, and with chords, too, all with a healthy amount of delay and reverb, which provides an extra tail of sustain behind the notes.

These techniques won't replace the sound of a real pedal steel player but if you don't have the luxury of having one in your band, it's nice to be able to have a similar texture. You need to know two things to imitate a steel guitar:

1. What notes to play
2. How to articulate the notes you choose to play using a volume pedal, reverb, and delay using all of the standard articulation devices.

It is no accident that this topic is presented after you learned a lot of money maker vocabulary earlier in this Level. The money makers you learned around the pattern III octave shape work well for imitating pedal steel. Now, create parts over this progression from Unit 6 Rhythm Guitar using the money maker ideas you learned along with a volume pedal to fade into individual notes, double stops, and chords.

A Major Progression

A		D	
E		A	

The parts don't have to be complicated at all. The steel part's role is to provide texture. The most important thing is to listen for what the song needs. A good motto to have is: *"stay out of the way of the lead vocalist or lead instrument"*.

To put that into some kind of formula, you might think about it this way: When the lead vocal or lead instrument is singing or playing, you should lay out or play simple and/or sustained rhythms so you don't compete for the center of attention. But in the spaces between phrases where the lead vocal or lead instrument does not play, you can fill in with motifs that compliment what they just sang or played. Again, this doesn't have to be complicated or flashy. It is really a matter of using taste and good judgment. You learn taste and good judgment by listening to well-produced songs.

Write simple songs and record yourself playing the basic rhythm guitar part. Listen back with the ear of a producer who is always asking, "What does this song need right here?" Then experiment creating other parts and record them over the basic rhythm track. This will be the focus of the next Unit.

MONEY MAKERS

Licks in Pattern II Minor Pentatonic

In this module you will work in the Pattern II minor pentatonic shell. You will learn the same way in this pattern as you did the Patterns IV, V, and I.

Pattern II Minor Pentatonic Scale

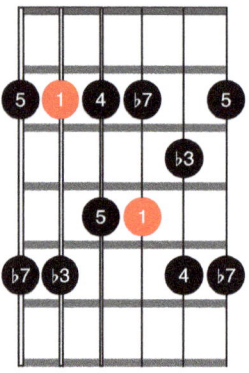

First let's learn some of these mini-licks now.

Pattern II Blues Lick 1

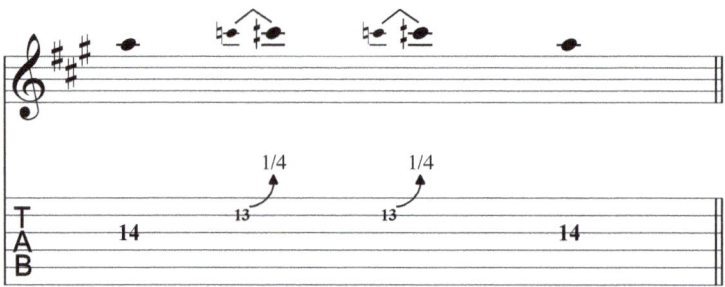

Pattern II Blues Lick 2

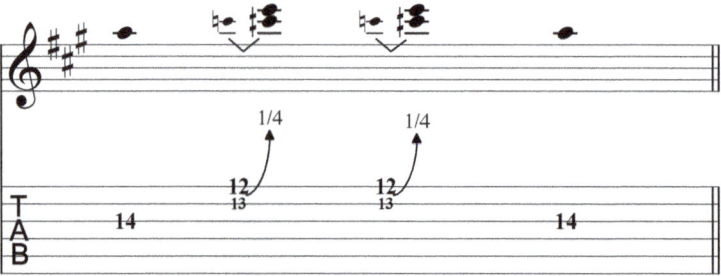

Pattern II Blues Lick 3

Pattern II Blues Lick 4

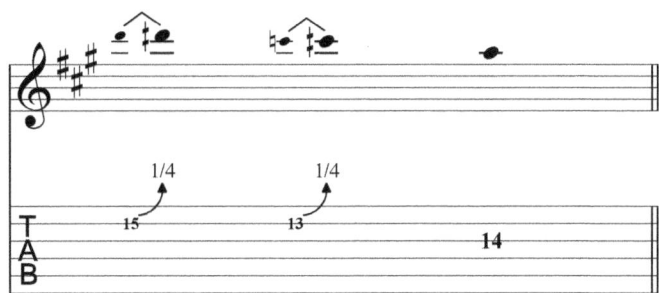

On the next page, you will see a demo solo that uses these licks so you can see how they work in the context of a solo.

Level 3 Unit 9 • Money Maker Demo

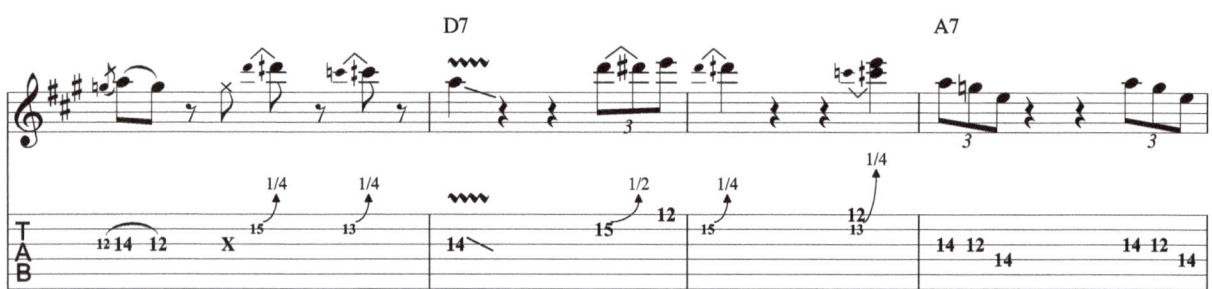

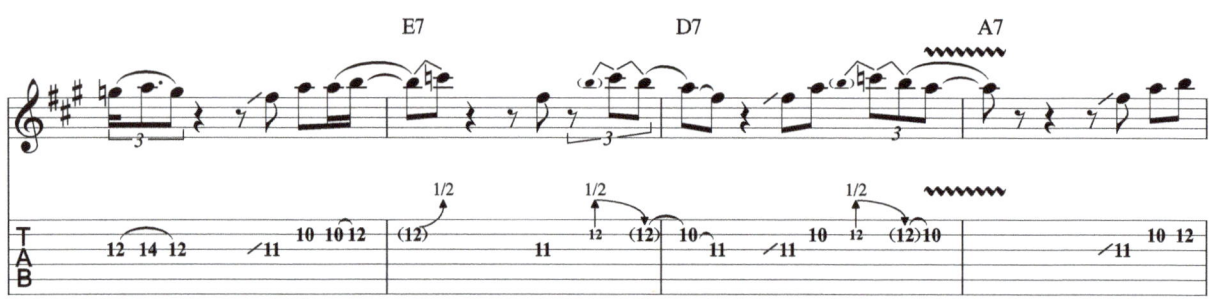

©2020 Fretboard Biology • fretboardbiology.com

Fretboard Biology
Level 3 • Unit 9: Money Makers

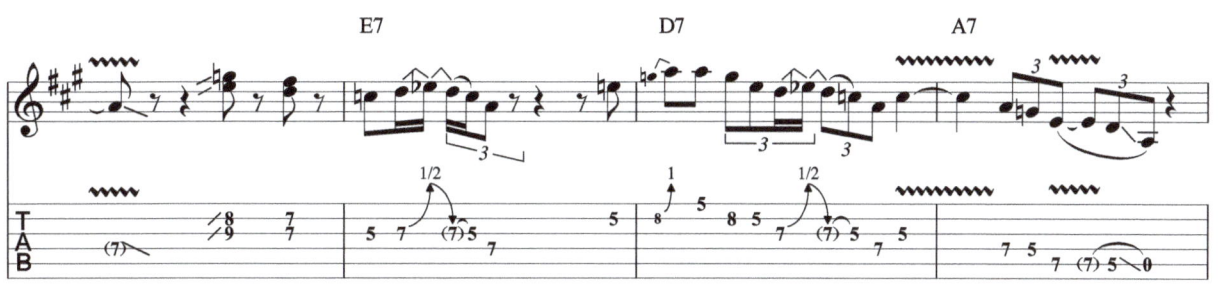

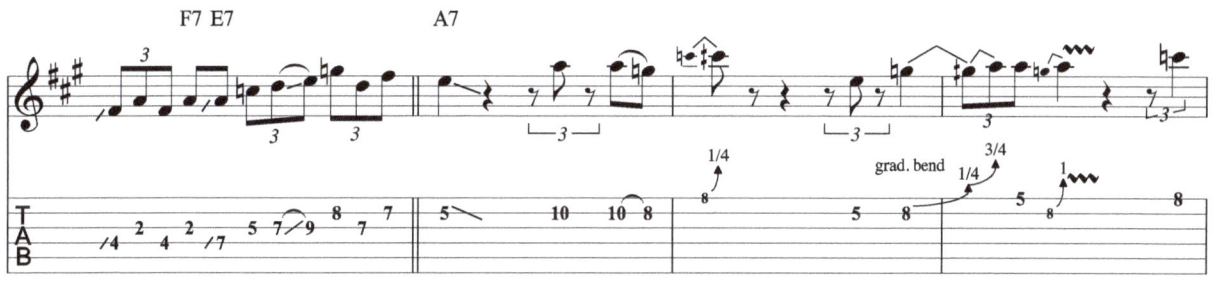

*Played as straight 8th notes.

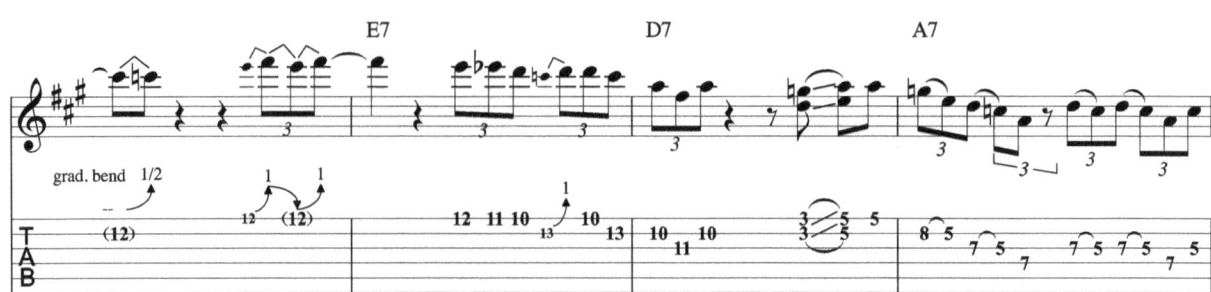
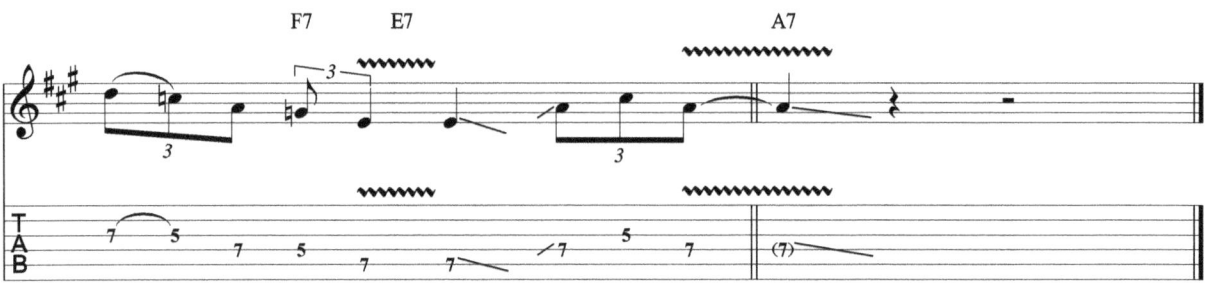

IMPROVISATION

In Units 1 through 8 you worked on chord-tone soloing. In each example, I suggested the specific arpeggios you should use based on the ones you had just learned. Those are the Patterns I and III major 7 and dominant 7, and Patterns II and IV minor 7 and minor 7(♭5). Throughout these Units, you likely encountered some logistical challenges when trying to move smoothly from arpeggio to arpeggio in a few of the examples. Let's fix that now.

In the Unit 9 Fretboard Logic module you learned the "in-position" arpeggio organization system. This system solves the problem of having to move out of position to find the next arpeggio in a diatonic progression. Try using the in-position system with a progression.

Here's a progression in F major:

F Major Progression

If you were to play a key-center solo, you could just use the Pattern I F major scale and I suggest you first do that to get acquainted with the changes.

Analyze this progression using the knowledge you learned in the Theory Module to determine the number of each chord. This progression is in the key of F major so you know that the Gmi7 is the IImi7 chord, the C7 is the V7 chord, and the Fma7 is the Ima7 chord

F Major Progression

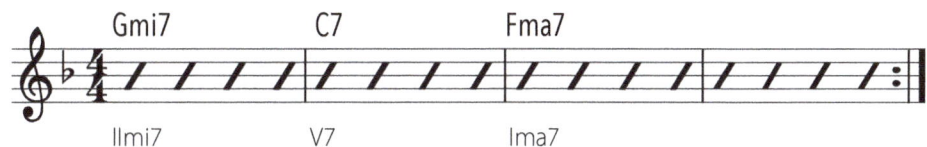

Using In-Position Arpeggios

Next use the chord-tone approach with this progression, but this time using the "in position" system. To start, look at the pattern I major scale harmonized in 7th chord arpeggios. With the in-position system, all of the arpeggios in a key can be played within a single scale pattern.

Pattern I In-Position Arpeggios

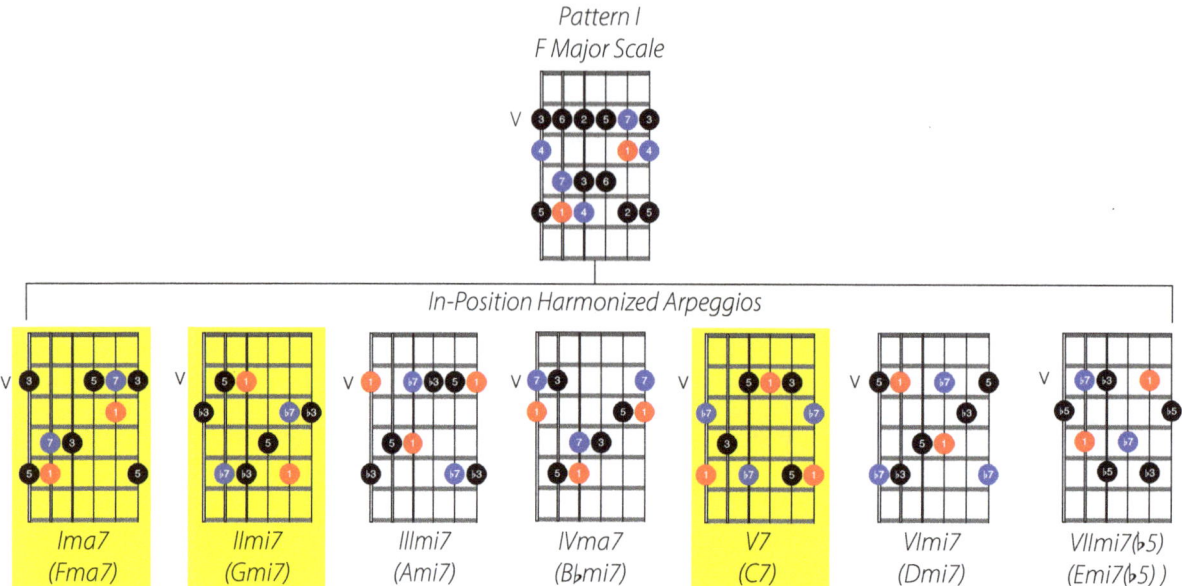

Now take a closer look at this II - V - I progression. Stay in Pattern I F major, which is in 5th position.

- Gmi7 is the IImi7, and in Pattern I, the IImi7 arpeggio's root is on the 4th string.
- C7 is the V7, and in Pattern I, the V7 arpeggio's root is on the 6th string.
- Fma7 is the Ima7, and in Pattern I, the Ima7 arpeggio's root is on the 5th string.

F Major Progression

Notice how convenient it is to be able to play all the arpeggios within one octave shape. You are able to use arpeggios to play chord tones throughout the progression without ever having to move out of position.

Fretboard Biology — Level 3 • Unit 9: Improvisation

I can't stress enough what an important step it is to locate arpeggios within the same pattern. Learning to play chord tones in solos using the in-position system will take some time. This needs to be part of your improvisation practice routine from now on. Keep at it and you will get better and smarter every week.

The "in-position" system for organizing arpeggios can be applied to each of the five major scale patterns, but I strongly suggest that to start you should only use patterns I and III for a while; perhaps a year or more. Be good to yourself and don't think you have to get all of this right now. That is impossible.

Level 3 Unit 9 • Improv Demo

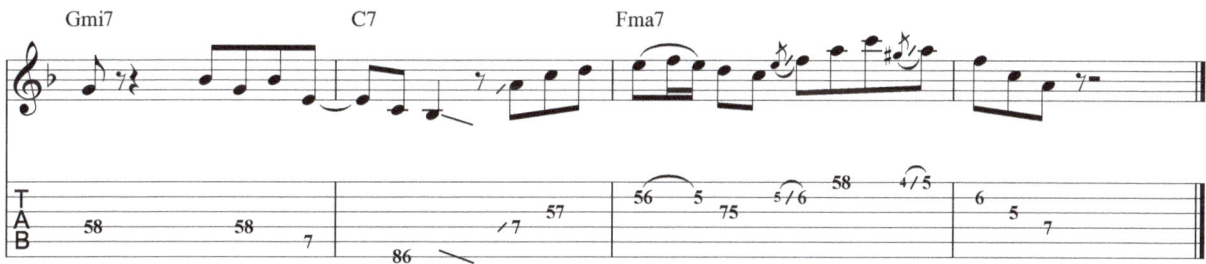

©2020 Fretboard Biology • fretboardbiology.com

PRACTICE

Theory

- ❑ Go to the tabs below the Theory video on the website and complete the quiz.
- ❑ Learn about Blues melody and how the scale and chords relate to each other.

Fretboard Logic

- ❑ Learn the Pattern I major in-position arpeggios.
- ❑ Learn the Patterns I, III, and V dominant 7th chords.

Technique

- ❑ Learn and practice the diatonic 7ths sequence exercise.

Rhythm Guitar

- ❑ Learn and practice how to imitate steel guitar.

Money Makers

- ❑ Learn common Pattern II minor pentatonic licks.

Improvisation

- ❑ Practice soloing over the progression in F major using pattern I major in-position arpeggios.

UNIT 10

Learning Modules

> **Theory** - Level 3 summary

> **Fretboard Logic** - Pattern II minor in-position arpeggios, Patterns I, III, and V minor 7(♭5) chords

> **Technique** - Technique summary

> **Rhythm Guitar** - Country rhythm guitar

> **Money Makers** - Pattern III minor pentatonic licks

> **Improvisation** - Using Pattern II in-position arpeggios in E minor

> **Practice** - Continue practice routine development

THEORY

You are now at the end of Level 3 in your study of Theory. It is important to emphasize that being a complete musician has three components: talent, hard work, and literacy.

You now have the ability to analyze major and minor diatonic chord progressions. You can identify the key and function of each chord. You also know about the unique harmony of the Blues. As familiar as it is, it was your first venture outside the world of diatonic harmony.

In the next Level and beyond you will learn about the common exceptions to diatonic harmony. In fact, it is more the exception to see songs where all the chords and melody notes are diatonic. Exceptions to diatonic harmony is the norm.

The more you learn more about music theory, the better equipped you will be to make good musical decisions. Having a lot of musical knowledge doesn't automatically translate into making good music. That comes from talent, experience, and a musical awareness that is gained from a lot of listening and practice. Listening to great music helps you develop the skill to make good musical choices because you learn what works. Pay close attention and emulate what you hear. Record your performances and identify where you made good as well as bad musical decisions. This is how you get better.

In Level 4 Theory, you will learn about modal interchange, which is the mix of parallel keys. You will also study inversions and slash chords.

Keep going. Work hard. There's so much more to learn! We'll see you in the next Level!

FRETBOARD LOGIC

Arpeggios

In the last module you learned about organizing arpeggios "in position". This is an important step and an essential concept for integrating chord tones into solos. Remember, it is difficult to use chord tones in solos if you know arpeggios as individual entities sprinkled around the fretboard. It is best if you can find all the arpeggios of a key in the exact same position. You worked with the harmonized major scale in the last module. In this module, you will learn the same concept in the minor scale and organize the seven arpeggios of the harmonized minor scale within a single octave shape.

Use the Pattern II minor scale to explore this. First, look at the minor scale and review the numbers of the scale degrees: 1, 2, ♭3, 4, 5, ♭6, ♭7, and the octave.

C Minor Scale

Next, review the quality of the chord built on each scale degree:

The Harmonized C Minor Scale with 7th Chords

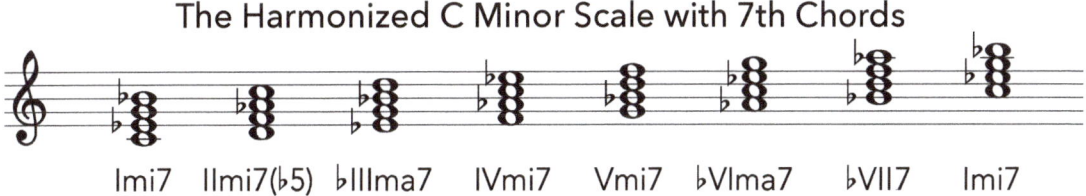

The goal is to be able to play all of the arpeggios of the harmonized minor scale within the Pattern II octave shape. This octave shape is movable to any key.

Pattern II Minor Scale

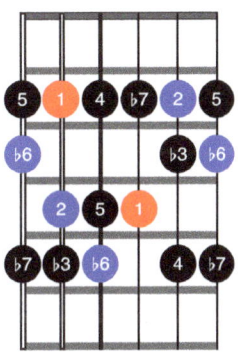

This is the harmonized minor scale:
- I – minor 7
- II – minor 7(♭5)
- ♭III – major 7
- IV – minor 7
- V – minor 7
- ♭VI – major 7
- ♭VII – dominant 7

The source of notes for the arpeggios built on each scale degree is the natural minor scale, with the exception of the V7 chord, which is often played in place of the diatonic Vmi7. If you can play all the notes of a scale within one octave shape, then you can play all of the seven arpeggios that result from harmonizing the scale.

Imi7 Arpeggio (In-Position)

In pattern II of the minor scale, the tonic is played on the 5th string with the 1st finger. The quality of the chord built on the 1st scale degree is minor 7. A minor 7 arpeggio played with your 1st finger on the 5th string is a Pattern II shape.

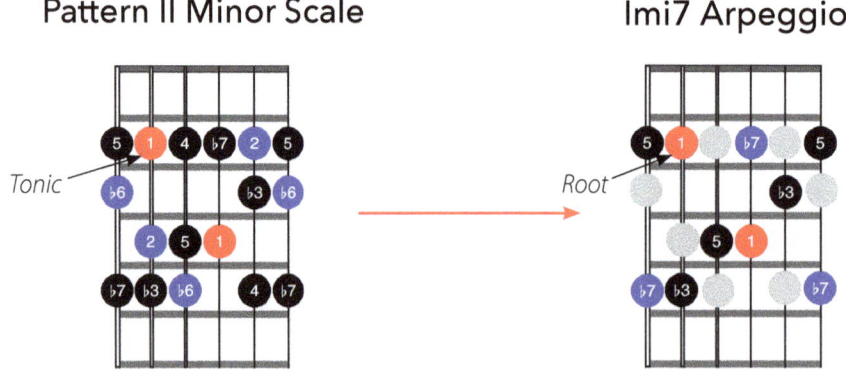

IImi7(♭5) Arpeggio (In-Position)

In Pattern II of the minor scale, the 2nd scale degree is played on the 5th string with the 3rd finger. The quality of the chord built on the 2nd scale degree is minor 7(♭5). The minor 7(♭5) arpeggio played with your 3rd finger on the 5th string is a Pattern I shape, but that is not what is important. What is important is that it lays right in the Pattern II minor scale.

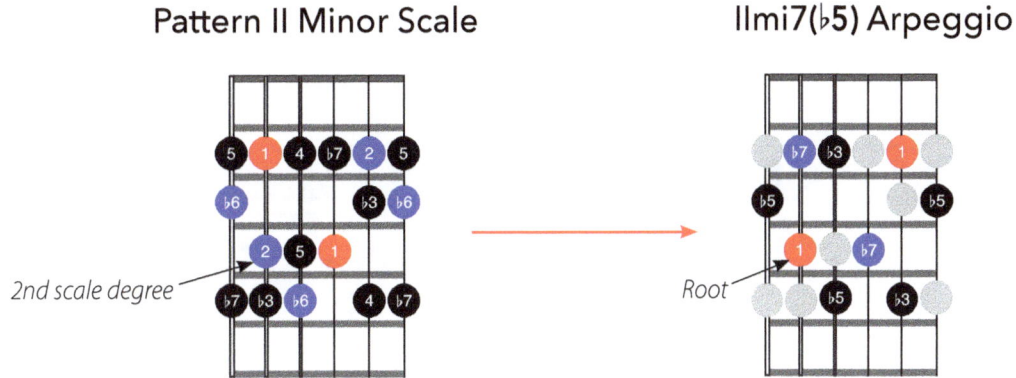

♭IIIma7 Arpeggio (In-Position)

In Pattern II of the minor scale, the flatted 3rd scale degree is played on the 5th string with the 4th finger. The quality of the chord built on the flatted 3rd scale degree is major 7. The I major 7 arpeggio played with your 4th finger on the 5th string is a Pattern I shape, and it lays right in the Pattern II minor scale.

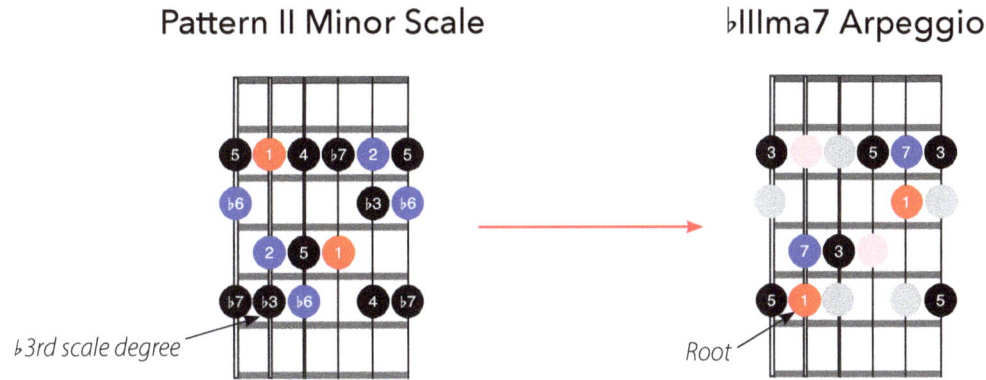

IVmi7 Arpeggio (In-Position)

Find the 4th scale degree. It is played on the 4th string with the 1st finger, right. The quality of the chord built on the 4th scale degree is minor 7. The V minor 7 arpeggio played with your 1st finger on the 4th string is a Pattern V shape, and it lays right in the Pattern II minor scale.

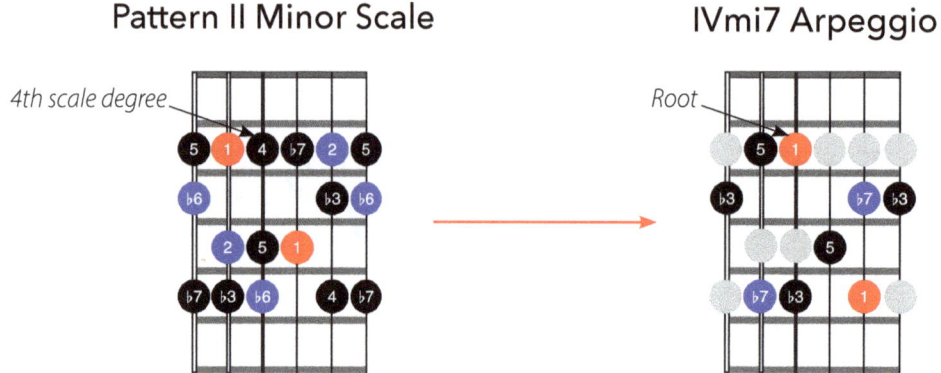

Vmi7 Arpeggio (In-Position)

Find the 5th scale degree. It is played on the 4th string with the 3rd finger. It can be played down an octave within the octave shape on the 6th string. The quality of the chord built on the 5th scale degree is minor 7. The minor 7 arpeggio played with your 1st finger on the 6th string is a Pattern IV shape and it fits in the Pattern II minor scale.

Remember it is common for a dominant 7th chord to be played instead of the diatonic minor 7. Find the dominant 7th arpeggio with a root on the 6th string. That is a Pattern IV dominant 7 arpeggio. Here it is:

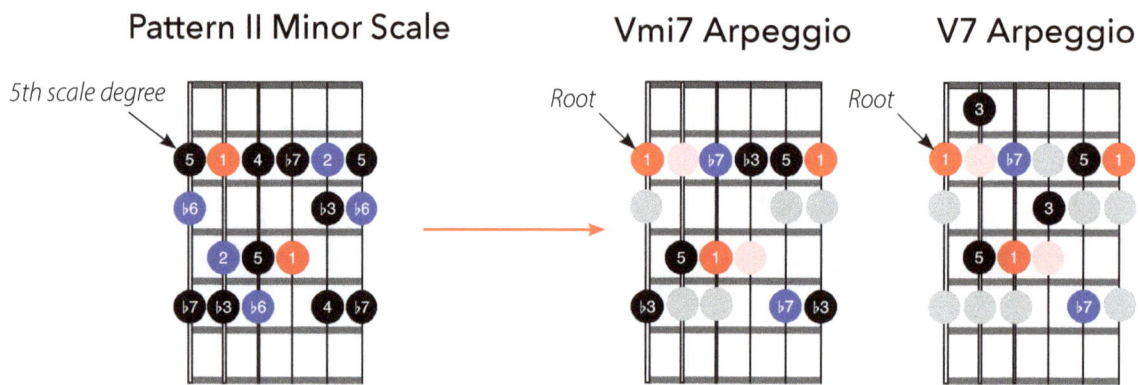

You should know both the diatonic V minor 7 and V dominant 7 chord.

♭VIma7 Arpeggio (In-Position)

Find the flatted 6th scale degree on the 6th string with the 2nd finger. The quality of the chord built on the flatted 6th scale degree is major 7. The major 7 arpeggio played with your 4th finger on the 6th string a Pattern IV shape and it fits in the Pattern II minor scale.

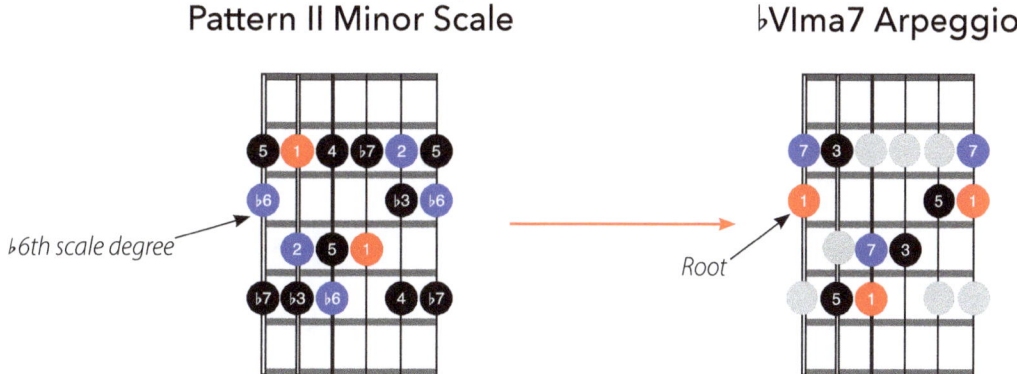

♭VII7 Arpeggio (In-Position)

And, finally, find the flatted 7th scale degree played on the 6th string with the 4th finger. The quality of the chord built on the flatted seventh scale degree is dominant 7. The dominant 7 arpeggio played with your 4th finger on the 6th string is a Pattern III shape and it fits in the Pattern II minor scale.

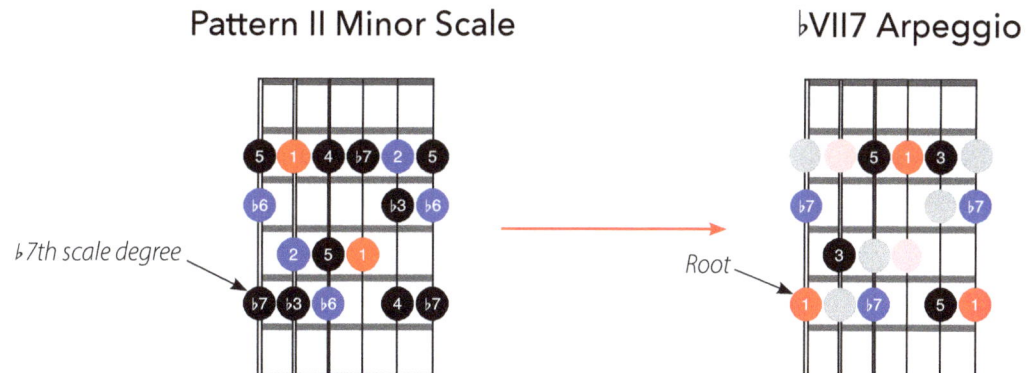

Look at how all seven arpeggios of the harmonized minor scale fit inside the minor scale, with the exception of the V dominant 7 chord. They all fit because of the source of notes for harmonizing the minor scale is the scale itself.

Pattern II Minor In-Position Arpeggios

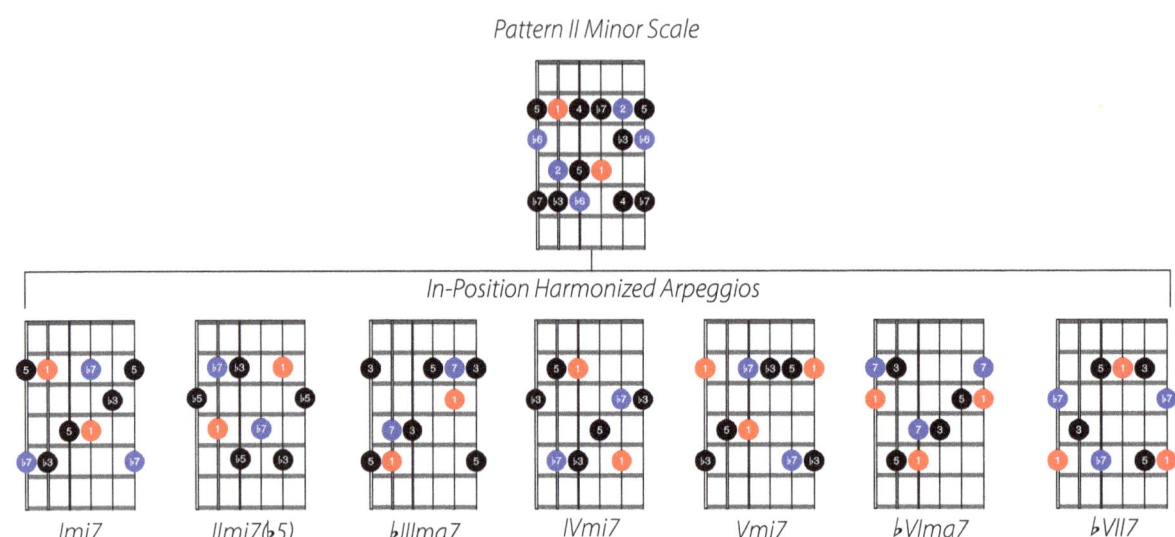

As with major scales, the goal is to be able to play all of the arpeggios of the harmonized minor scale within the Pattern II octave shape. This saves you from the inefficiency and physical challenge of jumping around the fretboard. This process can be replicated in minor patterns I, III, IV, and V as well. In the Improvisation module for this Unit you will put this organization system to work.

I suggest you practice your arpeggios "in position" in minor as well the major patterns. Perhaps on Monday, Wednesday, and Friday you can practice the harmonized major scales in the five octave shapes. Then on Tuesday, Thursday, and Saturday you can practice the harmonized minor scales in the five octave shapes. By practicing these harmonized scales with arpeggios in position, you will cover all of the 20 arpeggios you have learned.

Take a broad view of the "in-position" approach. In most situations when you solo, you are trying make instantaneous decisions and see the target notes in advance. Thinking "in position" helps you see the target notes you want to play in advance, and in the location on the fretboard where already are.

Consider playing the Blues and thinking in position. You recently learned about Blues harmony and Blues melody in the Theory Modules. You learned you can use the key-center approach and force the Blues scale over the I7, IV7, and V7 chords even though the major 3rds of each of those chords are not in the scale. But if you want to expand your approach and use chord tones, you need to see the arpeggios of the I7, IV7, and V7 chords.

Using the C Blues in pattern IV as an example, superimpose the pattern IV dominant arpeggio over the Blues scale based on the tonic. The root, 5th, and ♭7 of the I7 arpeggio are in common with the scale and the major 3rd is not, but you see the I7 arpeggio in position.

Next, look at the IV7 chord. The 4th degree of the scale is played on the 5th string. Superimpose a pattern II dominant 7 arpeggio over the Blues scale from the 4th of the scale. The root, 5th, and ♭7 of the IV7 arpeggio are in common with the scale and the major 3rd is not, but you can see the IV7 arpeggio in position.

Finally, look at the V7 chord. The 5th degree of the scale is played on the 5th string. Superimpose a pattern I dominant 7 arpeggio over the Blues scale from the 5th. The root and ♭7 of the V7 arpeggio are in common with the scale and the major 3rd and 5th are not, but you can see the V7 arpeggio in position.

Organizing arpeggios in-position is very logical. Carry this idea forward with everything you do as you integrate more chord tones into your solos.

Chords

You have learned the most common movable minor 7th and minor 7(♭5) chords which are derived from the patterns II and IV barre chords. To complete your knowledge, learn the practical minor 7th and minor 7(♭5) chord shapes for the patterns still left to learn: Patterns I, III, and V.

Here are the Pattern I minor 7 and minor 7(♭5) chords. Place these in the Pattern I Family Tree under the minor triad chord.

Pattern I Minor 7th Chord   Pattern I Minor 7(♭5) Chord

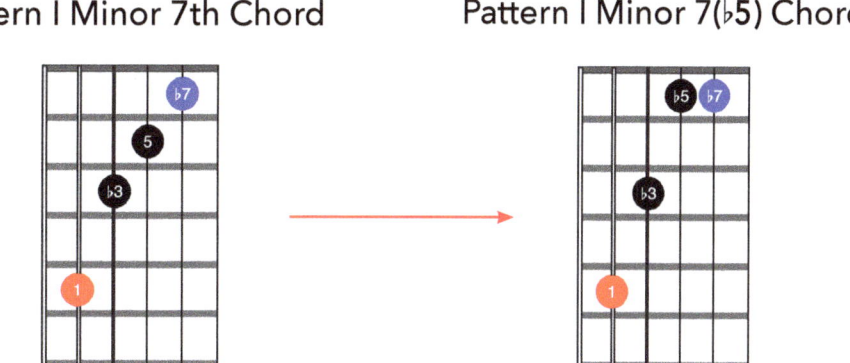

Next, let's look at the Pattern III minor 7 and minor 7(♭5) chords. Place these in the Pattern III Family Tree under the minor triad chord.

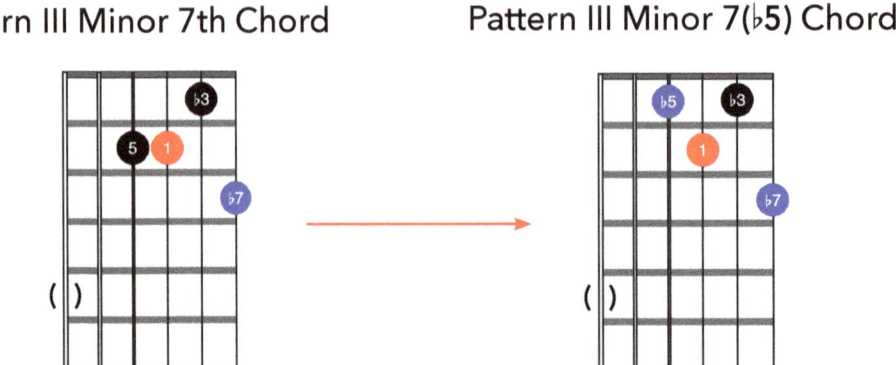

Finally, let's look at the Pattern V minor 7 and minor 7(♭5) chords. Place these in the Pattern V Family Tree under the minor triad chord.

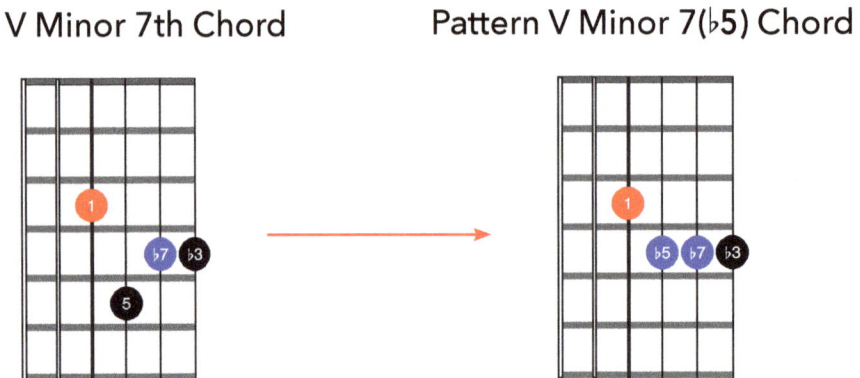

Octave Shape Family Trees

You now have an understanding of the octave shape Family Tree and how all scales, arpeggios, and chords relate to each of the five octave shapes. Be sure to study the octave shape Family Trees in the Appendix so that you can see how all 7th chords and arpeggios are derivatives of their triad counterparts.

There is more to come in the next Levels. There are more scales like the modes and others that can be derived from the pentatonic shells. There are more chords and arpeggios that can be derived from the triad and 7th shapes.

Stay organized in your practice! It's critical.

TECHNIQUE

There is an endless supply of scale and interval sequences – more than any human could learn and practice in a reasonable practice routine.

The point here is not to go through every possible combination of notes to create a million sequence exercises. The point is to introduce you to some of the more common sequence exercises that will help you develop your dexterity.

Don't budget a disproportionate amount of time on the sequences. Work on them, but don't worship them. I have seen too many guitar players who can blaze through scales and exercises, but once they are on the gig, they are lost because they spend all their time exercising and not developing their vocabulary. Remember, these exercises are like going to the gym. You will probably never play a full interval sequence on a gig. They are not music. Practicing them is simply a means of improving your technical abilities on the guitar. They are important, but are only one piece of the overall puzzle.

We are now at the end of the Technique section for Level 3. If you made it this far, and you have been doing the work and not just watching the videos, you should notice a real difference in your playing.

RHYTHM GUITAR

Putting it All Together

In this last module of Country rhythm guitar, imagine you're in a recording session or rehearsal for a live show and the song is a clean slate. There's only a drum part, bass part, and some chords. Your job is to create the guitar parts. There are a couple of approaches to layering parts above the bass and drums. It is standard procedure to record a strumming part first. This establishes a harmonic bed on which other parts can be laid. A fingerpicking part could come next. Those first two steps could be done in reverse order; a fingerpicking part followed by a strumming part. After that, parts like the steel guitar and/or fills can be recorded to frame the lead vocal or other instrument.

Listen to the audio track associated with the video on the website. This track has a straight 8th feel, is in the key of D and three chords: D – A – G

D Major Progression

In place of a vocal track, the melody is played by harmonica. Think of it as the lead voice that the other parts need to support.

Guitar 1 - On top of the bass and drums, first play a boom-chick rhythm guitar part with electric or acoustic guitar.

Guitar 2 - Next add a fingerpicking part on acoustic or electric guitar.

Guitar 3 - With these foundational parts played, create a steel part that compliments the lead harmonica part by filling in around it as well as tastefully overlapping in places.

Creating parts that complement the lead voice is a lot of fun, but can also challenging. It's kind of a dance with the lead voice. You want to play creative phrases that support without interfering or overshadowing. "Good taste" is hard to quantify and define. You just know it when you hear it. Mastering the art of layering parts takes practice, but if you are good at it, singers, musical directors, and producers will love you. Never forget: rhythm guitar is always about the song, not how interesting the guitar part is. If you keep that in mind, you'll have your best chance of getting called back for the gig.

This ends our series of Modules about Country rhythm guitar. Remember your role as a rhythm guitarist. Stay employed! That means play what the leader wants to hear which is usually what the song needs.

MONEY MAKERS

There are two goals in this module. First you will learn some vocabulary inside Pattern III minor pentatonic. Then you will use all the vocabulary you have learned in this Level and work through the 12-bar Blues, road-testing how it can all fit together in a single solo.

First, look at Pattern III minor pentatonic. We'll work in this pattern the same way we did the others. We'll do this as we did in previous Units.

Pattern III Minor Pentatonic Scale

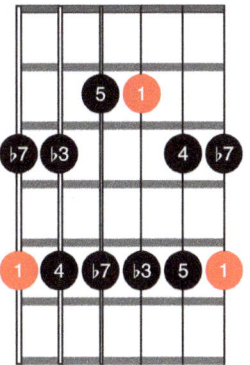

Like in the previous Money Makers modules, let's start by learning these mini-licks.

Pattern III Blues Lick 1

Pattern III Blues Lick 2

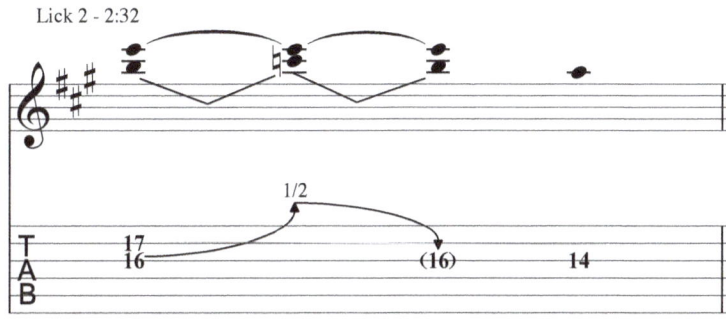

Pattern III Blues Lick 3

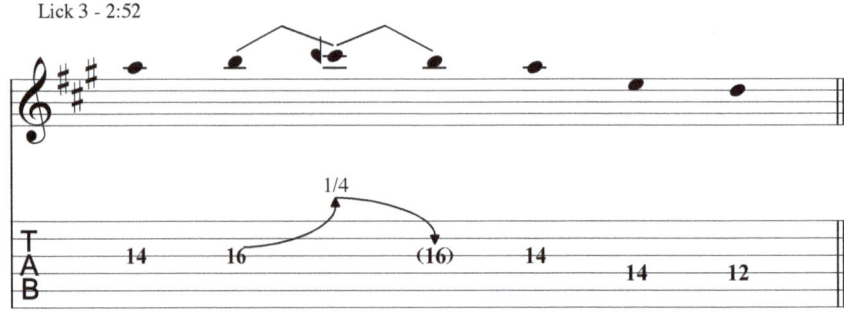

Pattern III Blues Lick 3

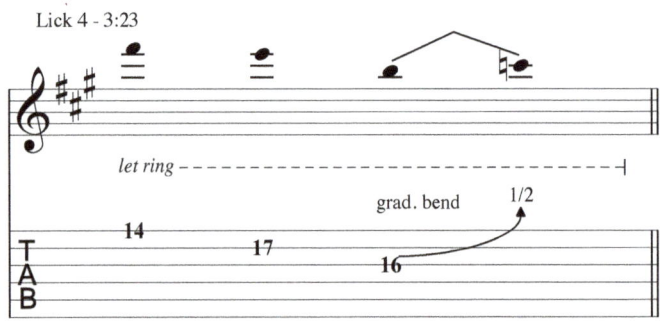

This is the last Money Maker module for Level 3. Practice mixing and blending as much of the vocabulary as you can. This kind of practice should stay with you a long, long time. On the next page, you will see a demo solo that uses these licks so you can see how they work in the context of a solo.

We'll see you in Level 4.

Level 3 Unit 10 • Money Maker Demo

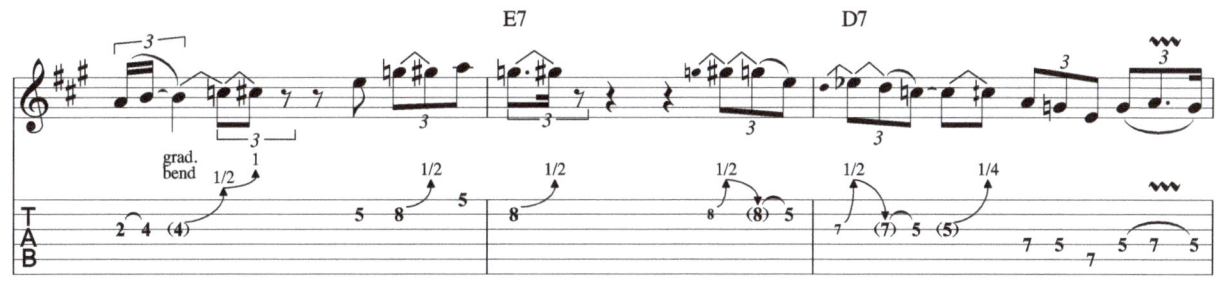

©2021 Fretboard Biology • fretboardbiology.com

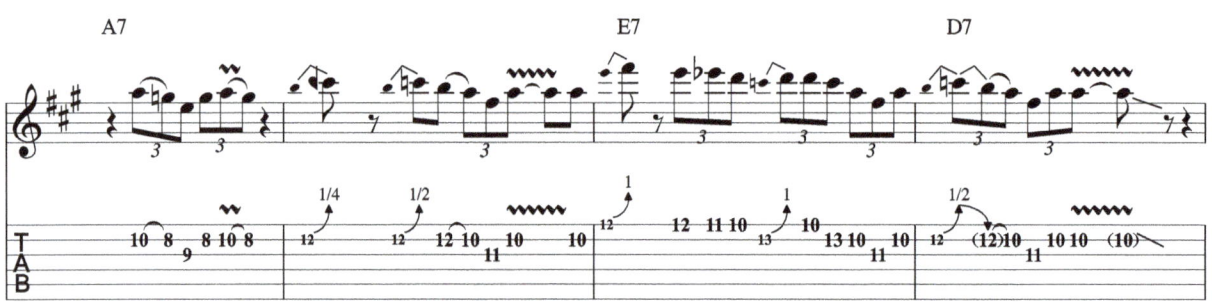
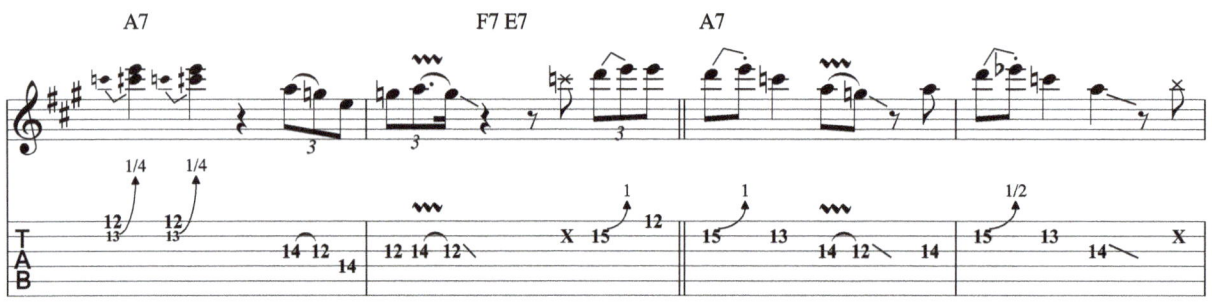
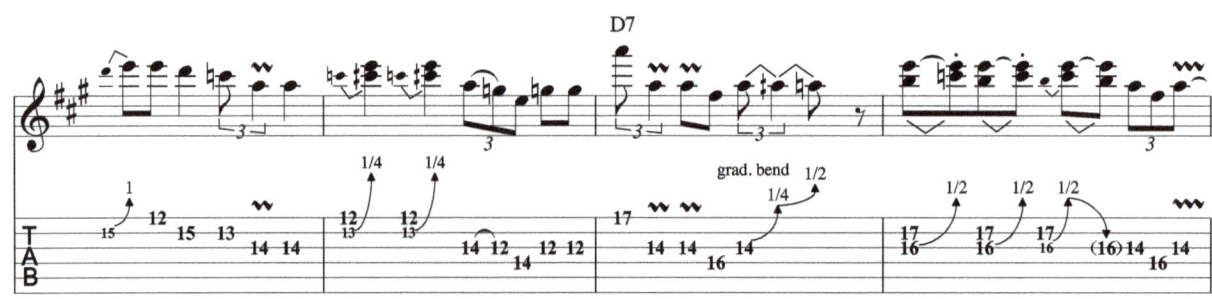

Fretboard Biology — Level 3 • Unit 10: Money Makers

IMPROVISATION

In the Fretboard Logic module you learned the in-position arpeggio organization system for minor keys. Now, put the in-position system to work in a progression with three chords.

Here's a progression in E minor:

Start by playing a key-center solo over the track using the Pattern II E minor scale to get a feel for the changes.

Analyze this progression using the knowledge you learning in the Theory modules to determine the number of each chord. Because this progression is in the key of E minor, you know that the Emi7 is the Imi7 chord, the Cma7 is the ♭VIma7 chord, and D7 is the ♭VII7 chord.

Using In-Position Arpeggios

Use the chord-tone approach with this progression, but this time use the "in-position" system. Look at the Pattern II minor scale harmonized in 7th chord arpeggios. Like with major keys, all of the arpeggios in a minor key can be played within a single scale pattern.

Here they are inside the Pattern II E minor scale

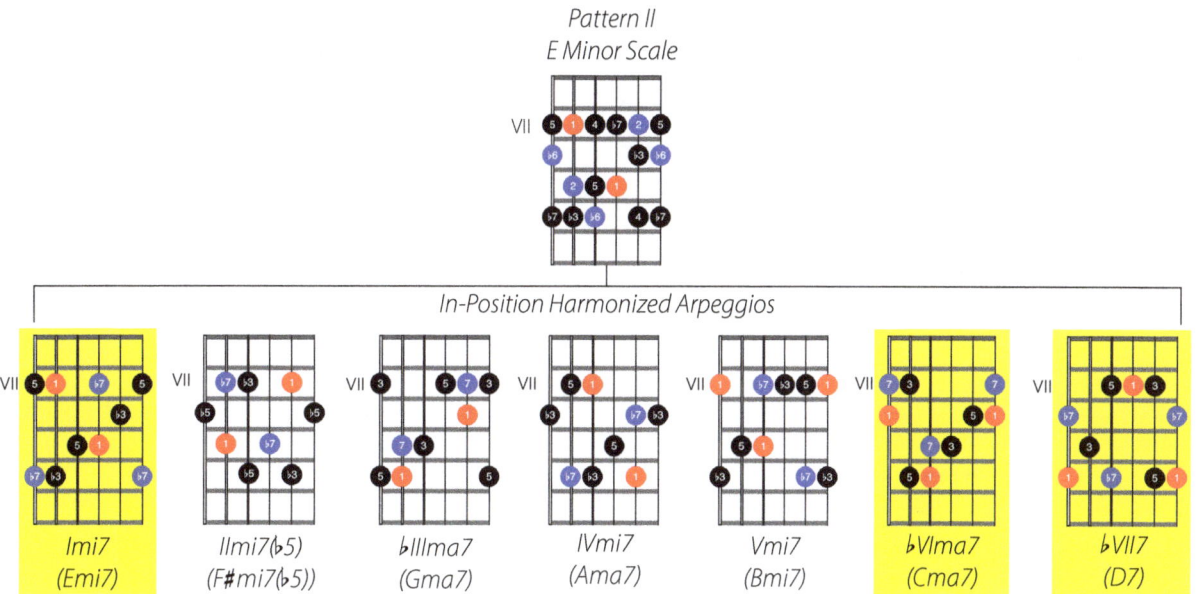

Now, take another look at this I–♭VI–♭VII–I progression, staying in the Pattern II E minor scale, which is in 7th position.

- Emi7 is the Imi7, and in Pattern II, the Imi7 arpeggio's root is on the 5th string.
- Cma7 is the ♭VIma7, and in Pattern IV, the ♭VIma7 arpeggio's root is on the 6th string.
- D7 is the ♭VII7, and in Pattern III, the ♭VII7 arpeggio's root is on the 6th string.

Notice how convenient it is to be able to play all the arpeggios within one octave shape. You are able to use arpeggios to play chord tones without ever having to move from 7th position.

Start by playing just the arpeggios over the chords in the progression. Then take another segment of your practice and create short motifs that blend chord tones and scale tones. An example of how to do this is on the next page.

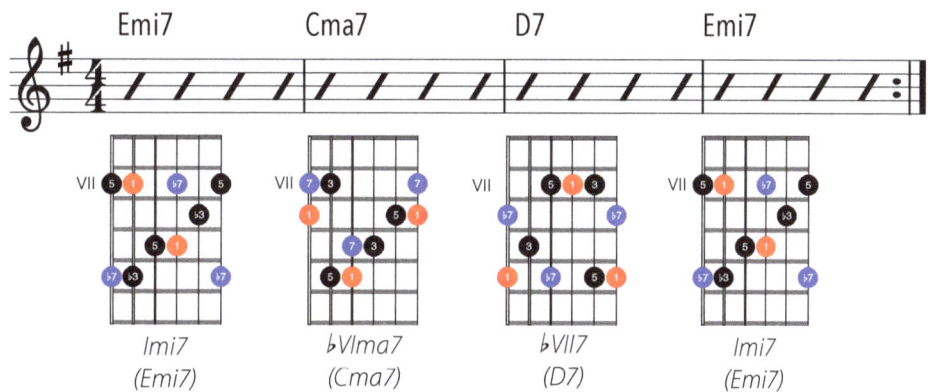

Level 3 Unit 10 • Improv Demo

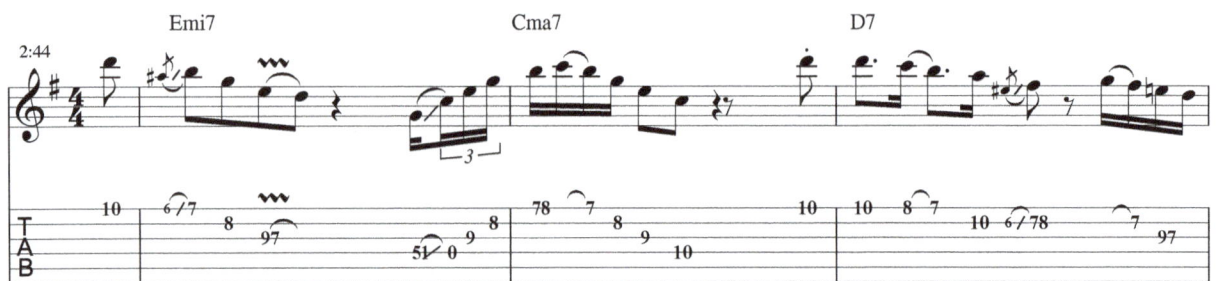

You can play arpeggios in-position in each of the five minor scale patterns but I strongly suggest you just use Patterns II and IV for a while, maybe a year or more. Be good to yourself and don't think you have to get all of this right now. It's impossible.

This concludes the Level 3 Improvisation modules. You have learned how to use chord tones in soloing. Eventually you want to return to being a key-center soloist – but a smarter soloist and with a heightened sense of awareness about where the chord tones are for each chord. After all this work with chord tones it may sound strange to hear that you will return to key-center soloing. Chord tones are part of the scale and can be used as a frame on which to base your lines and can be connected by the other notes of the scale.

Analyzing progressions is important to making good note choices and I recommend that you approach every song where you solo with these steps:

1. Determine the key.
2. Practice a key-center solo over the progression.
3. Analyze the progression, which means determining the function (the number) of each chord.
4. Map out the arpeggios for each chord in position using Pattern I and III for songs in a major key or Patterns II and IV for songs in a minor key.
5. Exercise the arpeggios over the progression.
6. Blend chord tones with key-center soloing.

Learning to make good note choices takes a long time. Using arpeggios in-position to play chord tones is a huge step. Over time and with a lot of repetition you will become more skilled. Chord-tone soloing does not mean that you use only chord tones. It means that you incorporate chord tones in your lines. Keep at it.

PRACTICE

Fretboard Logic

- ❑ Learn the Pattern II minor in-position arpeggios.
- ❑ Learn the Pattern I, III, and V and minor 7(♭5) chords.
- ❑ Look at how the new information from this Unit relates to the everything else in the octave shape Family Tree.

Rhythm Guitar

- ❑ Practice playing various guitar parts in Country rhythm guitar.

Money Makers

- ❑ Learn common Pattern III minor pentatonic licks.

Improvisation

- ❑ Use the Pattern II minor in-position arpeggios to play chord tones over the progression in E minor.

Appendices

> **Appendix 1** - Theory Exercise Answer Keys
> **Appendix 2** - Octave Shape Family Trees
> **Appendix 3** - Chord Chart
> **Appendix 4** - In-Position Arpeggios
> **Appendix 4** - Interval Sequences

Progression Analysis Exercise
LEVEL 3 : UNIT 3 - ANSWER KEY

Step One: Make a tentative determination of the key.
Step Two: Based on this, determine the number (function) of each chord.
Step Three: Confirm and label the key and function of each chord.

EXAMPLE:

Key: D

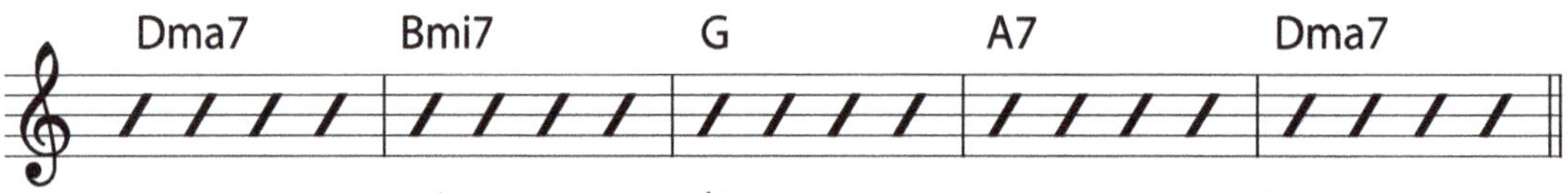

Dma7	Bmi7	G	A7	Dma7
Ima7	VImi7	IVma	V7	Ima7
☒ Tonic	☒ Tonic	☐ Tonic	☐ Tonic	☒ Tonic
☐ Subdominant	☐ Subdominant	☒ Subdominant	☐ Subdominant	☐ Subdominant
☐ Dominant	☐ Dominant	☐ Dominant	☒ Dominant	☐ Dominant

Key: C

Cma7	Dmi7	G7	Cma7
Ima7	IImi7	V7	Ima7
☒ Tonic	☐ Tonic	☐ Tonic	☒ Tonic
☐ Subdominant	☒ Subdominant	☐ Subdominant	☐ Subdominant
☐ Dominant	☐ Dominant	☒ Dominant	☐ Dominant

Key: D

Dma7	Bmi7	Emi7	A7	Dma7
Ima7	VImi7	IImi7	V7	Ima7
☒ Tonic	☒ Tonic	☐ Tonic	☐ Tonic	☒ Tonic
☐ Subdominant	☐ Subdominant	☒ Subdominant	☐ Subdominant	☐ Subdominant
☐ Dominant	☐ Dominant	☐ Dominant	☒ Dominant	☐ Dominant

©2021 Joe Elliott • FretboardBiology.com

Fretboard Biology — Appendix 1 : Theory Answer Keys

LEVEL 3 : UNIT 3 — Progression Analysis Exercise

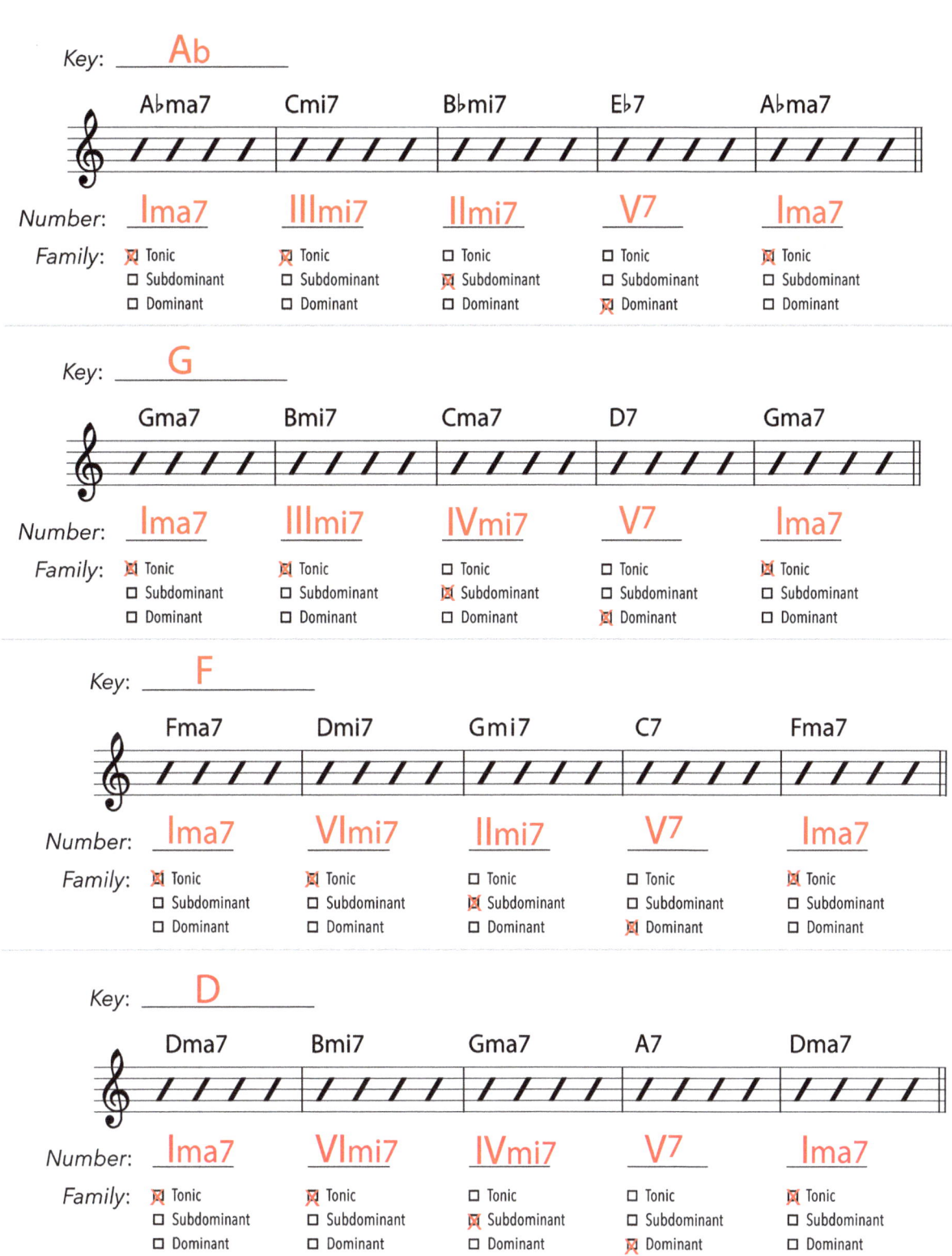

LEVEL 3 : UNIT 3 — Progression Analysis Exercise — 3

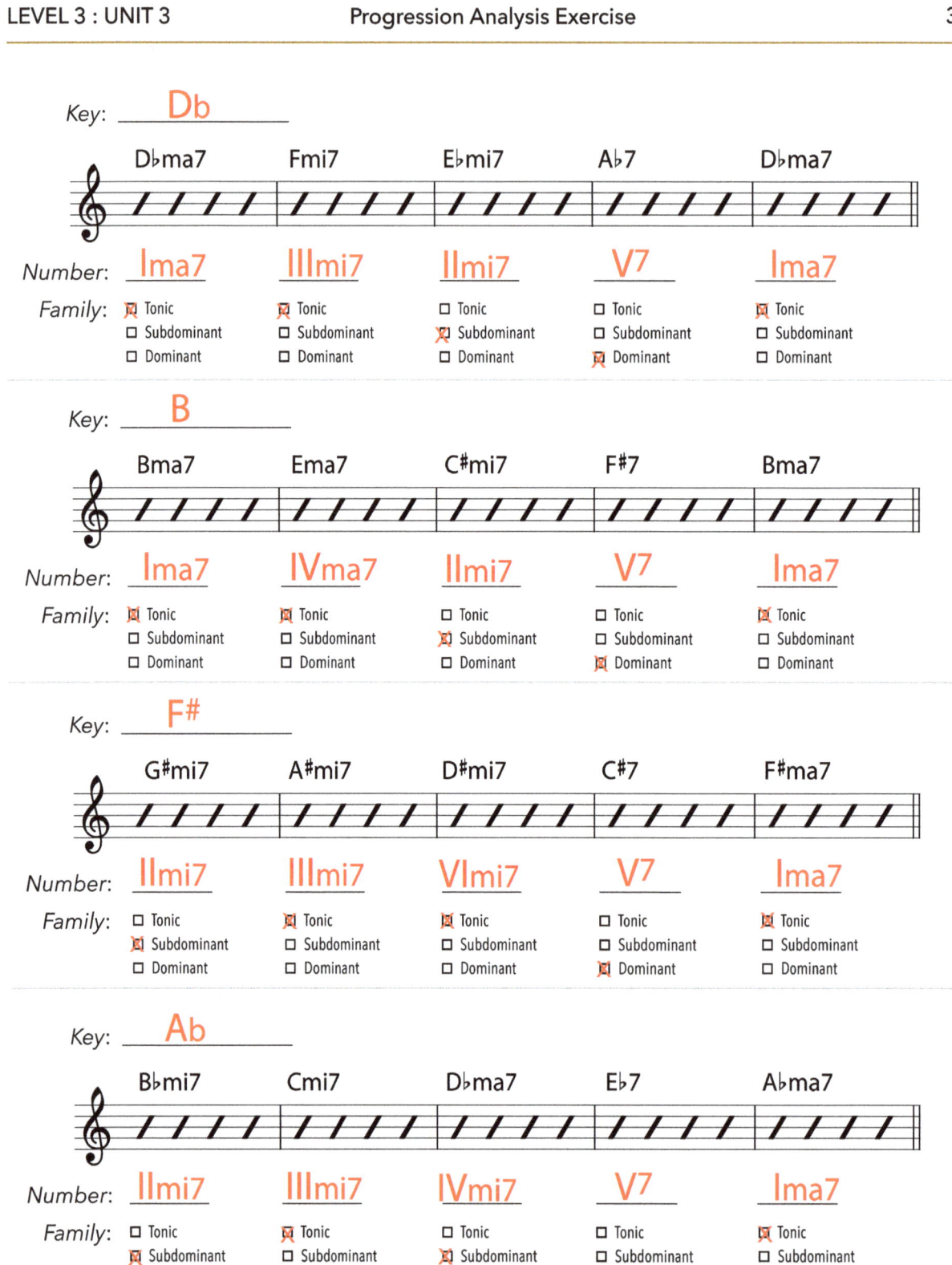

Fretboard Biology — Appendix 1 : Theory Answer Keys

Progression Analysis Exercise

LEVEL 3 : UNIT 4 - ANSWER KEY

Step One: Make a tentative determination of the key.
Step Two: Based on this, determine the number (function) of each chord.
Step Three: Confirm and label the key and function of each chord.

EXAMPLE:

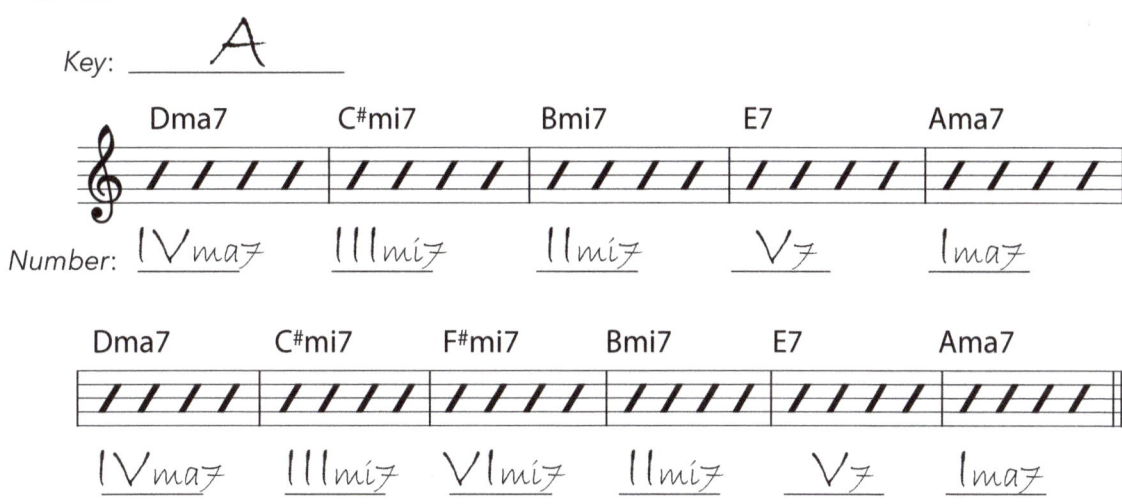

Key: A

| Dma7 | C#mi7 | Bmi7 | E7 | Ama7 |
| IVma7 | IIImi7 | IImi7 | V7 | Ima7 |

| Dma7 | C#mi7 | F#mi7 | Bmi7 | E7 | Ama7 |
| IVma7 | IIImi7 | VImi7 | IImi7 | V7 | Ima7 |

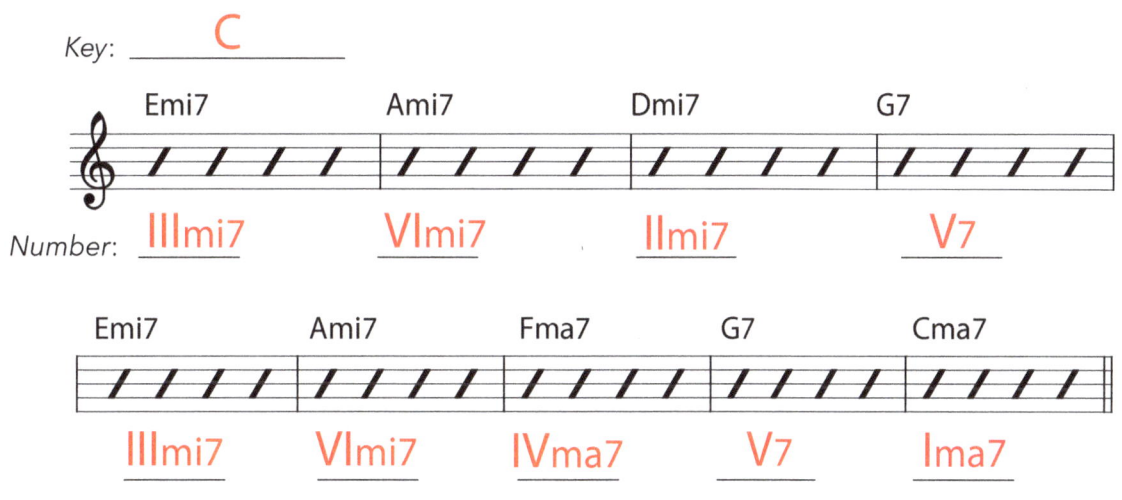

Key: C

| Emi7 | Ami7 | Dmi7 | G7 |
| IIImi7 | VImi7 | IImi7 | V7 |

| Emi7 | Ami7 | Fma7 | G7 | Cma7 |
| IIImi7 | VImi7 | IVma7 | V7 | Ima7 |

LEVEL 3 : UNIT 4 — Progression Analysis Exercise

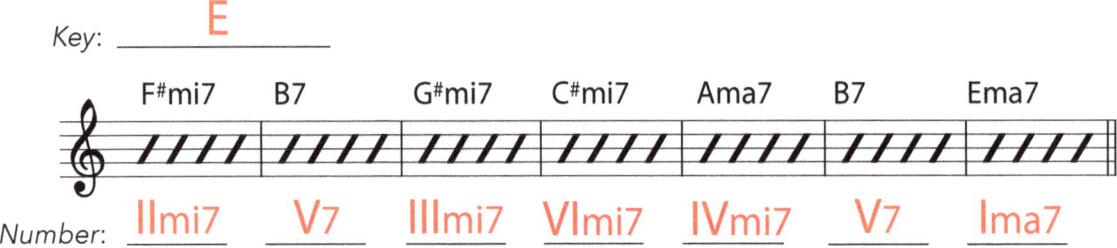

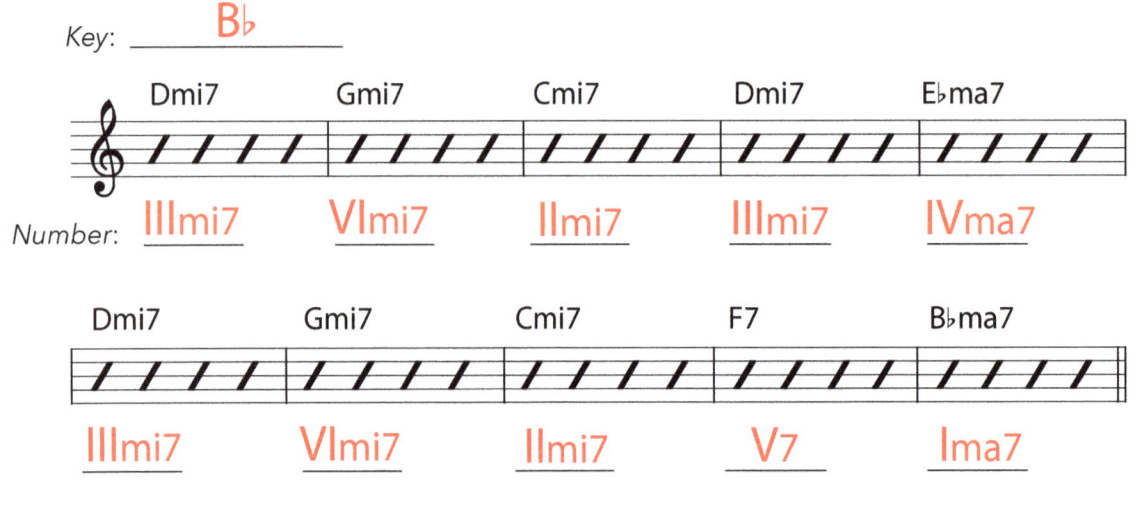

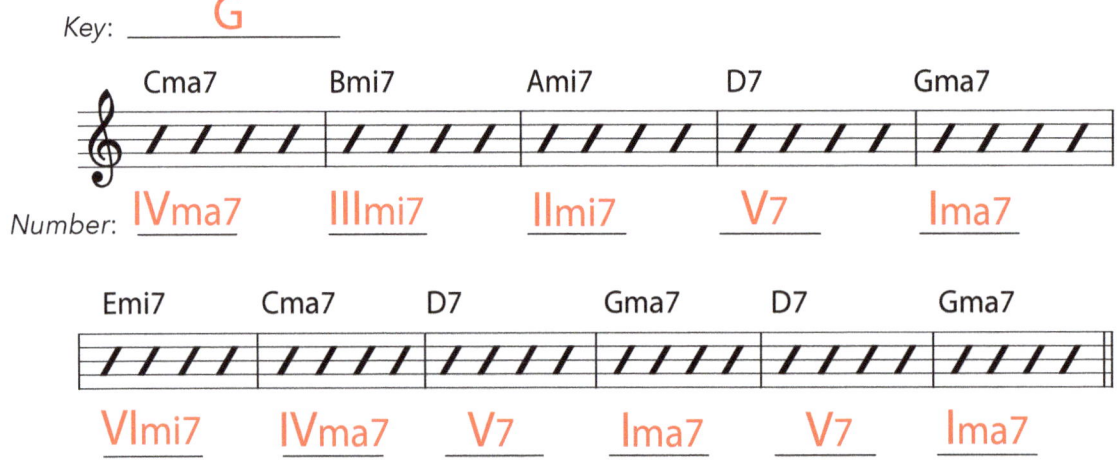

Fretboard Biology — Appendix 1 : Theory Answer Keys

LEVEL 3 : UNIT 4 — Progression Analysis Exercise

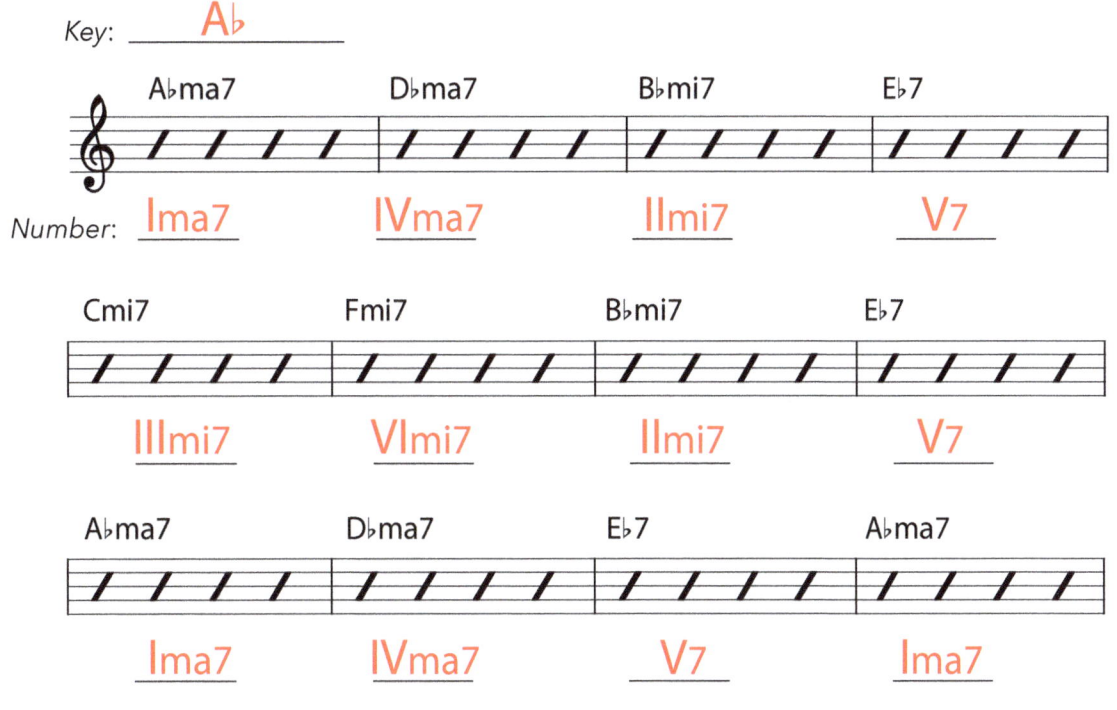

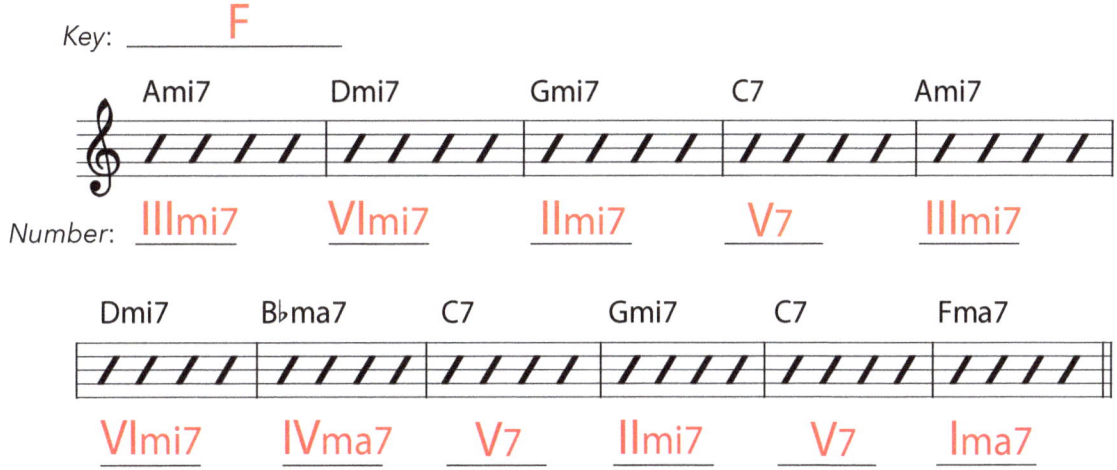

©2021 Joe Elliott • FretboardBiology.com

Appendix 1 : Theory Answer Keys

Progression Analysis Exercise

LEVEL 3 : UNIT 6 - ANSWER KEY

Step One: Make a tentative determination of the key.
Step Two: Based on this, determine the number (function) of each chord.
Step Three: Confirm and label the key and function of each chord.

EXAMPLE:

Key: F#mi

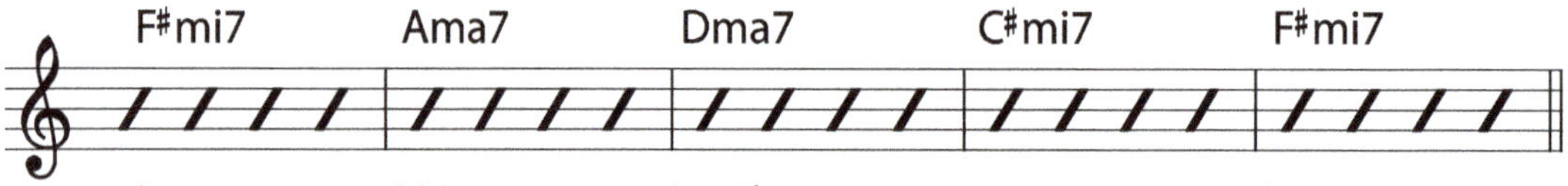

	F#mi7	Ama7	Dma7	C#mi7	F#mi7
Number:	Imi7	bIIIma7	bVIma7	Vmi7	Imi7
Family:	☒ Tonic ☐ Subdominant ☐ Dominant	☒ Tonic ☐ Subdominant ☐ Dominant	☐ Tonic ☒ Subdominant ☐ Dominant	☐ Tonic ☐ Subdominant ☒ Dominant	☒ Tonic ☐ Subdominant ☐ Dominant

---

Key: **Ami**

	Ami7	Fma7	Emi7	Ami7
Number:	**Imi7**	**bVIma7**	**Vmi7**	**Imi7**
Family:	☒ Tonic ☐ Subdominant ☐ Dominant	☐ Tonic ☒ Subdominant ☐ Dominant	☐ Tonic ☐ Subdominant ☒ Dominant	☒ Tonic ☐ Subdominant ☐ Dominant

Key: **Emi**

	Emi7	D7	Cma7	Bmi7	Emi7
Number:	**Imi7**	**bVII7**	**bVIma7**	**Vmi7**	**Imi7**
Family:	☒ Tonic ☐ Subdominant ☐ Dominant	☐ Tonic ☐ Subdominant ☒ Dominant	☐ Tonic ☒ Subdominant ☐ Dominant	☐ Tonic ☐ Subdominant ☒ Dominant	☒ Tonic ☐ Subdominant ☐ Dominant

©2020 Joe Elliott • FretboardBiology.com

Fretboard Biology — Appendix 1 : Theory Answer Keys

LEVEL 3 : UNIT 6 — Progression Analysis Exercise

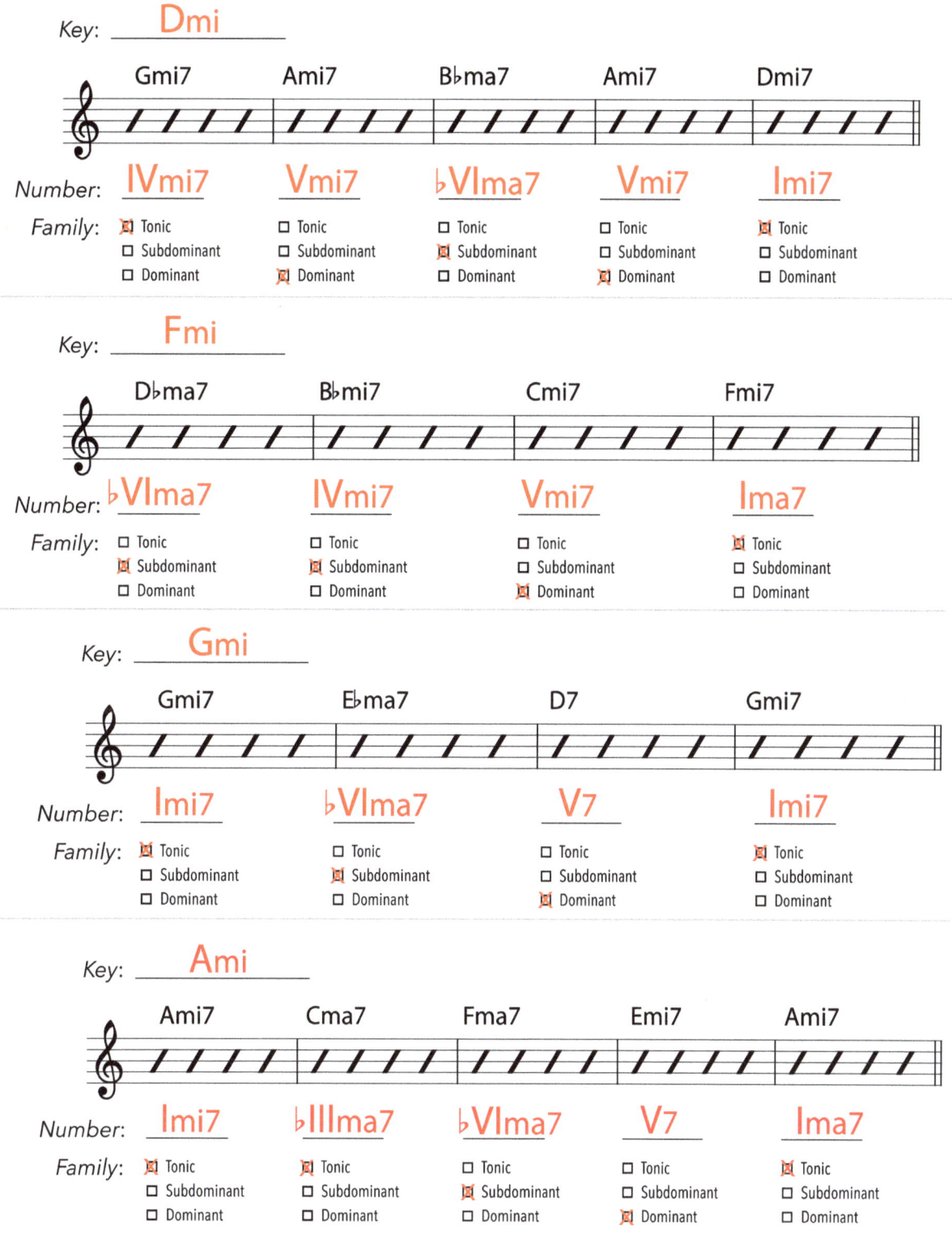

LEVEL 3 : UNIT 6 — Progression Analysis Exercise

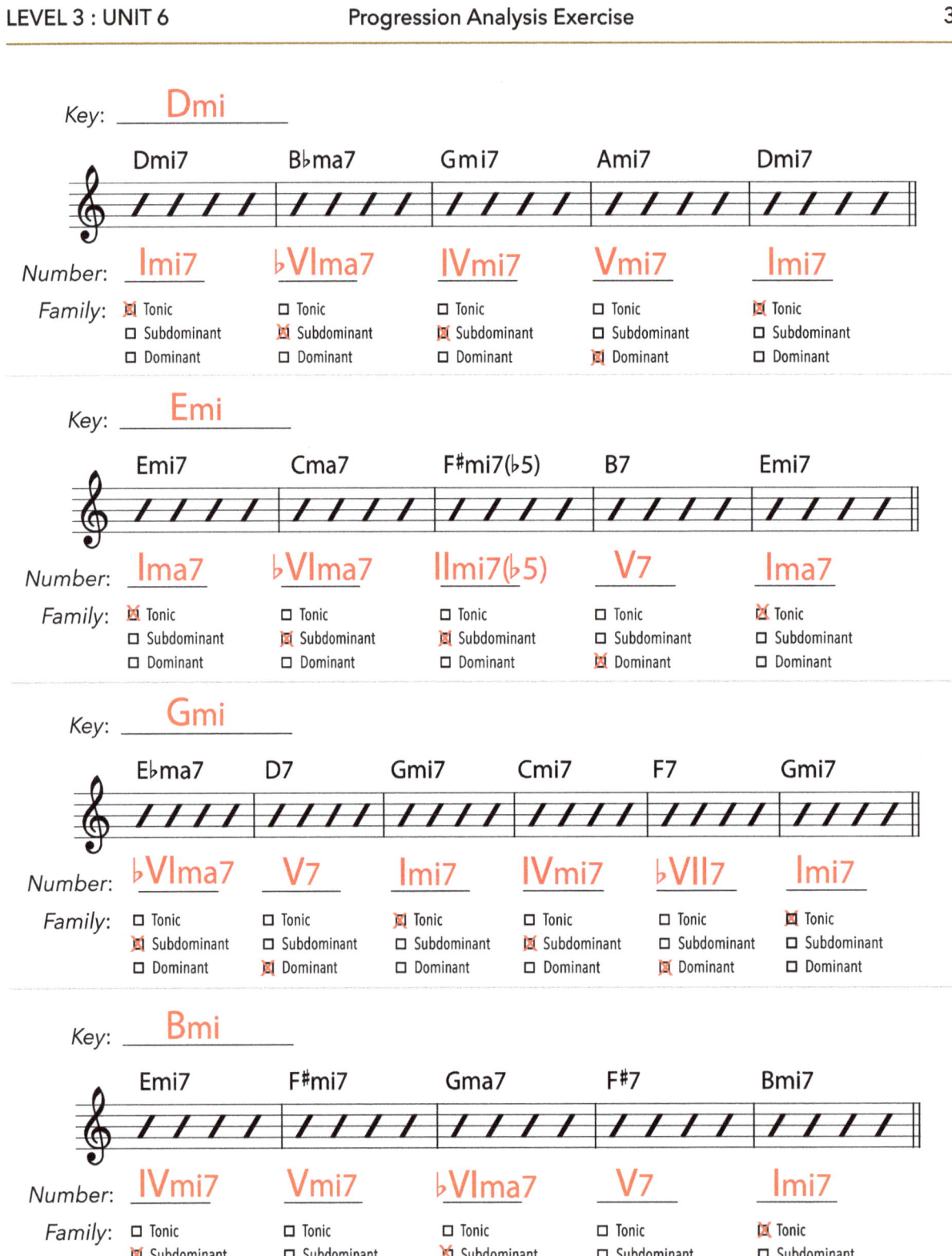

Fretboard Biology
Appendix 1 : Theory Answer Keys

Progression Analysis Exercise
LEVEL 3 : UNIT 7 - ANSWER KEY

Step One: Make a tentative determination of the key.
Step Two: Based on this, determine the number (function) of each chord.
Step Three: Confirm and label the key and function of each chord.

EXAMPLE:

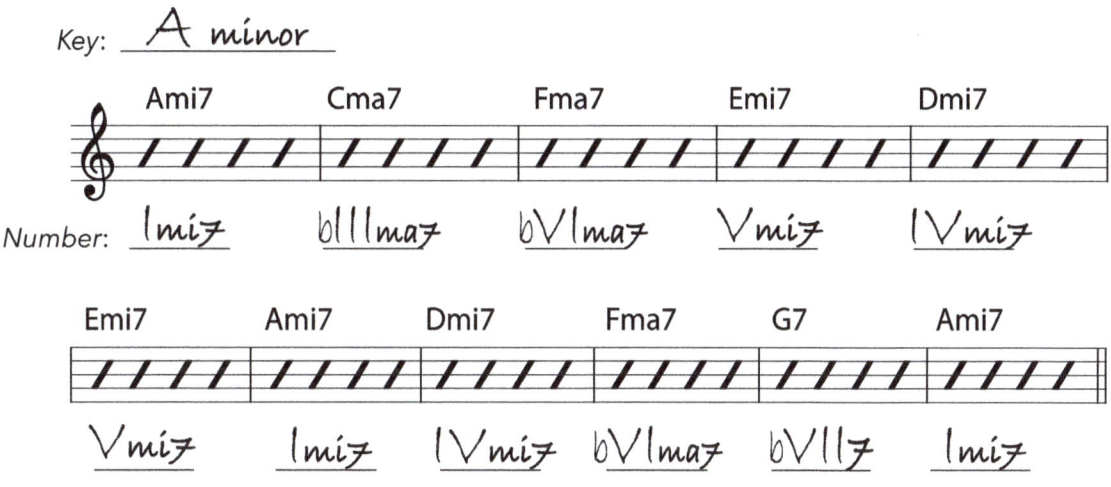

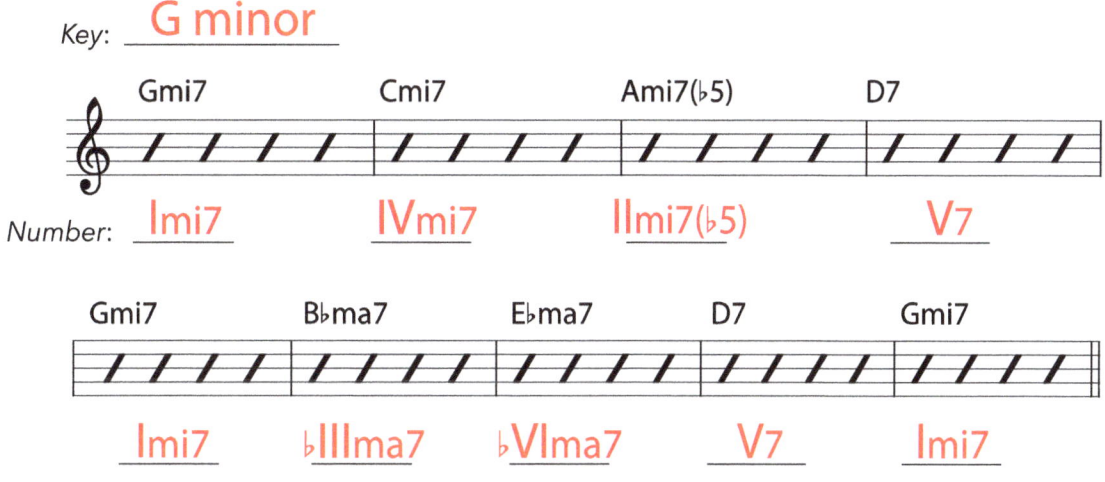

©2020 Joe Elliott • FretboardBiology.com

LEVEL 3 : UNIT 7   Progression Analysis Exercise

Key: **C# minor**

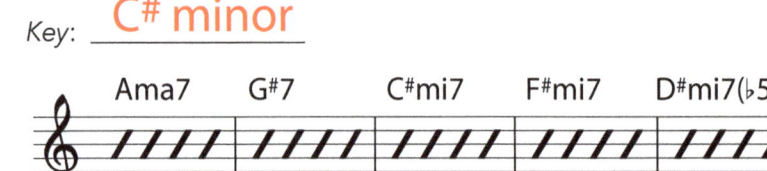

Ama7	G#7	C#mi7	F#mi7	D#mi7(♭5)	G#7	C#mi7
♭VIma7	V7	Imi7	IVmi7	IImi7(♭5)	V7	Imi7

Key: **D minor**

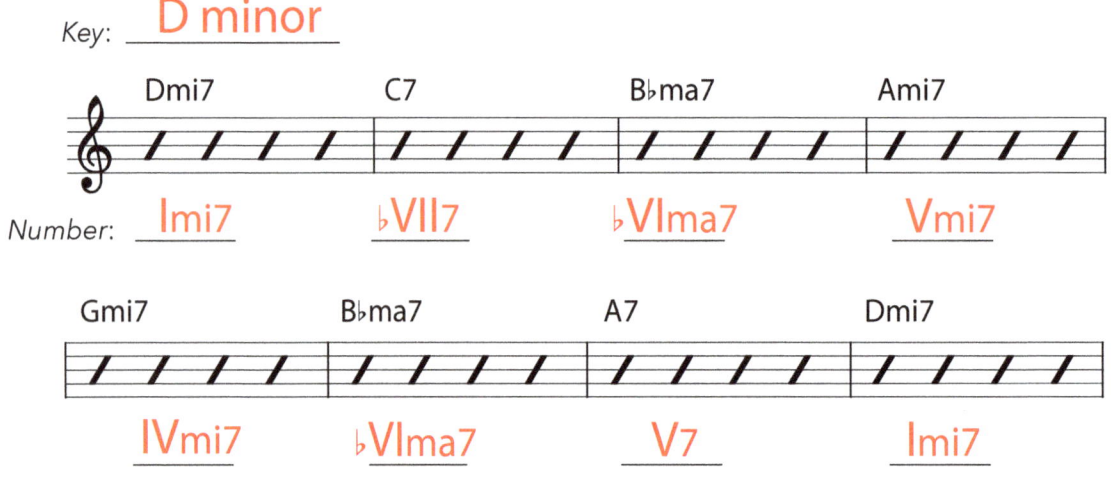

Dmi7	C7	B♭ma7	Ami7
Imi7	♭VII7	♭VIma7	Vmi7

Gmi7	B♭ma7	A7	Dmi7
IVmi7	♭VIma7	V7	Imi7

Key: **F# minor**

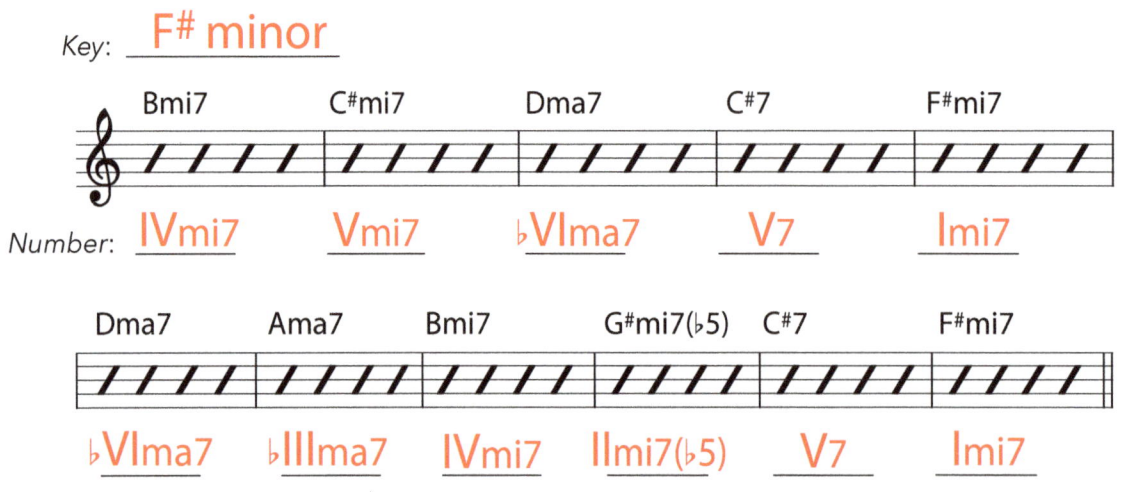

Bmi7	C#mi7	Dma7	C#7	F#mi7
IVmi7	Vmi7	♭VIma7	V7	Imi7

Dma7	Ama7	Bmi7	G#mi7(♭5)	C#7	F#mi7
♭VIma7	♭IIIma7	IVmi7	IImi7(♭5)	V7	Imi7

©2020 Joe Elliott • FretboardBiology.com

Fretboard Biology — Appendix 1 : Theory Answer Keys

LEVEL 3 : UNIT 7 — Progression Analysis Exercise — 3

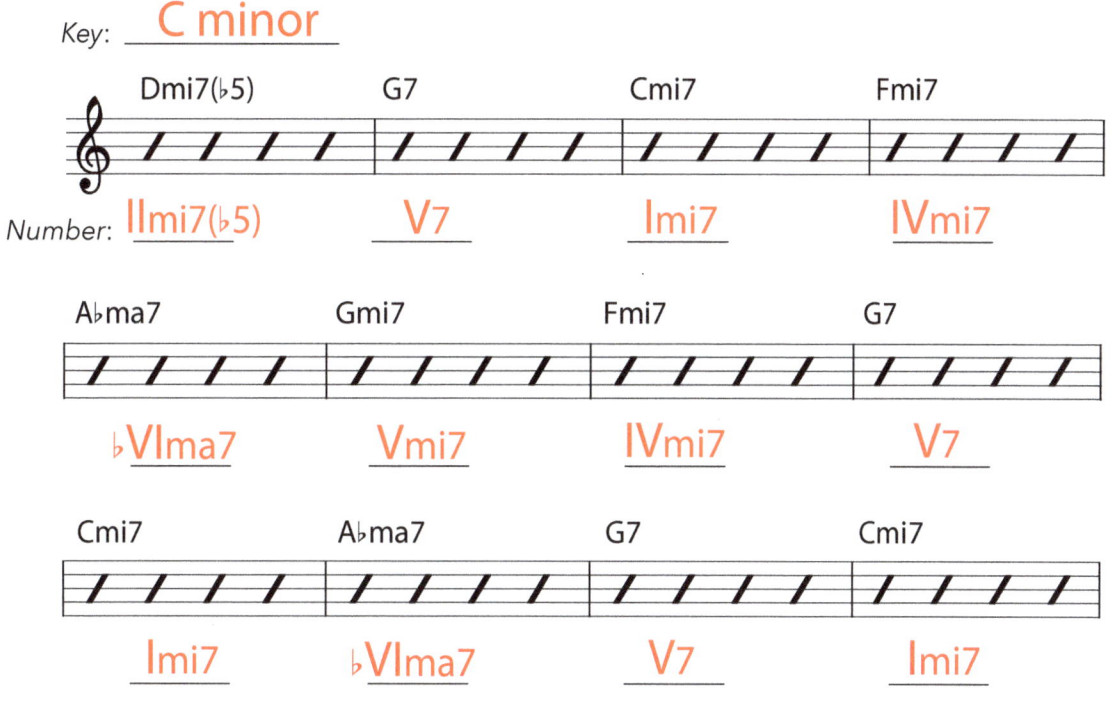

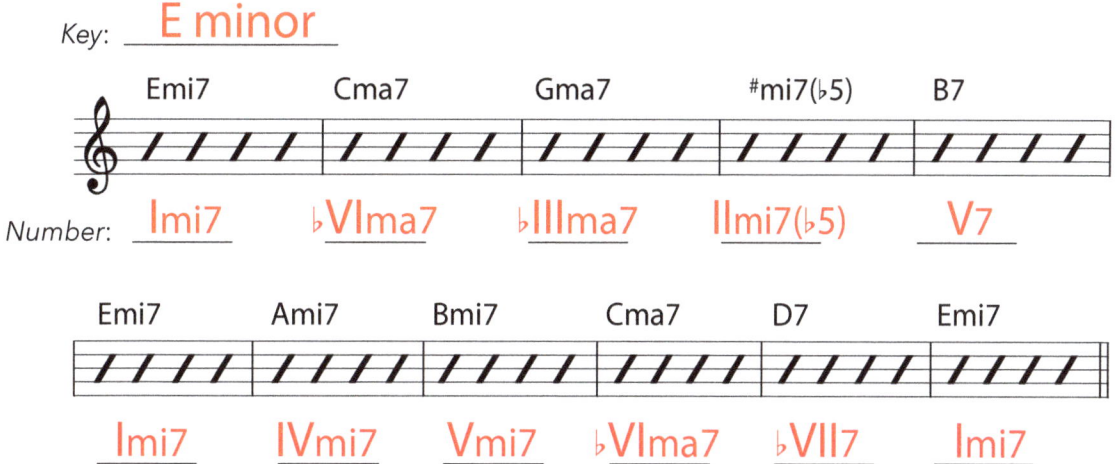

Pattern I Family Tree

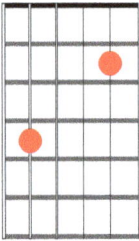

MAJOR

Pentatonic Scale
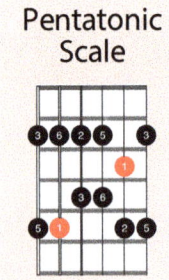

Ionian (Major) Scale
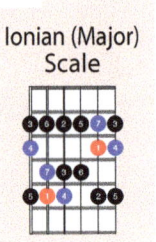

Triad Arpeggio / Augmented Arpeggio
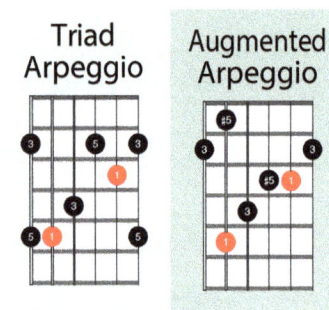

Major 7 Arpeggio / Dominant 7 Arpeggio
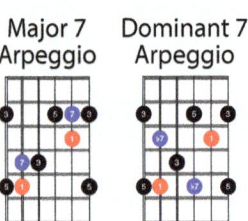

Triad Chord / Augmented Triad
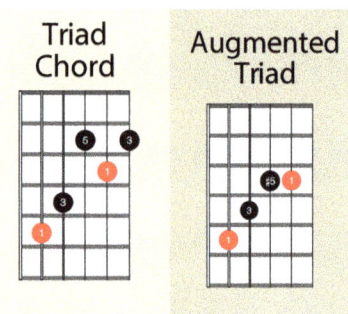

Major 7 Chord / Dominant 7 Chord
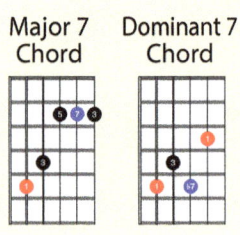

Suspended Chords (Sus 2, Sus 4, 7Sus 4) / Suspended Arpeggios (Sus 2, Sus 4)
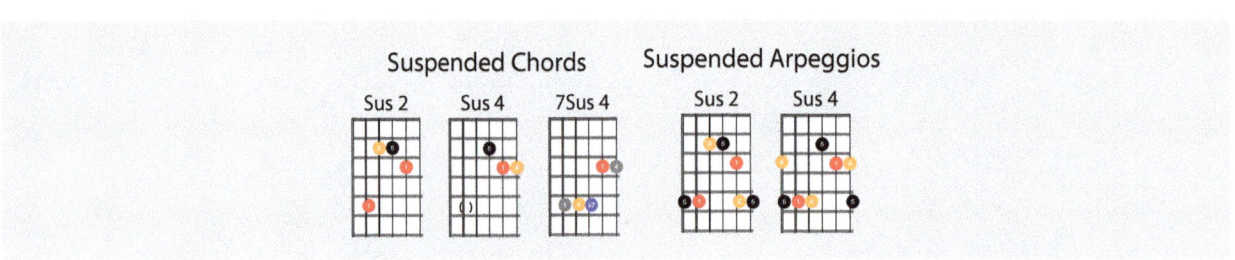

Pattern I Family Tree

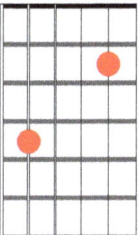

MINOR

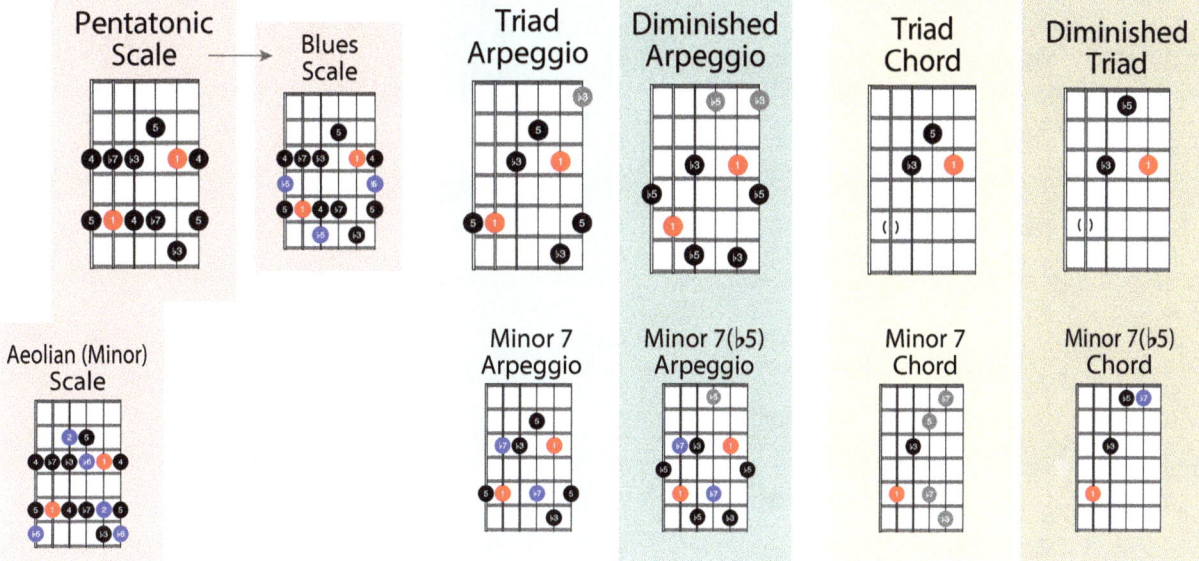

Pattern II Family Tree

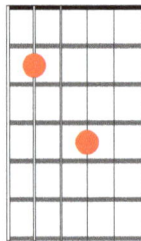

MAJOR

Pentatonic Scale
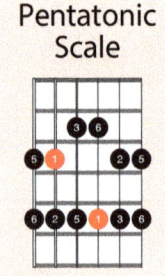

Ionian (Major) Scale
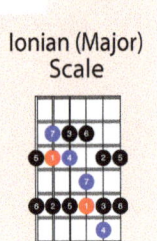

Triad Arpeggio / Augmented Arpeggio
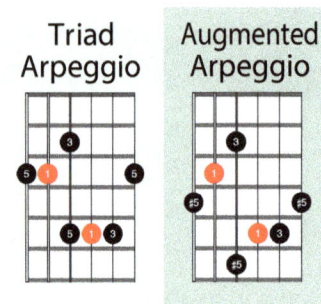

Major 7 Arpeggio / Dominant 7 Arpeggio

Triad Chord / Augmented Triad
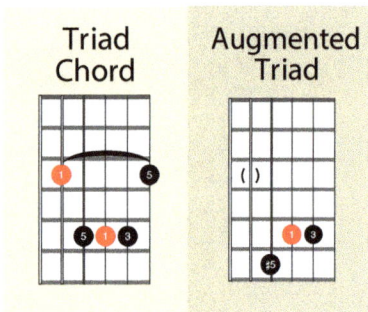

Major 7 Chord / Dominant 7 Chord
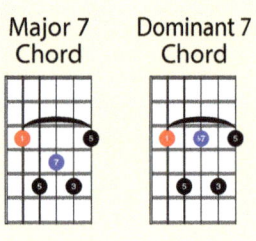

Suspended Chords / Suspended Arpeggios
Sus 2 — Sus 4 — 7Sus 4 — Sus 2 — Sus 4

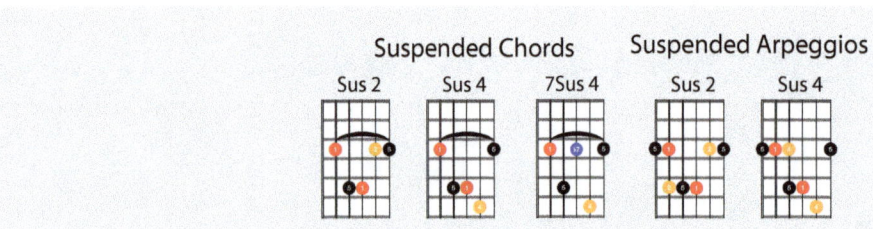

Pattern II Family Tree

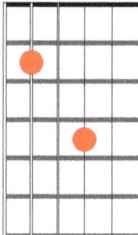

MINOR

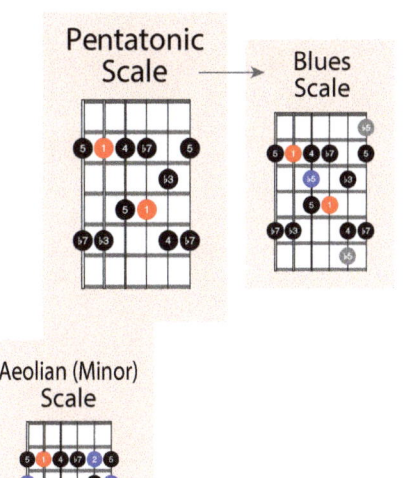
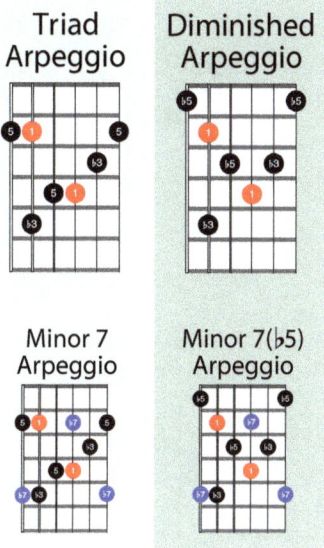
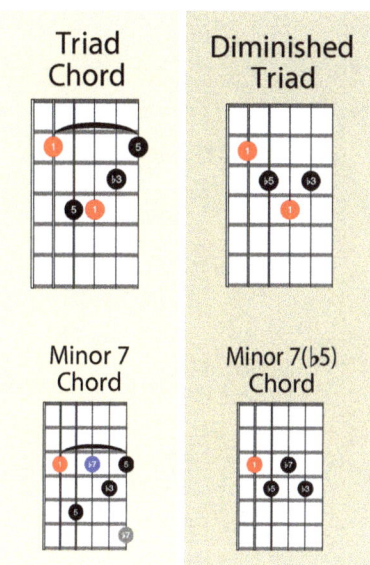

Pattern III Family Tree

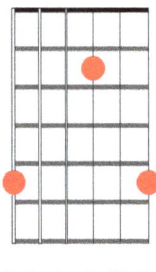

MAJOR

Pentatonic Scale	Triad Arpeggio	Augmented Arpeggio	Triad Chord	Augmented Triad

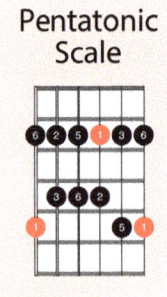 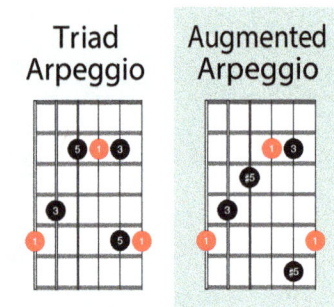 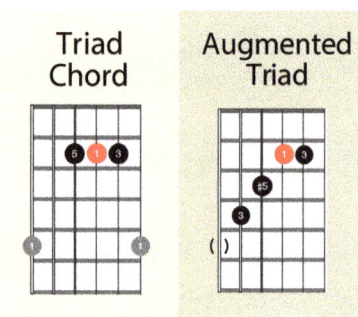

Ionian (Major) Scale	Major 7 Arpeggio	Dominant 7 Arpeggio	Major 7 Chord	Dominant 7 Chord

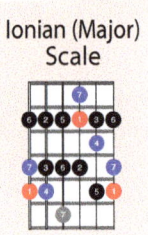  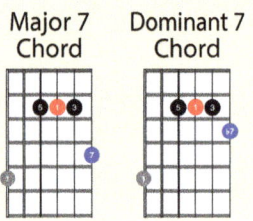

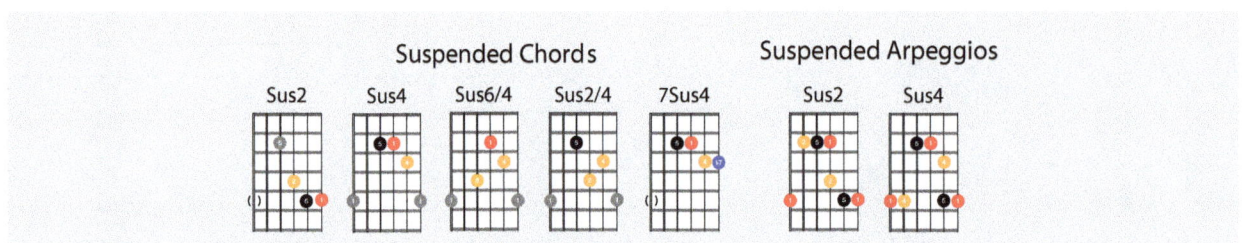

Pattern III Family Tree

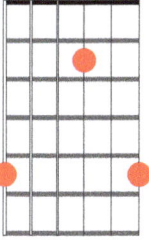

MINOR

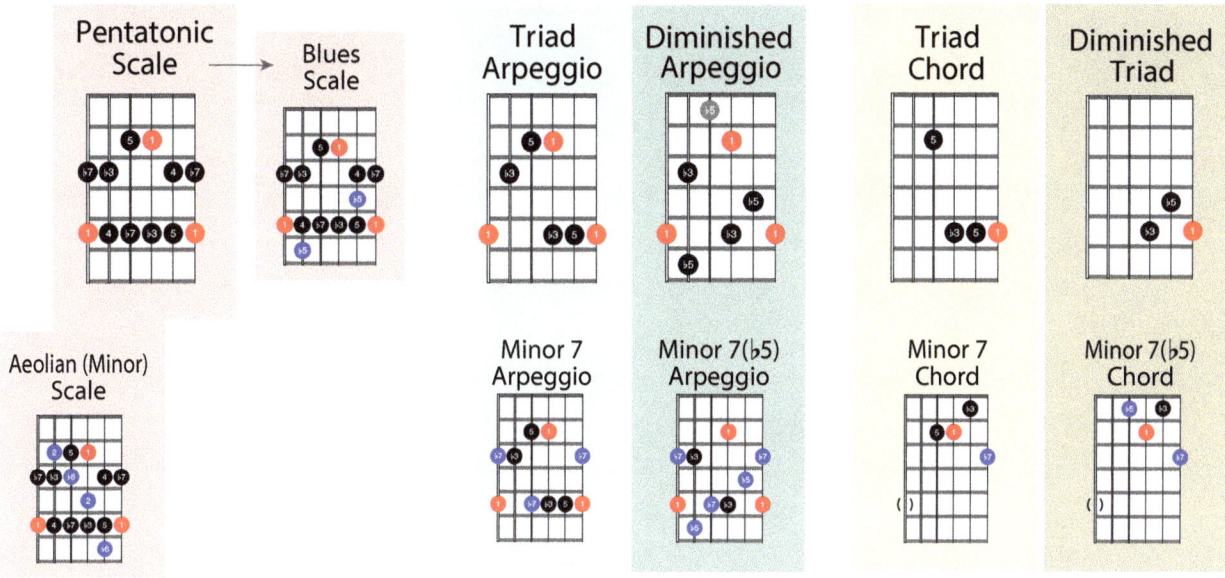

Pattern IV Family Tree

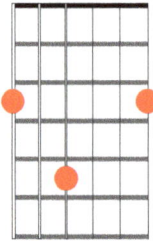

MAJOR

Pentatonic Scale	Triad Arpeggio	Augmented Arpeggio	Triad Chord	Augmented Triad

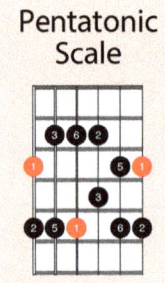 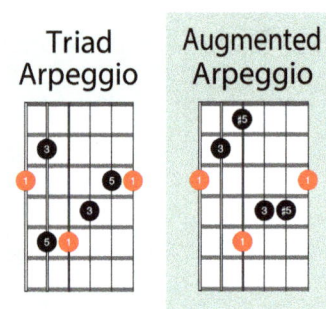 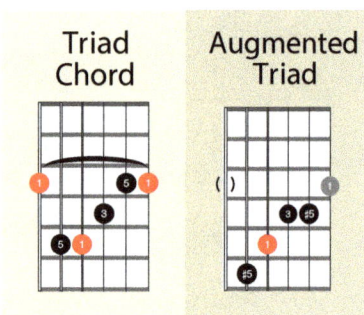

Ionian (Major) Scale | Major 7 Arpeggio | Dominant 7 Arpeggio | Major 7 Chord | Dominant 7 Chord

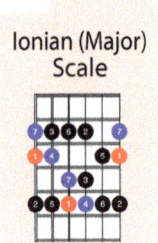  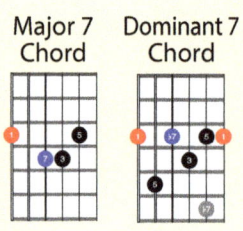

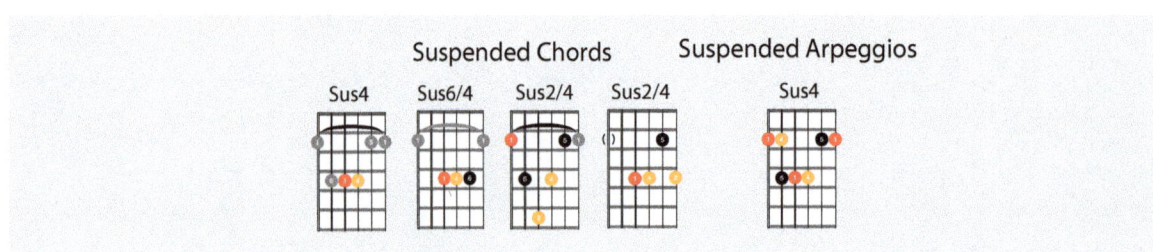

Pattern IV Family Tree

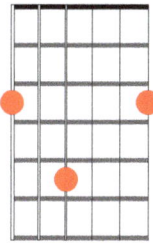

MINOR

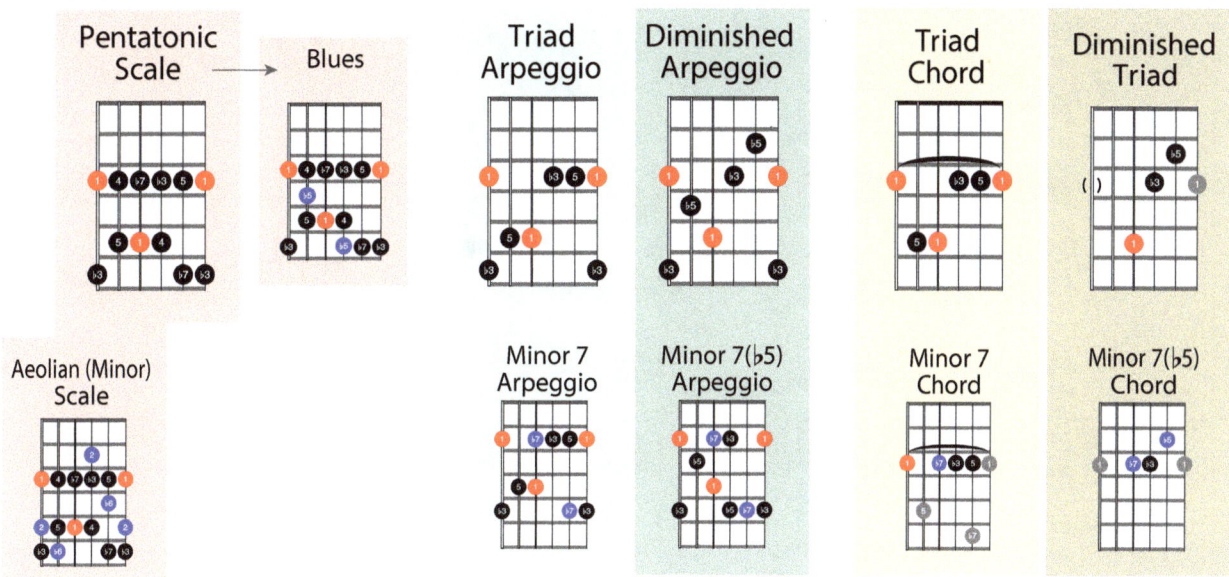

Pattern V Family Tree

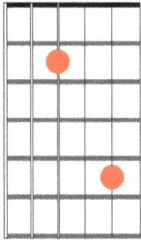

MAJOR

| Pentatonic Scale | Triad Arpeggio | Augmented Arpeggio | Triad Chord | Augmented Triad |

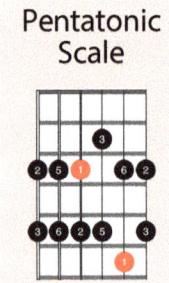
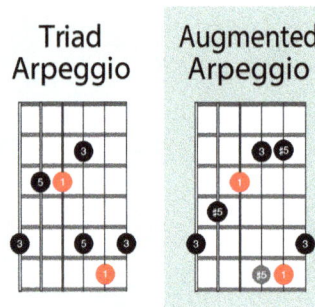
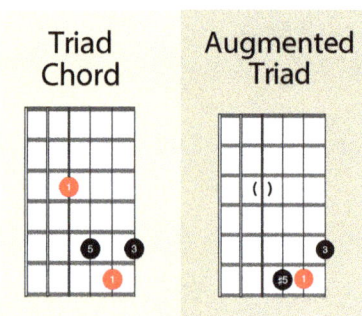

Ionian (Major) Scale · Major 7 Arpeggio · Dominant 7 Arpeggio · Major 7 Chord · Dominant 7 Chord

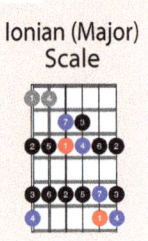
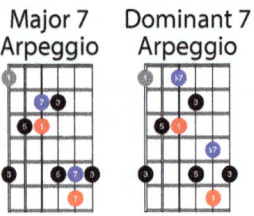
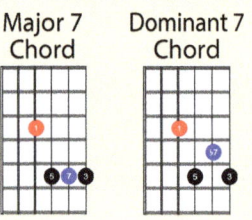

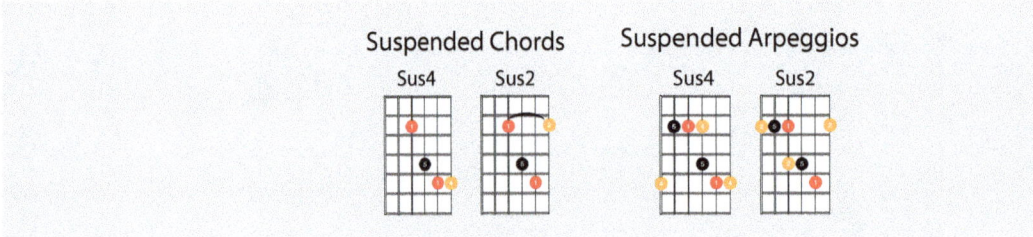

Pattern V Family Tree

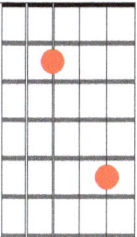

MINOR

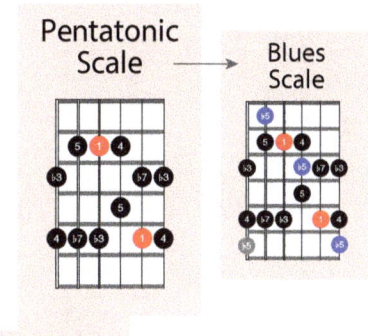

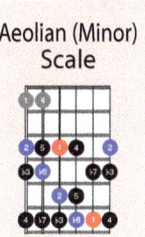

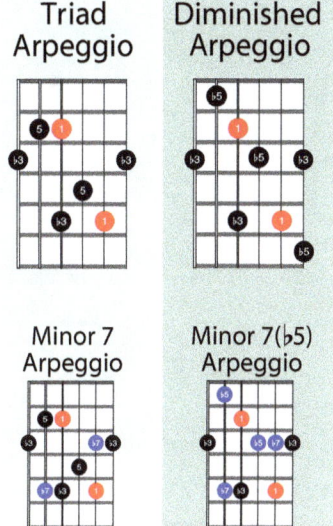

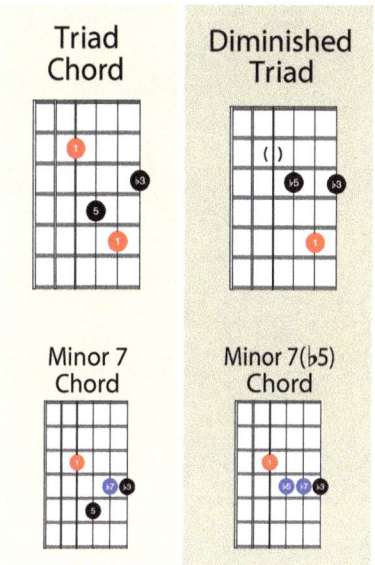

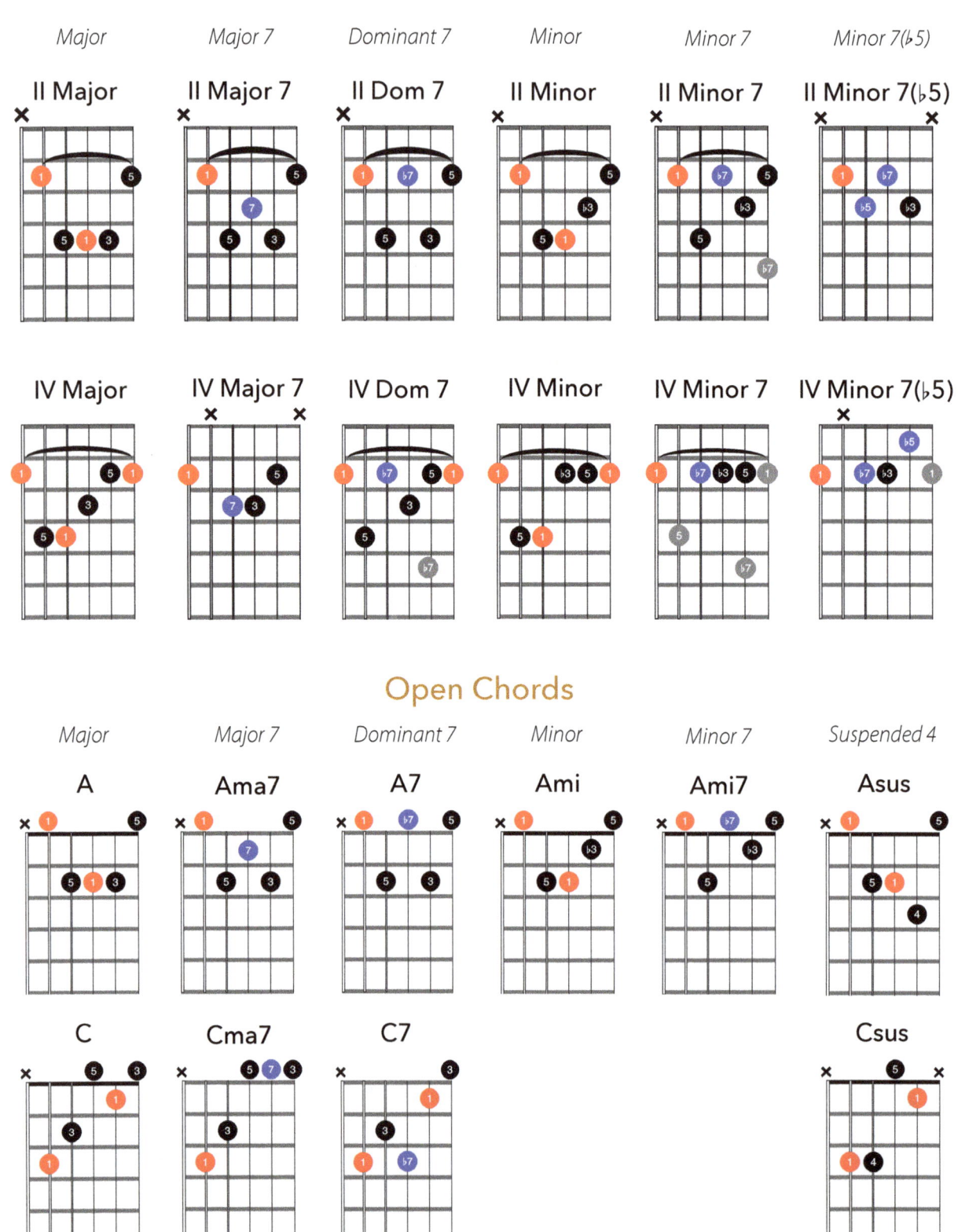

Appendix 3: Chord Chart

Open Chords (cont.)

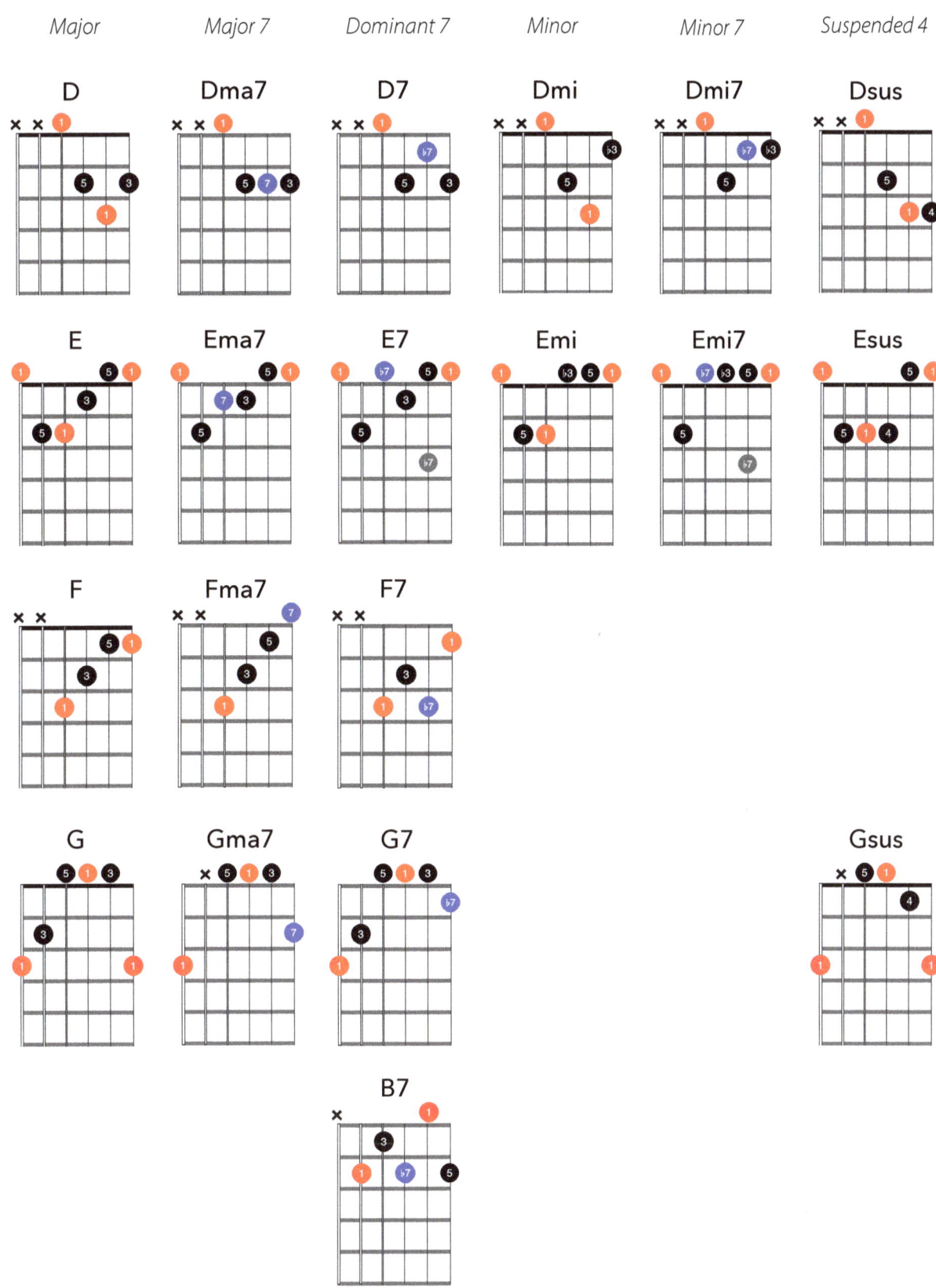

Major In-Position Arpeggios

Pattern I Major In-Position Arpeggios

Pattern I Major Scale

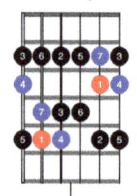

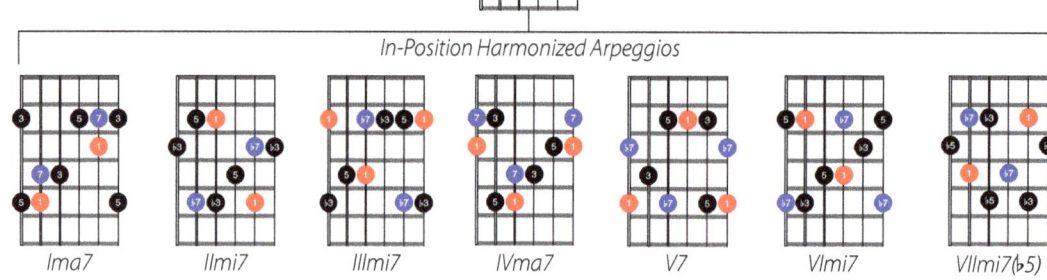

Pattern II Major In-Position Arpeggios

Pattern I Major Scale

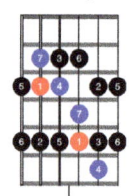

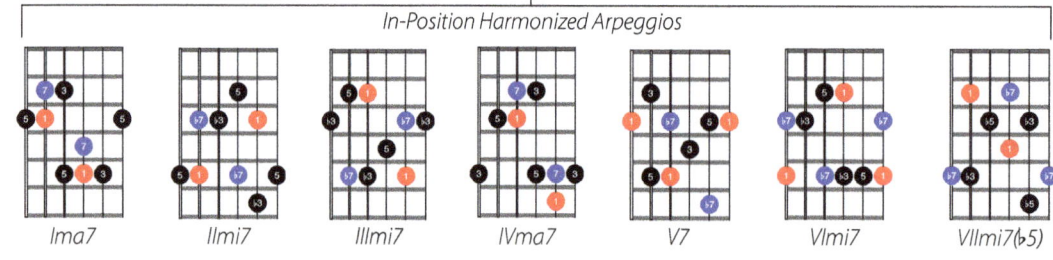

Pattern III Major In-Position Arpeggios

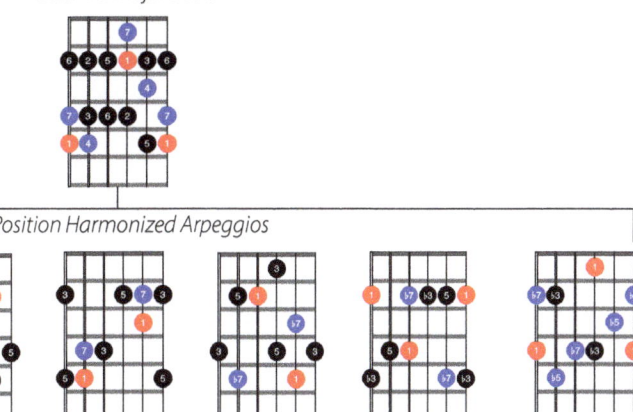

Pattern IV Major In-Position Arpeggios

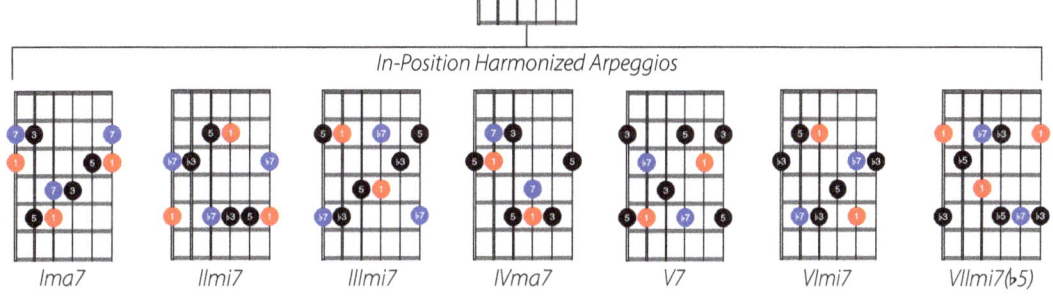

Pattern V Major In-Position Arpeggios

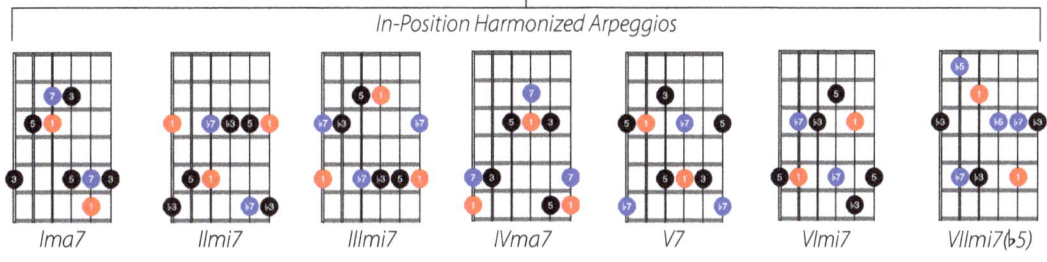

Minor In-Position Arpeggios

Pattern I Minor In-Position Arpeggios

Pattern I Minor Scale

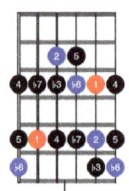

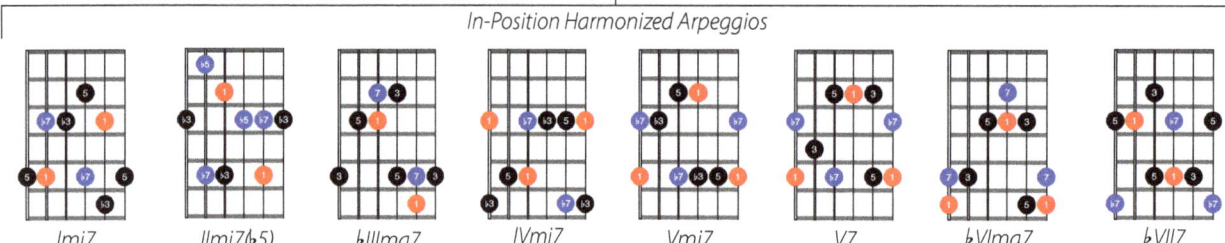

Pattern II Minor In-Position Arpeggios

Pattern II Minor Scale

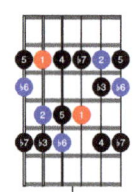

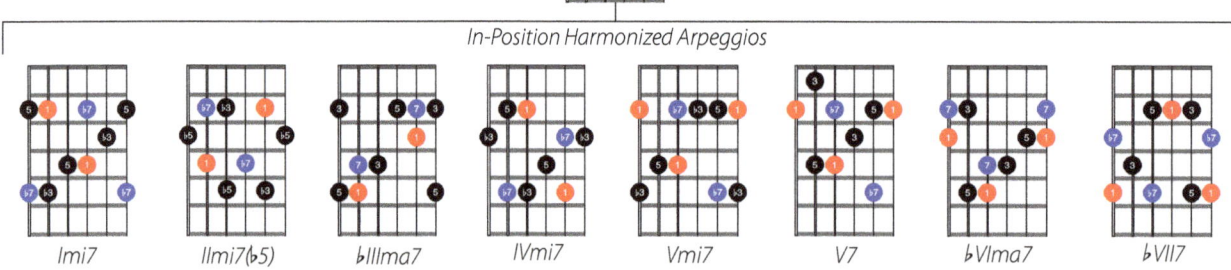

Pattern III Minor In-Position Arpeggios

Pattern III Minor Scale

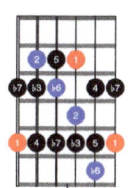

In-Position Harmonized Arpeggios

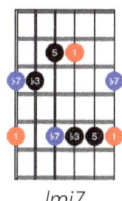 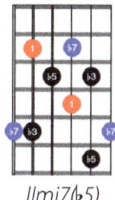 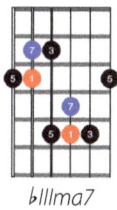 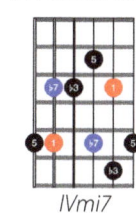 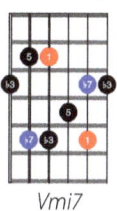  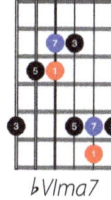 

| Imi7 | IImi7(b5) | bIIIma7 | IVmi7 | Vmi7 | V7 | bVIma7 | bVII7 |

Pattern IV Minor In-Position Arpeggios

Pattern IV Minor Scale

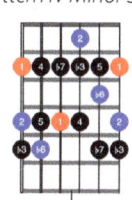

In-Position Harmonized Arpeggios

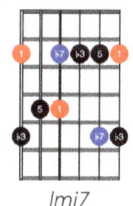 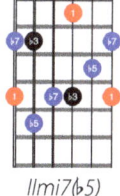 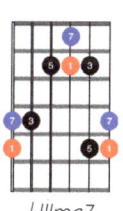 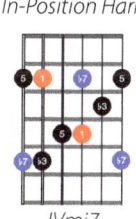 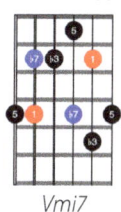 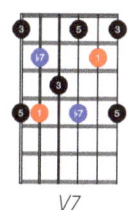  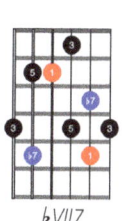

| Imi7 | IImi7(b5) | bIIIma7 | IVmi7 | Vmi7 | V7 | bVIma7 | bVII7 |

Pattern V Minor In-Position Arpeggios

Pattern V Minor Scale

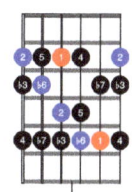

In-Position Harmonized Arpeggios

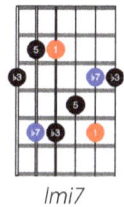 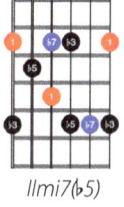 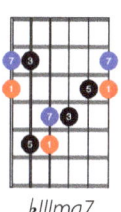 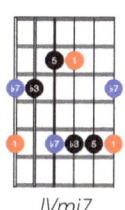 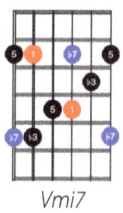 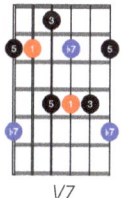 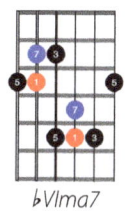 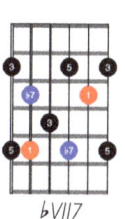

| Imi7 | IImi7(b5) | bIIIma7 | IVmi7 | Vmi7 | V7 | bVIma7 | bVII7 |

Unit ___ Practice Routine

Date:	Routine #	\multicolumn{10}{c	}{DAY}
Exercise	Time/Reps	1	2	3	4	5	6	7	8	9	10

Unit ___ Practice Routine

Date:	Routine #	DAY									
Exercise	Time/Reps	1	2	3	4	5	6	7	8	9	10

FRETBOARDBIOLOGY
COMPREHENSIVE GUITAR PROGRAM

FRETBOARDBIOLOGY
COMPREHENSIVE GUITAR PROGRAM

About Joe Elliott

Joe Elliott is an American guitarist, author, composer, and music educator.

Joe's professional experience as an educator includes 23 years of teaching at Musicians Institute (MI) in Hollywood, California, at the Guitar Institute of Technology (GIT). Joe has taught numerous clinics throughout the U.S. While at MI, Joe wrote and edited courses for GIT and MI's Baccalaureate programs. He spent three years as GIT Department Head and nine years as Vice President and Director of Education at Musicians Institute. He spent seven years as the Guitar Department Head and Director of Academic Administration at McNally Smith College of Music in St. Paul, Minnesota. He is currently the co-founder, CEO, and Director of Education of the guitar education website FretboardBiology.com and Music Biology, Inc.

Joe has authored several instructional books for guitar, including *An Introduction to Jazz Guitar Soloing* and *The Fretboard Biology* series of books, and has co-authored *Ear Training* with Carl Schroeder and Keith Wyatt.

Joe has released two solo guitar albums, *Joe's Place* and *Truth Serum*, as well as an instrumental country album, *Country Grit*, is currently a composer for APM Music in Los Angeles, and has composed numerous scores for television and film.

www.ingramcontent.com/pod-product-compliance
Lightning Source LLC
Chambersburg PA
CBHW051119110526
44589CB00026B/2973